REINDEER AND GOLD

by
Keith A. Murray

D1218355

Occasional Paper #24
Center for Pacific Northwest Studies
Bellingham, Washington 98225

ISBN # 0-929008-22-7
Copyright
Center for Pacific Northwest Studies
Western Washington University
Bellingham, WA 98225
August, 1988

For Karleen

TABLE OF CONTENTS

ILLUSTRATIONS

PREFACE

The Yukon and Alaska gold rushes of 1898 and 1899 have been the inspiration for hundreds of colorful tales of adventure and hardship, of riches and poverty, of ruthless villains and of unselfish heroes. Some of the stories about the north country are only partially true, but have become a part o American folklore nevertheless. Some other tales are entirely true, but are not known. None is more colorful than the story of sixty-eight men from Lapland, who came with their families, seven thousand miles from their Norwegian homes, to Alaska in 1898 as employees of the United States Army, hired to carry freight and mail by reindeer to the remote outposts o Alaska. Some of these men, who were expert reindeer herders, came to teach the Eskimo how to care for the deer. Not long after they reached the northern Pacific coast, they were transferred to the Reindeer Service, under the Department of the Interior, and moved to the Bering Sea. Soon after that they arrived at the Unalakleet River, and one of their number discovered gold on the Seward Peninsula not far from where Nome is now located. He became a millionaire, and others of the herders became moderately wealthy. These gold discoveries were responsible for the swarms of American citizens who came to Nome from Canada and the lower forty-five states, and mined enough gold to repay the purchase price of Alaska many times over.

The account of the Reindeer Expedition and its part in the Nome gold rush has been buried in official government reports for three quarters of a century. Several accounts of the Klondike gold fields have made allusions to the men from Lapland and to the role of the reindeer herders in the Nome experience. As the stirring events of the turn of the century recede farther into history, however, the project that brought the herders to Alaska has been almost entirely forgotten, except for a mention or two in Seattle histories, or an occasional footnote in scholarly papers published in relatively obscure historical journals.

In the early 1950s, however, a handwritten journal in the Norwegian language came to light which told the complete story of the two-year adventure as seen through the eyes of Carl Sacariasen, one of the Norwegian cooks for the expedition.[1] Since the journal had never been translated, its existence was unknown except to a few persons, mostly members of Sacariasen's immediate family at Quincy and Portland, Oregon, and Norwegian friends living on Puget Island in the Columbia River. Sacariasen began his journal when he was hired to work for the Reindeer Service in Norway in January 1898, and he ended it in the fall of 1899 when thousands of gold-seekers crowded into Nome and he left.

The journal disappeared sometime in the 1920s, when its author loaned it to a Mrs. Hendrickson of Puget Island who was visiting friends in Quincy. She asked to read it at her leisure, and took it home putting it with her other Norwegian books. Unfortunately, she died in May 1933, and her family knew nothing about the journal. They stored her Norwegian books in a bookcase in the basement, where nothing was disturbed for the next few years. Her daughter and son-in-law bought the place, built a new house and moved Mrs. Hendrickson's things into their own home. In 1948, exceptionally severe flooding in the lower Columbia valley required that Puget Island be evacuated. Among the things that the new owners rescued was the Sacariasen *Journal*.[2] Mrs. Hendrickson's daughter, Agnes Sjogren, found it when she went through her mother's library, but did not know who Carl Sacariasen was. She read it aloud to her husband in its original language. Later, in 1955, as a student at Western Washington University, she told me that she knew about the reindeer expedition to Alaska because she had a diary about it. When I asked her for more information, she sent me several pages that she had translated to let me read. I urged her to complete the translation of the entire diary, which she finished in the summer of 1958.

At that time, neither of us knew where Sacariasen lived, or whether he was still living. By chance, in May 1958, the Portland *Journal* carried a feature story about Leonhard Seppala, who had made a heroic mid-winter dash by dog sled to Nome in 1925 to take diphtheria antitoxin for use in a severe epidemic there. The reporter asked him why he was in Portland, and he replied that he had come to visit his friend Carl Sacariasen.[3] Immediately after receiving a copy of the newspaper from Mrs. Sjogren I wrote a letter to

Sacariasen which shortly afterward brought the answer that he was indeed the author of the journal, and he also asked me where I had obtained the manuscript, which he had lost many years before. As a result, Mrs. Sjogren was able to return the original journal to him, and in turn we received his permission to use it as the basis for a published story of the Nome gold rush.

In 1971 another bit of information came to light when the Finnish-American Historical Society of the West published the journal of Wilhelm Basi of the same expedition, under the title *Diary on 1898 Yukon Rescue*.[4] Basi was Carl Sacariasen's cousin. They were partners in the Alaskan adventure, and they remained close friends in both farming and church work in the subsequent years spent in the Columbia valley of Oregon and Washington. From the two journals, reports written by various officials of the Reindeer Service in various government publications, and records of the Department of the Interior of Alaskan Affairs at the turn of the century, it has now become possible to reconstruct what happened to bring such an unlikely set of individuals from Finnmark Province, Norway, to Seattle, Haines (Alaska), and finally to the Bering Sea and the Seward Peninsula, where they struck gold.

I met Sacariasen only once, and found him a charming person. He was eager to have the story told, and his family cooperated as well. Mrs. Sjogren has been of great help, for without her translation the heart of the story would be missing. Carl read her translation and approved it as a true rendering of what he wanted to say. Professor Sverre Arrastad of the Scandinavian Language Department of the University of Washington read the translation as well, and made excellent suggestions for ways to put idiomatic Norwegian into English, especially some of the expressions Sacariasen used that Mrs. Sjogren found difficult to put into common American speech.

I would like to thank Karleen Strain for taking time, effort, and expense to make contacts for me in Poulsbo, Washington, which helped me to know what happened to some of the herders after 1900. Also, I appreciate the assistance of the Bureau for Faculty Research at Western Washington University, who prepared the manuscript for me.

Finally, I should like to thank my wife, Shirley, who after our marriage, got me interested in finishing this project, and urged me to do additional research and writing on what I had started twenty years before. She felt that people who had all but forgotten about events in '98 could catch some of the excitement that Americans in and around Puget Sound felt long ago when they heard key words like "Bonanza Creek," "Klondike," "Nome," or "the Yukon River," by reading the Sacariasen adventure story.

Keith A. Murray

NOTES

[1]Sacariasen, Carl Johan, *Reiseminder i Alaska*. (Translated from the Norwegian by Agnes Hendrickson Sjogren.) Typewritten unpublished manuscript in the Center for Pacific Northwest Studies, Western Washington University, Bellingham, Washington. Hereafter cited as *R. i A.*

[2]Letter, Agnes Hendrickson Sjogren, Reno, Nevada, to Keith A. Murray, May 13, 1979.

[3]Mattila, Walter. "He's the Greatest Musher." Portland *Journal*, May 1958; letter, Murray, Keith A., to Rev. Carl J. Sacariasen, May 13, 1958, and reply, June 11, 1958.

[4]Basi, Wilhelm. *Diary on 1898 Yukon Rescue*. Portland Finnish-American Historical Society of the West. Historical Tract Issue, 6:4, September 1971. Hereafter cited as *Basi*.

Chapter One

INTRODUCTION

Any historical event is, of course, the end result of previous actions and decisions made by many men and nations over years or even centuries. The "relief expedition" of 1898, sponsored by the United States War Department and completed by the United States Reindeer Service (an agency of the Department of the Interior), was not a wild dream spawned in the mind of an impractical and hysterical missionary, as was charged at the time, but was rather a result of American involvement in Alaskan affairs that began when the United States purchased Alaska from Russia on March 30, 1867.[1]

Americans who supported the bill to purchase Alaska did so with the vague hope that it might pay off sometime in the future as a purely speculative enterprise, which of course it did. Until such a payoff was evident, however, neither citizenry nor government were enthusiastic about appropriating large sums of money to learn about the vast land of "Walrussia" or to develop it in any way. The natives had lived for generations without any assistance from any government, and no one in America proposed to change this state of affairs. The few white citizens living in the Great Land were mainly Russians who had stayed after 1867, or United States military personnel stationed around Sitka. The other tiny forts along the Alaskan seacoasts constituted virtually all the points of contact Americans had with the native Alaskans. Throughout the entire period between 1867 and 1884, when civil government finally came to Alaska, the native population was almost completely ignored, and most of the other resources in "Seward's Folly" were unknown. There was neither civil nor criminal law established for the Purchase. In 1868 some customs fees were collected in Sitka, but most of Alaska could be reached by traders who seldom stopped to pay any kind of duty on their imports. Occasionally the Customs Collector might drop in on a native village for an inspection, but this happened so seldom that it was no great hardship to the "smugglers" who came by.

Commercial harvesting of seals began within two years of the American takeover of the Pribilof Islands, however. An enterprise calling itself the Alaska Commercial Company began to slaughter the seal in the Bering Sea in the summer of 1868. As was the ruthless custom of the time, no one thought about any kind of conservation, and the Company had only the vaguest authority to kill the animals legally.[2] The Secretary of Treasury notified the Secretary of the Interior whose department had the presumed official control of sealing what had been going on for the previous two years, but the letter got lost in the maze of bureaucracy, and nothing happened.[3] Governor A.T. Swinford also complained about the "malfeasance" of the Company[4] and eventually in 1887 the Government stirred itself to check out the taking of animals without compensation to the natives or significant fees to the taxpayers of the United States.[5]

The Army relinquished control of Alaska to the Navy in 1879, but the Navy did little better than the Army had done. Congress continued to hold back any appropriations for Alaska, and protecting native or animal life had an exceedingly low priority on their list of urgent legislation. The naval officers found it easy to do nothing, since nothing was expected of them. They travelled very little, and complained of their lack of resources and ships. The Governor complained that the naval commander in Alaska was in league with the Treasury Department and the "Whiskey Ring" to smuggle liquor to the natives on naval vessels. In addition, the ships that the navy sent to Alaska, according to Swinford, made trips to Nanaimo, British Columbia to buy coal for $3.50 a ton in order to sell it for $11 in Sitka. The offices kept the profits themselves in the process.[6]

As early as 1871, while the Army still officially controlled Alaskan affairs, Major-General Oliver O. Howard, commander of the military department of the Northwest, suggested that Christian missionaries might be encouraged to locate in Alaska, and serve as a point of contact between Indians or Eskimo and whites. Partly as a belated response to Howard's suggestion, Dr. Sheldon Jackson, a Presbyterian missionary operating over several territories in the Rocky Mountains of the United States, travelled to Alaska to find what conditions were like there. Jackson had intended to go to Idaho, but the Nez Perce war of 1877 diverted him to Alaska. He was so impressed with what he found that he spent much of the rest of his life there.

He obtained the services of Mrs. Amanda R. McFarland from Lapwai, Idaho, who opened a mission at Fort Wrangell in August, 1877, without books, school building, helpers, money, or friends. She stayed, however.[7] The following year, 30-year-old John G. Brady came to establish the second mission which he located at Sitka.

Jackson was an uninspiring man in personal appearance, barely five feet tall, but he compensated for his poor image with boundless energy and a fiery temper.[8] He had been born in New York, and was educated there and in New Jersey. As a child he had been ill a great deal, and he gave the impression of weakness when one first saw him, for he was always bothered by poor vision. Yet this tiny man had held his first religious and educational responsibility in Indian Territory, teaching Indian children to read. For the next twelve years he wandered over Montana, Wyoming, Utah, Colorado, New Mexico, and Arizona ministering to whites and native Americans alike.[9] When he went to Alaska in 1877 he was already forty-three years old, but he entered into his new responsibilities with characteristic drive and enthusiasm. More than this, he had not only energy but an even greater talent for butting into the affairs of unscrupulous government officials or corporation agents determined to advance their own interests at the expense of the Indians, Aleuts, or Eskimos. He was a crusty individual, and had the weakness of considerable vanity, but he was totally honest and did not hesitate to fight those who would exploit the natives.

Missionary endeavor is not in good repute today. These earnest individuals are pictured in popular stereotypes as totally ignorant of the customs of the native population, unfamiliar with their language and guilty of imposing an alien religion on the hapless aborigines almost by force. Those who feel righteous indignation over missionary activities do not know of the things Sheldon Jackson did to preserve native culture.[10]

In 1884, Congress belatedly established the rudiments of civil government for the Russians, Eskimo, Indians, and the handful of Americans living there.[11] The Organic Act of 1884 provided for a Governor to be appointed by the President, a District Court, a District Attorney, and one policeman for nearly a million square miles of land with thousands of miles of coastline to patrol. If anyone was arrested, this lone policeman had to take the accused person to Portland, Oregon for trial. Understandably, there were few arrests!

This same year Sheldon Jackson moved to Alaska as a permanent resident. His first act as a missionary was to establish another mission at Haines among the Chilkats, and he also founded an industrial training school for native boys at Sitka on land donated by John Brady, who had resigned from the Presbyterian missionary service and was operating a store he called The Sitka Trading Company. Jackson not only recruited Presbyterian missionaries and teachers, but also helped missionaries from other denominations in America and Europe to work with the native peoples. More importantly, he waged a one-man campaign on behalf of Alaska native rights by delivering more than nine hundred talks before church, educational, and civic groups in the older parts of the United States. In addition, he described the geography and economic importance of the Purchase. In the process, he acquired the reputation of being the chief authority on Alaska's problems and its potential value to the nation. As a result, President Grover Cleveland followed the suggestion of the United States Commissioner of Education, and appointed Jackson General Agent for Education in Alaska in April 1885.[12] Jackson held this position almost until his death in May 1909.

As soon as he received his appointment, the new General Agent travelled along the coasts of southeastern Alaska and the Bering Sea on the cutter *Bear* visiting villages and talking to other missionaries. He urged the federal government to honor its promise made at the time of the Purchase, to replace Russian teachers with Americans, and to change the attitude expressed by a congressman who complained that Alaska would be ". . . a constant annual expense for which there [would] be no adequate return . . . no value as a mineral country . . . its timber of poor quality . . . its fur trade of insignificant value . . . the fisheries of doubtful value."[13] Jackson disagreed with this evaluation based on his personal observations.

Jackson believed strongly that the Indian children needed to learn how to cope with western civilization. Accordingly, although he had no money, no means of dependable transportation, and no government schools of any kind to administer, Jackson set out to transform Alaska, with only an official title to give him authority.

While he went about the Great Land learning all he could about conditions of the natives there, he reported what he learned about cases of dishonesty and neglect of duty of various Americans. He also believed that many of the Eskimo in northern Alaska were dying of malnutrition because the whale, walrus, and seal that formed their customary diet were being slaughtered by whalers and fur hunters. These people had never even considered conservation. Even the aquatic birds and salmon were decreasing in number. Breechloading, repeating rifles had driven away or killed the inland caribou. When Jackson talked with the Captain of the *Bear*, Michael A. Healy, he learned that in contrast to the assumed misery of the Alaskan natives, the Chukchi people in Siberia who owned Asiatic reindeer herds were relatively prosperous.[14] As a result, four years later Jackson concluded that the job of bringing immediate public education to Alaska without sufficient funds was too big a job, and that there would of necessity be a delay in starting government supported education. He proposed in his report of December 1890 to the United States Commissioner of Education, W.T. Harris, that until there was money enough to build and staff schools for all Alaskan children, every effort should be made to buy Siberian reindeer, bring them to Alaska, and teach the Eskimo there to herd them as the Siberians did.

Not everyone was in favor of what Jackson was trying to do. When Governor J.H. Kincaid first learned in 1885 that Jackson had received a Presidential appointment, he protested the foolishness of entrusting education of white children to a missionary.[15] Indian education might be handled by churches, but "American" children were different. Jackson refused to agree. Commissioner Eaton supported him, and at once there was conflict. Another group that opposed Jackson's appointment was that of young businessmen in Alaska. They did not like drunkenness among the Indians, but they didn't want Jackson to talk about it. "They feared that every time statements appeared in print referring to Indians and prohibition in Alaska, capital was frightened away and immigration was discouraged."[16] It did not take long for Jackson's opponents to try to get him removed. As early as mid-summer 1885 he was arrested for building a fence around his Indian school in Sitka without getting a proper permit, and his bond was set for $2,000 which was more than his entire yearly income.[17] As late as June

1899, during the busiest year of his life, a Juneau grand jury indicted Jackson on the charge of negligence of duty, unwise expenditures of government funds, infrequent visits to Juneau, and lack of adequate schools in Alaska. One author suggests that this indictment was the result of the struggle between John Brady and Sitka business interests against the entrepreneurs of Juneau over the permanent location of Alaska's capital as much as hostility to Jackson.[18]

Congress, however, paid little attention to Jackson's suggestions. His enemies in Juneau thought he had lost all remnants of his reason. A member of Congress, Louis E. McComas, introduced a bill on December 19, 1890, proposing to build Agricultural Experiment Stations in Alaska and making funds available to carry this out; also to allow Jackson to buy deer in Siberia. While the McComas bill was reported favorably by the Committee of Education, it was not voted on by the whole House.[19] Senator Henry M. Teller of Colorado, who was acquainted with Jackson, proposed to appropriate $15,000 for such a project, and it passed the Senate, but the two-house Conference Committee that rewrote the final appropriation bill dropped it from the measure.[20]

Dr. Jackson then appealed by way of newspapers in New York, Boston, Philadelphia, and Chicago for private contributions to learn whether Siberian deer could be brought successfully to Alaska. He also appealed for funds through several religious publications. He was gratified by the response. Contributions totalling $2,146, received in small sums, were sent to him by those who read of his appeal.[21] With this money Jackson bought barter goods consisting of such items as lead, axes, saws, tin pans, files, and knives. He asked for the use of the *Bear* in travelling to Siberia. He also requested that the State Department apply for permission from the Russian government to deal with the Chukchi. He obviously was held in high regard among national leaders, for the Departments of the Interior, Treasury and State cooperated, the Russian authorities agreed to let him try, and he was on his way.[22]

Now his Juneau enemies stood up and jeered at his scheme. They referred to him as "Shellgame" Jackson, and his project as "the education of reindeer." His efforts to continue native education under religious auspices with the cordial support of Brady were referred to as the work of "Jesus

Christ and Company."[23] Some delcared that the Chukchi would not sell their deer. This proved to be partly true, for the native shamans, the religious leaders among the Siberian Eskimo, opposed the sales vigorously, and after he had traveled almost fifteen hundred miles from village to village, Jackson was able to buy only sixteen deer.[24] Other opponents said the deer wouldn't survive the trip on the *Bear* even if he could buy a few. This proved to be false, for the animals remained aboard the cutter for three weeks, and went through one severe storm without a single loss. Still other crepe-hangers claimed that the wild dogs of Alaska would kill all reindeer, or else the nomadic Eskimo there would destroy them for food. Dogs proved to be no problem except in unusual circumstances. The Eskimo did require considerable education before they learned to stop hunting and killing the deer, but they did learn, and the later deer herds did increase in numbers.[25] Jackson landed his first small herd on Amaknak and Unalaska Islands in the Aleutians and they were uncared for since he had neither funds nor herders to look after them. Two years later, all had died.

Senator Teller, who had been President Chester Arthur's Secretary of the Interior, continued to urge support for Jackson's plan to change the Eskimo from hunters and fishermen to herders of reindeer. While his bills did not pass, his support was highly appreciated by Jackson. When the *Bear* returned from its second trip to Siberia in 1892 with more than a hundred deer, Jackson chose a site at Port Clarence for herders to live while they taught the natives, and built a house there, as well as warehouses and accommodations for the apprentice Eskimo herders whom he hoped would soon arrive to learn about animal culture. He named the spot the Teller Reindeer Station.[26] After the herd was moved to Unalakleet in 1898, this became known as the Teller Mission (Lutheran) and was later called the Brevig Mission.[27]

Still depending on private contributions, Jackson brought 171 deer in 1892, as well as four Chukchi herders to show the Alaskan Eskimo how they took care of them.[28] The Siberians proved unsatisfactory, however, and the Superintendent at Teller, W.T. Lopp, soon sent them home.[29] As general promoter of the project, which he did in addition to his duties as General Agent for Education, and head of the Presbyterian missionary work in Alaska, Jackson was convinced that he had to find another way to teach the natives to change their way of life.[30] He finally concluded that Laplanders who had lived with reindeer for centuries and who had already had contact with Europeans, would be more successful teachers than the Chukchi.

On March 3, 1893, Congress finally made its first small appropriation of $6,000 to support Jackson and his plan for feeding the Eskimo.[31] The Reindeer Service officially became an agency of the Department of the Interior, and Jackson was appointed its director. He knew nothing about reindeer, but then neither did anyone at Teller Station. His duties seemed to make no changes from what he had already been doing as General Agent of Education and a Presbyterian missionary. It did pay a small salary in addition to his educational appropriation. He continued to receive private contributions as well, which that year gave him another thousand dollars. He used this to employ William T. Lopp as supervisor of the apprentice program in addition to his duties as Superintendent of the Teller Station. Jackson listened to the advice of Rasmus B. Anderson, former United States Minister to Denmark, who told him that if he wanted to get Lapps for his project, he should try to hire William J. Kjellmann,[32] a thirty-seven year old Norwegian immigrant, now an American citizen, to be his agent in Lapland. Kjellmann had been a herder himself, and knew both Norwegian and Finnish as well as the Lapp dialect, in addition to English, and who also knew the countryside of Lapland well.[33] He had once been a salesman of reindeer supplies before he came to America. Kjellmann was living at that time in Mt. Horeb, Wisconsin.

Kjellmann was to prove an invaluable addition to the Service and played a major role in subsequent events. He sailed for Finnmark, then part of Norway and Sweden, on the liner *Majestic* in mid-February, 1894, and reached his destination early in March. When he disembarked he gave several of the local people some gifts of American food, and told them he wanted five of them to return with him to Alaska.

He spent nearly a week with the herders. He found that his main difficulty was that none of the Lapps had ever heard of anyone who had gone to America, and they scarcely knew where Alaska was. He overcame all objections, however, when he promised that he would personally bring home anyone who went with him, and after a year of service should decide that he wanted to return home.[34]

Before Kjellmann left for Norway, Jackson had instructed him to try to hire someone of the Roman Catholic faith among the Lapps. The Superintendent was sensitive to criticism that the reindeer he had brought from Siberia were being used only to give publicity to the Protestants and, while he shrugged off most criticism, he tried to avoid unnecessary bickering if he could. Finding a Catholic in Lapland was very difficult, however, but Kjellmann heard of one family of Lapps who claimed to have been baptized into that church. Their eighteen-year-old son, Frederik Larsen, agreed to go with Kjellmann. Another member of the first people hired was Johan Speinsen Tornensis, who stayed with the reindeer service through the rest of the 1890's.

Kjellmann's first group left Hammerfest on April 17, and four weeks later were on a train in America headed for Alaska. They visited Kjellmann's family in Wisconsin briefly, then turned west. Altogether there were five families and two single men who went with him. Early in June they reached Seattle. As there was no direct link with Alaska from Seattle at that time, the entire group, including their dogs, travelled to San Francisco where they took passage for Teller Station. When they reached Teller, Kjellmann, now promoted to Superintendent there, found fifteen young Eskimos living in the quarters provided for them, already involved in the training program, though there was no one to instruct them properly.

When they reached the Station, Lopp returned to his missionary work, and Kjellmann took up his new duties. He revised the training program somewhat, and took a census of his herd.

This herd now numbered 568 animals. Four hundred thirty-one had been brought from Siberia by Jackson in the previous two years, and there was a natural increase of 127 fawns.[35] The apprentices were to be given six deer if they stayed a year, eight more if they stayed two years, and ten more for each year they stayed in the program. They were also allowed to keep the natural increase. The Lapps were to be given one hundred deer as a loan, which they could keep for five years, and return a hundred animals at the end of that time. They were allowed to keep the natural increase as a reward for their efforts.

Four years later in the decade, some of the deer were distributed to the mission stations of the Swedish Evangelical mission at Golovnin, and to the Episcopal churches on the Yukon, as well as to the Congregational mission at Cape Prince of Wales. Later yet, Moravian, Methodist, and Presbyterian missions received deer.

According to one writer, the Lapps had to change the whole philosophy of the Eskimo from a killer to that of a protector of animals. one Lapp said:

> Men do not take care of deer, but deer take care of men . . . Your job is to follow the deer, then, and not try to make them follow you. Can't you see why this is so? They are more important than you. They can live without you, but you cannot live without them. With all your game killed off by these new rifles, what will you live on next winter if you do not keep your deer? See? You do not know what you will live on.[36]

In January 1895 the first Eskimo was pronounced ready to own his own herd, and a small number of deer were given to him. This became the precedent which in the next two years provided several Eskimo with their own deer.[37] The most successful of these men was Charlie Antisarlook, also called Antesilook and Antachaluk. After his death in 1900, his part-Russian wife, Mary Antisarlook, managed the considerably enlarged herd.[38] His was a complete success story.

At this point the tempo of Alaskan activities accelerated. Jackson was now more than sixty years old, but his energy seemed boundless. Although very little in his educational duties or the reindeer project called for it, Jackson was asked by the Secretary of Agriculture to travel to the upper Yukon valley to check out the agricultural possibilities of that region. He had been elected to the office of moderator of the General Assembly of the Presbyterian Church, the highest position that Jackson would hold in his denomination, but by the summer of 1897 in response to the request of Agriculture, he was on his way up the Yukon. What he did not know was that in August 1896 George Washington Carmack and his Indian brother-in-law "Tagush" Charlie had looked into the sands of Bonanza Creek near the Klondike River and found the gold that had escaped others who had searched for the precious metal. The rich deposits of placer gold lay in an eight hundred square mile area just east of the Alaska-Yukon border, and in the upper Yukon valley in Alaska itself. The only way to reach this gold field was up the Yukon River from its mouth on the Bering Sea, or over the Chilkoot Pass or White Pass at the head of Lynn Canal. During the fall of 1896, dozens of prospectors gathered equipment to try to get to the Klondike in the spring.

William Kjellmann went with Jackson on the flat-bottomed steamer *Portus B. Weare*. This steamer had carried almost a half million dollars in gold dust downstream on its previous trip, and that was all the crew and passengers could talk about. Naturally Jackson and Kjellmann heard them talking, and their interest in agriculture changed abruptly to concern for the future of Alaska now that a gold rush was underway. When they reached Dawson City in July 1897, they found themselves in the midst of a gold craze. They remained in Canada for only one day, then returned to St. Michael to make their report.[39]

Although there is considerable dispute about the source of the rumor, Jackson is popularly credited with telling the world that there were between four and five thousand prospectors in Dawson and Circle City who might be starving before the next winter ended, because the river would be useless for freighting after it froze, and there was no other means of bringing in supplies. It appears, however, that the first warnings of a food shortage in the Yukon came from the Secretary of the Interior himself, and not Jackson.[40] Nevertheless, Jackson's enemies later spread the story that he had given a false alarm when there was no emergency, and this idea seems to have been widely accepted. It is true, however, that he was quoted in Congress as saying that it would be an easy matter to supply freight in Dawson with harness-broken reindeer purchased in Lapland, if it were necessary.[41] Secretary of War, R.A. Alger, supported by professional military advice, stated that he believed a disaster was very imminent. For about two months the newspapers of the United States published occasional stories predicting trouble. A small amount of relief supplies was gathered in Portland, Oregon, to be sent to the presumably suffering miners.[42]

In the fall of 1897, the idea was given considerable support when it became known that several hundred whalers were trapped in the ice of the Arctic Ocean near Point Barrow, by an unusually early freeze. Since some of the whaling ships were so badly damaged by the ice that they had to be abandoned, and since the ships did not have enough food to remain in the

11

Arctic for two years, it seemed that starvation was a likely fate for the crews of the ships. Captain George F. Tilton on the steam whaler *Alexander* reached San Francisco on November 3, and told of the impending tragedy. While actually the whalers were in no immediate danger, President McKinley called a cabinet meeting on November 8, and expressed concern about the events at Point Barrow. Someone proposed that the Reindeer Service save the lives of the whalers.

The story of the rescue operations which resulted in an overland expedition in mid-winter from the Teller Reindeer Station with animals from their herd and that of the Eskimo apprentice Antisarlook who lived near Cape Nome has been told elsewhere, and does not need to be repeated here.[43] What is important to this story is that the Service received publicity that it had not had in its previous seven year existence.

The attention and concern of the nation for the imperiled whalers supported the ideas of those who had been predicting starvation at Dawson. On December 15, a bill was introduced into Congress to appropriate money to the War Department to buy food for the American prospectors in the Yukon. Since most of the Americans were at or near Dawson, and since this community was in Canada, some congressmen balked at spending United States military funds for any purpose whatever in a foreign country. When Joseph Cannon, then chairman of the House Appropriations Committee, had a conference with Sheldon Jackson, however, and emerged from the interview declaring himself in favor of the bill, opposition declined to a mere whisper, for Cannon was very influential. The bill passed.[44] It was entitled: "An Act authorizing the Secretary of War at his discretion, to purchase subsistence stores, supplies, and materials for the relief of the people who are in the Yukon River country, to provide means for their transportation and distribution, and making an appropriation of $200,000 therefor."

Secretary of War Russell A. Alger then instructed Dr. Jackson, who was still in Washington, D.C., to purchase five hundred harness-broken reindeer, sleds, reindeer moss for food for the animals, and harness. He further directed Jackson to go to Norway himself, to hire drivers and herders to care for the animals that would be brought to Alaska, and to wait in Norway until he was told what to do next. Jackson was willing to add this chore to the rest of his governmental and religious activities, but he suggested that he be allowed to buy enough extra deer to repay the missions, the Teller herd, and Antisarlook for animals they had contributed for the relief expedition to Point Barrow and the isolated whaling ships.[45]

Fortunately for the efficiency of the operation, Kjellmann was already in Norway when President McKinley signed the bill. According to his promise, he had gone there in October, taking four herders he had hired three years previously who had asked to be allowed to go home.[46] Kjellmann picked up his mail in Trondheim, and Jackson cabled him there asking him to begin hiring many times the replacements he had originally planned to take to Alaska. Since probably at least sixty Lapp herders and their families would be too difficult to persuade to go with him, he was told to hire as many Norwegians as he needed to make up the difference, and also to buy as much of the other supplies as he could obtain before Jackson arrived to join him. He was urged to speed all arrangements, for soon Jackson would be arriving in Lapland to bring everyone, the animals and the freight, back to America.

Uncharacteristically for a government operation in 1897, but quite characteristic of Sheldon Jackson, he got the army authorities to act swiftly and decisively. Within a week after he wired Kjellmann, he found Lieutenant D.B. DeVore, who had been assigned to go with him as disbursing officer and to assume nominal command of the operation, and succeeded in having DeVore meet him in New York to leave promptly for Europe. Exactly one week after Congress passed the bill and two days after the President signed it, Jackson and DeVore were on the Cunard liner *Lucania*. They left New York on Christmas morning, 1897. Six days later they were in Liverpool.[47]

When Jackson reached London he found a wire from Kjellmann asking that he send money immediately, for the Lapps demanded cash before they would sell him anything. Jackson went to several London bankers, though their institutions were closed for the New Years Day holiday, and they said they could not help him, but suggested that he send Kjellmann a check! This would have taken days to arrive, and Jackson was not accustomed to that much inefficiency. Impatiently, he had to wait until the next day to obtain the money.

13

Next, he learned that the United States Department of Agriculture had regulations against any Norwegian or Swedish cattle being imported into the United States. This was designed to prevent competition with American beef, but it included reindeer. He rushed to the United States Embassy in London to work out the details of overriding the regulation, then spent the rest of the day with the Undersecretary for Agriculture for Great Britain. This man suggested that if DeVore chartered a ship that had never been used for transporting cattle it might satisfy the Agricultural inspectors, especially since Congress and McKinley were heartily in favor of what Jackson was doing.

Jackson left for Norway the same night. Presumably he decided he could rest aboard the ship. The two men reached Oslo on January 6, and by ten in the morning Jackson was conferring with Henry Bordevich, the United States Consul there. He was carrying a draft for $1,000 to send to Kjellmann, which he finally got sent north by telegram on January 8. DeVore returned to Glasgow to charter a passenger vessel that had never carried cattle, and Jackson took a train to Trondheim. When he arrived he bought bales of reindeer moss, which took him only a short time, then went aboard the *Vesteraalen* for Trömsoe, where he arrived at five in the morning on January 11. He did not wait to rest, but boarded the small steamer *Sigurd Jarl* for Hammerfest, which he reached at 2 a.m. on January 12. At this time of year darkness continued for twenty-four hours a day. In spite of the snow and the darkness, Jackson hired a rowboat to take him from Hammerfest to Alten at the head of Altenfjord. Here he found the admirable William Kjellmann waiting for him. It was January 13, 1898, and less than three weeks from the time Congress took action.

Kjellmann had not waited to get the money in his hands, but had borrowed 1,000 kroner on his own promissory note, which allowed him to begin his purchases. He, too, had bought 250 tons of reindeer moss. He hired two of the Lapps who wanted to go home, Per Rist and Samuel Kemi, to go with him as he picked up the supplies and herders he needed for the Alaskan adventure.

According to Jackson's own account, the normal winter snowfall turned into a blizzard, which did not let up for weeks. In spite of the storm, he urged Kjellmann to rush his purchases, for already twenty-one days had gone by, and according to those who feared famine in Dawson, they had only until the end of February before the fear of disaster would become a reality.

Kjellmann had many of the traits of his employer. For him it was hurry, hurry, hurry, until he finished what he set out to do. In the next two weeks he traveled more than two hundred sixty-five miles on foot and by sled, traveling as far as Finland before he turned back. He spent his spare time buying sleds, harness, reindeer, and hiring men. By now Rist and Kemi had caught some of his enthusiasm, and while they did not return to Alaska, since both were past fifty years of age, they did become excellent salesmen for him, and were able to get the required beasts and men in a surprisingly short time.

DeVore, meanwhile, unaware of the severe blizzard in Finnmark, wired Jackson impatiently asking when he should come to pick up the deer. He had chartered the Allen liner, *Manitoban* in Glasgow, and the crew of that ship began to build pens on the deck to hold the animals while they crossed the Atlantic.

Several more days passed while the arctic storm increased in violence. Jackson began to worry when Kjellmann did not return within a couple of days, which seemed to the impatient missionary long enough to buy five hundred deer and hire sixty-eight men. He did not know how far his agent had had to travel to fill the needed quota. On January 26, however, Jackson wrote:

> Mr. Kjellman [*sic*] started on the 25th to return to the coast, reaching Bosekop [Alten] on the 28th in the midst of a furious storm, the most severe of the winter. That storm, which had been raging almost without cessation for three weeks, piling the snow in great banks along the fences, filling lanes full above the fence tops, and obliterating all evidences of roads or tracks in the open country, had been gradually increasing in severity until on the 26th, 27th, and 28th of January it had turned into a blizzard, culminating on the 28th in the worst day of the season. The hotel at Bosekop, a strong log building, with a substantial stone foundation, in a sheltered spot, trembled under the furious blasts of wind and snow. At midday, houses a block away could not be seen through the driving snow. All traffic was suspended in the street; and yet on the

mountains, where the cold was much greater and the wind swept with the force of a hurricane, were four herds of reindeer, and between one and two hundred men, women, and children [*actually 110*] in open sleds, facing the blizzard as, on different roads and widely separated sections, they were centering into Bosekop. While anxious lest they should be detained by the storm and perhaps some of the children perish, I received a call for the mayor, (*landsman*) of the village. Inquiring what were the prospects of the Lapps getting through, he shook his head, saying that nothing could face that storm for any length of time and live. I doubt whether any other race than the Lapp, that was cradled in the snow and inured from childhood to hardship, could have done so, or any other animal than the reindeer have brought them safely over the storm-swept and trackless mountains.

About noon, going to a window and with a knife scraping off the frost in order to get the sight of a thermometer hanging outside, I saw faintly through the whirling snow a solitary reindeer coming up the street, and soon after could make out a sled with a man encased in ice and snow. It was Mr. Kjellman, his great fur coat covered with snow and his face and whiskers encased in a mask of ice.[48]

Within a few hours all of the herds arrived with over sixty men, and with forty-two dependents. Not one person nor animal was lost.

The next four days were filled with confusion. Some of the new employees of the Reindeer Service had made their acceptance of Kjellmann's offer of employment conditional upon his permission to let them marry their sweethearts and take them to Alaska with them. Others, who were already married, were reluctant to leave their wives and children for an indefinite number of years, which in some cases actually became a lifetime. Kjellmann had been so impressed with the need for haste, that he readily granted them permission to add women and children to the group, which complicated the expedition considerably.

There were not only matrimonial and family arrangements to be settled, but others had to pay personal bills, since they were likely to be gone for a very long time, and others wanted to attend farewell parties which seemed to the impatient Jackson to be constantly occurring. During the daytime the herders put deer, sleds, harness, and bales of moss into a small warehouse near the structure that passed for the village dock. They got the deer into some kind of shelter, and waited for the *Manitoban* to arrive.

As soon as Kjellmann had reached him, Jackson wired DeVore to bring the ship to Altenfjord, and the relieved army officer directed the ship's captain to sail that afternoon. In spite of the storm that was still raging, it took the old liner only four days to reach Alten, and by the time it arrived on February second, everything was ready. After the stores were put in the warehouse, the herders de-horned the deer to prevent any injuries to them while they were aboard ship in case they should begin to fight. Apparently the War Department, which had ordered this operation, thought of them as being like cattle, but since these were all gelded male deer they were not likely to fight in any event. Some did panic while aboard ship and one was injured enough to cause it to be destroyed, but for the most part they were singularly docile and cooperating animals.

The crew of the *Manitoban* had finished building the stalls while they were steaming to Norway, and had also prepared passenger bunks of sorts below decks for the Lapps and the Norwegians. Jackson, DeVore, and Kjellmann were assigned to staterooms on the upper deck. Jackson did not record his reactions to what he found, or how he felt about the transportation DeVore had chartered. DeVore left no records at all that are available for this account, so we do not know what he thought. The ship was very old, the engines were constantly on the verge of breaking down, and the efficiency of the crew left much to be desired. With the need to make hasty arrangements, however, DeVore had done the best he could with the money made available to him and this was what they had to use.

The vessel had to be anchored offshore, for there was no way they could tie it to the tiny dock in such shallow water. All supplies, deer, and passengers, therefore, had to be put in barges and rowed out to the ship where the animals were loaded aboard, placed in the stalls, and all at the rate of one at a time. After the deck stalls were filled, the balance were lowered below, and placed in stalls in the dark cargo hold, along with the supplies they were taking with them. The herders worked as longshoremen from

17

early morning until after seven at night without any break except for a brief meal at noon. They became so tired that finally they refused to do anything more until the next day, even when Jackson offered to pay them extra wages for their overtime. The next morning they went to work again, and by dinnertime that evening, February 3, 1898, everything was loaded and the passengers were in their quarters. After a final inspection, Jackson at last declared himself ready to sail, and came aboard about midnight.

At four o'clock the next morning, the *Manitoban* got underway. In addition to the cargo and the deer, there were seventy-one men, nineteen women, (including six brides), and twenty-six children. Perhaps the most famous of the men Kjellmann had hired was Samuel Johannesen Balto, who had been with Nansen on the polar expedition of 1888. He had received a decoration from King Oscar II of Sweden and Norway for another achievement when he and five companions crossed the Greenland icecap on skis.

Not as well known as Balto were the two cousins, Carl Johan Sacariasen and Wilhelm Basi, whom Kjellmann had hired in the Langfjord district to work as cooks for the Norwegian contingent on the expedition. For the years that these men kept their journals, these diaries are the best accounts of the events in existence. It would appear from reading Sacariasen's *Reiseminder i Alaska* that he intended from the beginning that his adventures should be told. He recorded the trip to America, his impressions of the country, the way in which the relief expedition to Dawson went sour, his transfer to the Bering reindeer stations, and his adventures in the gold fields at Nome. Basi's account, while much less colorful and much shorter, adds details and is particularly valuable because he kept writing in his diary longer than his cousin Carl, and told something of what happened after they left Nome.

The two men told very little about themselves. There is a photograph in the Basi diary that shows the men and some friends just before they left Norway. Basi was a small man, but Sacariasen was a tall, well-built Viking with broad features and a friendly and intelligent face.

Basi wrote his journal in Finnish, and he also spoke Lapp and his native Norwegian as well. Both men wrote well, though Sacariasen was apparently not highly educated if improper grammatical usage and

18

misspelled words are any measure of education. He was certainly an intelligent person, however, though he had some severe prejudices against people of other ethnic groups when he left his home. He did not eliminate these from his comments until after he had been in Alaska for many months. His dislike extended beyond non-Norwegians to include a lively distaste for Sheldon Jackson or anything to do with him!

These two men left their small village of Talvig in the hills to the west of Altenfjord on February 1, in the midst of the storm that Jackson described in his report. Neither was married. Both were in their late twenties, and both were healthy and in high spirits.

Carl Sacariasen made his first journal entry the day he went aboard the *Manitoban* in Alten harbor.

NOTES

[1]National Archives Microfilm Publications. *Interior Department Territorial Papers: Alaska 1869-1911.* (Hereafter cited as IDTP:AK) "Letters Received Relating to the District of Alaska," Introduction.

[2]Letter, Agapius Honcharenko to Secretary of Treasury, October 12, 1885. IDTP:Ak Introduction p. 1 Recapitulating the wasteful practices of the Company.

[3]Letter, Secretary of Treasury to Interior, Feb. 3, 1869, and reply December 3, 1869. IDTP:AK. Roll 1 microcopy #430.

[4]Letter, Governor Swinford to Interior, October 30, 1885; *Loc. Cit.*

[5]Letter, A.T. Swinford to Interior, May 18, 1887. *Loc. Cit.*

[6]Swinford to Interior, November 1885. *Op. Cit.*

[7]Stewart, Robert Laird. *Sheldon Jackson, Pathfinder and Prospector of the Missionary Vanguard in the Rocky Mountains and Alaska,* New York: Fleming H. Revell Company, 1908, pp. 287-306. In his account Stewart says that Jackson was planning to start a mission in northern Idaho, but the Nez Perce War of 1877 made that impossible, and he went north to Alaska instead. He was aware of General Howard's suggestion to send missionaries.

Mrs. McFarland's husband had been a missionary at the Spalding Mission in Lapwai before his death.

[8]Miller, Max. *The Great Trek: The Story of the Five Year Drive of a Reindeer Herd Through the Icy Wastes of Alaska and Northwestern Canada.* Garden City: Doubleday, Doran & Company, Inc., 1936, p. 20.

[9]*Dictionary of American Biography.* Dumas Malone, ed. New York: Charles Scribner's Sons, 1932. v. 9. Robert Joseph Diven, "Sheldon Jackson."

[10]Hinckley, Ted C. "Sheldon Jackson as Preserver of Alaska's Native Culture." *Pacific Historical Review*, XXXIII:4. November 1964. pp. 411-424.

[11]Report, Governor A.T. Swinford, October 1888. Population: "Creole." (Russians born in Alaska or descendants of Russian-native marriages) 1,900; Aleut, 2,950; "Civilized Indians," 3,500; whites, 6,500; "Uncivilized" Indians and Eskimo, 35,000 (EST.); Total--49,850. IDTP:AK, Introduction.

[12]Lazell, J. Arthur. *Alaskan Apostle, The Life Story of Sheldon Jackson.* New York: Harper & Brothers, Publishers, 1960. p. 71.

[13]*Ibid.*, p. 63.

[14]Ray, Dorothy Jean. "Sheldon Jackson and the Reindeer Industry of Alaska." *Journal of Presbyterian History*, 43:2, June 1965. pp. 71-99. Ray concerns herself mainly with Jackson's presumed motives and the mistakes he made when first he introduced reindeer into Alaska. She cites William T. Lopp as her authority for Healy's suggesting that reindeer be imported for use by the Eskimo. (*Lopp Papers*, University of Oregon Library; also a handwritten note she found from Lopp in the *C.L. Andrews Collection*, Sheldon Jackson College, Sitka, Alaska.) Ray noted elsewhere that only a small fraction of the Eskimo were endangered by the slaughter of the walrus or caribou. In fact they were gaining in population numbers. Ray, Dorothy Jean, *The Eskimos of Bering Strait, 1650-1898*, Seattle: The University of Washington Press, 1975. pp. 226-227.

[15]Lazell, p. 71.

[16] *Ibid.*, p. 70.

[17]Letter, Jackson to John Eaton, August 26, 1885. IDTP:AK, Introduction.

[18]Nichols, Jeanette P., *Alaska. A History of its Administration, Exploitation, and Industrial Development during the first half century under the rule of the United States.* Cleveland: Arthur H. Clark Company, 1924. p. 167.

[19]Letter, W.T. Harris to Secretary of Interior, December 5, 1890. IDTP:AK (roll 2) "Letters Received Relating to the District of Alaska, January 21, 1890-December 21, 1892."

[20]Letter, Harris to Interior, May 7, 1891, *Loc. Cit.*

[21]52 Congress, 2nd Session. *Senate Miscellaneous Document #22.* "Report on Introduction of Domestic Reindeer into Alaska, 1893," IDTP:AK roll 3.

[22]54 Cong., 1 Sess., *Senate Document #111*, "Introduction of Domestic Reindeer into Alaska." 1895.

[23]Nichols. *Alaska.* pp. 108-112.

[24]Miller. *The Great Trek*, p. 21; Letter, Harris to Interior, February 13 and 15, 1892. IDTP:AK roll 2.

[25]Lantis, Margaret. *Human Problems in Technological Change, A Casebook.* Russell Sage Foundation, New York, 1952. pp. 127-148.

[26]54 Cong., 1 Sess., Senate Doc. #111. pp. 9-18; Colby, Merle, *A Guide to Alaska, Last American Frontier.* Federal Writers Project, New York: The Macmillan Company, 1939. pp. 386-387.

[27]Ray, "Sheldon Jackson," p. 72.

[28]Andrews, Clarence L. *The Eskimo and His Reindeer in Alaska.* Caldwell (Idaho): The Caxton Printers Ltd., 1939. p. 224.

[29]53 Cong., 3 Sess., *Senate Exec. Doc. #92.* "Introduction of Domestic Reindeer into Alaska."

[30]Ray, *Op. Cit.*, p. 80.

[31]52 Cong., 1 Sess. *Congressional Record.* May 23, 1893. p. 4546.

[32]The spelling of this name presents a problem. The official reports spell it Kjellman. The Sacariasen Journal consistently spelled it Kjellemann. Basi spelled it Kjellman. In the official reports of the "Eaton Station Log Book," however, he spelled his own name Kjellmann, and this is the form that will be used from here on.

[33]53 Cong., 3 Sess., *Senate Exec. Doc. #92.* pp. 9-11.

[34]54 Cong., 1 Sess., *Senate Document #111.* "Kjellmann Report." (1894 Expedition to Norway.) pp. 38-47.

[35]Harris, *Exhibit III*. "The Approach to the Interior of Alaska by Chilkat on the Southeast"; also *Exhibit F.1.*, IDTP:AK, roll 3.

[36]Miller. *The Great Trek*. p. 16.

[37]53 Cong., 3 Sess., *Senate Exec. Doc. #92*. p. 12; Ray, "Sheldon Jackson," p. 84.

[38]Mary Antisarlook Andrewuk died November 22, 1948, Ray, *Eskimos of Bering Strait*, f.n. p. 235.

[39]Lazell. *Alaskan Apostle*. pp. 135-137.

[40]Letter, Secretary of Interior, C.N. Bliss to Harris, September 21, 1897. DITP:AK roll 6.

[41]55 Cong., 2 Sess., *Congressional Record*. December 16, 1897. p. 210.

[42]55 Congress, 2 Sess., *Senate Document #14*. "Alaska Gold Fields," pp. 2-41.

[43]55 Cong., 3 Sess., *House Doc. #5*. "Report of the Commission on Education," v. 2. (Sheldon Jackson Report.) pp. 1775-1783; 55 Cong., 3 Sess., *Senate Document #34* Jackson Report, 1898. "Relief of the Whalers Imprisoned in the Ice Near Point Barrow"; 56 Cong., 2 Sess., *House Doc. #511* "Report of the Cruise of the U.S. Revenue Cutter *Bear* and the overland expedition for the relief of the whalers in the Arctic Ocean from November 27, 1897 to September 13, 1898"; Bertholf, Lt. Ellsworth P. "The Rescue of the Whalers, A Sled Journey of 1600 miles in the Arctic Regions." *Harpers Magazine*, v. 99, p. 3-24, June 1899; Andrews, Clarence Leroy. "William T. Lopp." *Alaska Life*, 1944, v. 7, #8, pp. 49-54; Brower, Charles D. *Fifty Years Below Zero, A Lifetime of Adventure in the Far North.* New York: Dodd Mead & Company, 1942, pp. 201-213; The Seattle *Times*, Sunday, April 9, 1944, "Arctic Rescue."

[44]55 Cong. 2 Sess., *Congressional Record.* December 18, 1897.

[45]Letter, Harris to Interior, December 23, 1897. IDTP:AK roll 5; 55 Cong., 3 Sess., *House Doc. #5* (Serial 3767). "Report of the Commissioner of Education, v. 2."

[46]Letter, Harris to Interior, October 3, 1898. IDTP:AK, roll 5.

[47]55 Cong., 3 Sess., *House Doc. #5* (Serial 3767). Jackson Report, "Commission to Lapland."

[48]55. Cong., 3 Sess., *House Doc. #5*. "Commission to Lapland," pp. 1789-1790.

Chapter Two

FOOD FOR THE "STARVING MINERS"

Finnmark Province, Norway, is a forbidding land at best, and in mid-winter it is no place to be traveling in the open. Even the local people stay close to their homes during January storms yet the men, women, and children that Kjellmann had hired to go to Alaska to aid the presumably starving miners at Dawson were approaching Altenfjord with their personal possessions and their reindeer in one of the most severe storms of the nineteenth century.

Carl Sacariasen, along with his cousin Wilhelm Basi, accepted Kjellmann's offer to go with the herders and deer, but they stayed in their own village until the last possible moment, hoping that the storm would be over before they had to leave. They knew that the *Manitoban* would be at Alten by the time they got there, but they waited as long as they could. Originally, they had planned to go by way of the fjord and the sea to reach the liner, but they gave this up when the storm became more violent. They were able to persuade four acquaintances in their village to help them carry their gear over the low hills to Talvig, twenty-eight miles away, and on February 3, 1898, the six men started out.

Long before they reached the top of the mountain, exposed to the elements and struggling along the snow-clogged trail, one of the helpers complained of frostbitten nose and cheeks. The party divided, giving him and one of the helpers most of the food they were carrying to make sure they returned home safely, while Carl and the others pushed on, carrying the supplies of the two travelers trying to reach Alten.

Night is almost continuous in February in this region of the Arctic, and long before they reached Talvig it was dark. For more than four hours they carried their heavy packs through the darkness and the falling snow, stopping only to check each other's faces and ears for signs of frostbite. They knew they must reach Talvig that night, and did not stop either to eat or rest until they arrived. About eight in the evening they reached their overnight stop, tired and hungry, but safe.

Carl knew he could not spend too much time that night in bed, for the two men had to reach Alten before the ship sailed. Accordingly, early the next morning he looked for some way to ride the rest of the way. He found a party headed the way he wanted to go, and the men were able to ride to the seaport, taking their supplies with them without having to carry them on their backs.

They reached Alten about noon.[1] It was a fortunate thing that they did, for they met Kjellmann standing at the water's edge supervising loading of the vessel. He spoke to Carl and told him to get aboard at once, for the ship would be leaving that evening.

Carl did as he was told. He was shown to a bunk, and he stowed his clothing, luggage, and other supplies beneath it. As swiftly as possible he was ready to leave for North America where he was to spend the rest of his life! With the excitement of the impending voyage it seemed only a few moments until darkness fell, although it was still early afternoon. By nine that night he admitted that he was tired enough that when he went to bed he dropped off to sleep almost instantly. The date was Thursday, February 3.

While he was asleep trouble erupted. Some of the Lapps had been drinking too heavily at their farewell parties, and refused to go aboard the ship. Jackson summoned police who came through the village, routed the Lapps out and told them either to get aboard the ship or be put in jail for disturbing the peace. To Jackson's consternation, he found a cargo of four kegs of whiskey had arrived from Hammerfest to help his employees along with their farewell party. He asked the police to confiscate the whiskey, which they did, and eventually the Lapps came aboard. Sacariasen did not hear a thing.[2]

During the night they sailed out through the fjord, and by morning they were in the open ocean. When Carl awoke he went on deck and saw where they were. He went through the ship getting acquainted with his surroundings.

The *Manitoban* had three decks. The upper deck was not comfortable enough for the long voyage, in Carl's opinion, and he also believed that the sanitary arrangements where the deer were kept in their stalls would become a problem. How right he was! Jackson, Kjellmann, and Lieutenant DeVore had staterooms on the middle deck, if their quarters could be dignified by such a term. Below was a moderately sized room where many of the herders and their families were supposed to stay during bad weather, and where they were to sleep, cook and eat the rest of the time. It was so dark in this area, called the steerage, that many of the young Lapp children as well as some of their parents became frightened thinking about what lay in store for them. Their nervousness and fright, combined with the rocking of the ship, produced the normal result. Many of the passengers became violently seasick. This probably was the situation in most of the transatlantic ocean vessels of the 1890's, but Carl found the sounds and odors of vomit too much for him, and went out on the upper deck to sleep with the deer. The alternative was to sleep in the storage areas where baggage, moss, and other reindeer were kept.

Sacariasen grumbled about the presumably palatial quarters Jackson and the other two men had as compared with the miserable places the herders and their families were supposed to use, but the "staterooms" were no great delight either. In Jackson's personal diary he complained bitterly about what he found. His berth was damp from condensation of warm air against cold walls. One end of the mattress was soaked. Little pools of water were everywhere on the floor, formed by leaks in the ceiling coming from the deck above where the deer were kept. As the days went by, especially with snow and rain continuously falling, water seeping through the deer manure continuously dripped from the roof, until it was ankle deep in his room. The odor was terrible. Eventually a makeshift catwalk of planks was nailed together to enable him to walk from his door to his bunk with relatively dry feet, but not surprisingly he suffered a furious attack of rheumatism in his knee, which almost prevented him from walking at all.[3] One suspects that Kjellmann and DeVore had no better accommodations than he.

The first day out each herder was assigned one pen as his responsibility. He was to feed and care for the animals and clean them regularly. No one knew how long the voyage would last, for this was not a scheduled route, and actually it would be twenty-four days before they arrived in New York.

In the afternoon of that first day at sea the sickness of the passengers eased enough so that the ship's steward came below with small bottles of soda water to sell to the Norwegians and Lapps for about ten cents each, which many of the people bought. This was almost twice what a similar drink would have cost in their home towns. This was a small annoyance, but it was the second thing Carl found to complain about. He was to find many more.

Like that dismal Saturday, the following two days were just the same. A heavy sea pushed by a strong east wind made many passengers sick again. Over a hundred people trying to live and comfort one another in the small saloon were far too many. When lunch was served in the cramped quarters on Monday, Sacariasen was totally humiliated. He confessed that "I, who had never before been so disposed, had to give in too." He was as seasick as the rest.[4]

Fortunately, some of the Lapps had brought a small amount of preserved reindeer meat with them, which a few of them shared with the seasick Norwegians. Immediately, the familiar food made Carl feel better, but this sensation did not last long. The shipboard menu was not the kind of fare that he knew, and he did not like what he was eating. He called it "loathsome" and it probably was. As a professional cook himself, he complained that the men in charge of preparing the food didn't know their business.

As they passed between Iceland and the Faroe Islands they had one day of good weather. The sun came out, and the air seemed much warmer. The passengers recovered temporarily from their seasickness, and things looked much brighter. Some of the men went to the deck to sleep for the night, as a better place than the foul-smelling saloon which had not been cleaned from the filth that had accumulated during the previous day's storm.

Unfortunately, the one pleasant day was only a lull. The following morning the cyclonic storm hit them again from the opposite direction, blowing from the west this time. Since the *Manitoban* could only proceed at eight knots under the most favorable conditions, and frequently averaged only a quarter of that, the wind slowed them to about three and a half knots, while the waves broke over the middle deck and the reindeer stalls. To prevent accidents no one was supposed to go on deck, but some of the men stubbornly refused to obey orders, and went out anyway. The deer were neither fed nor watered nor cared for with regularity while the storm lasted.[5] It lasted for an entire week.

The crowded, poorly fed, sick and frightened passengers were in a state of deep depression. Some played cards, but in the living area foul with the stench of vomit, slippery to walk over while the ship was pitching so wildly, there was little to be cheerful about.

On Friday, about noon, a tremendous wave broke over the ship, smashing the davits of one of the lifeboats, and shattering some of the deck hardware of the ship herself. Torrents of snow and hail hammered the ship, and several of the animals had to be taken below to prevent them from being injured. One of the herders, Ole Stensfjeld, was almost swept overboard, for he had gone up to the deck in spite of the terrible storm. Stensfjeld came back to the saloon, badly frightened, but reported that he had been able to hang onto something solid, though the water had covered him totally, and even his head was wet. He spent the rest of the day trying to dry his clothes the best way he could.

The following morning, in spite of the continuing hurricane, a group of women announced that they were going on deck for a breath of fresh air, but just as they entered the companionway a wave sweeping over the water-soaked deck spilled cold ocean down the stairs onto them and they retreated in panic.

Their second Sunday aboard was no better. No one enjoyed eating while the ship tossed about, or breathing the foul air of the steerage, or thinking about the possibility that they might all be drowned. After dark that night another lifeboat was shattered by a huge wave, and several of the reindeer stalls were smashed, but fortunately they were empty of reindeer by this time.

The wet and miserable Jackson was still in bed trying to get his aches and pains under control so that he could go down to see what condition his herders were in. It is just as well that he didn't. As the storm continued, the wretched passengers began to care little about what happened. Carl believed that the ship's cook was making the food as unappetizing as possible out of sheer spite, and after a brief inspection tour of the galley he found the galley to be filthy. Probably if the seasick passengers had been hungry they would not have been so critical of the food, but with days and days of crowding, inadequate sleep, seasickness, boredom, and fright, it is a wonder that there was no violence aboard and that they took out their frustration only on the cook. Since no one had given more than the most minimal care to the deer, their excrement was deep along the edges of the deck, and people going outside for fresh air continuously tracked through it. Sacariasen noted that this included the cook, who had to go outside his galley to the ice-room, past the deer, consequently tracking considerable amounts of filth down the stairs, contributing to the general mess.

Eventually, Kjellmann came down to listen to their complaints. He promised to try to do something about better food and greater cleanliness, but there was little he could do until the storm let up. One desperate Lapp woman bathed her child in a soup kettle, and that ruined what little appetite Carl had remaining, for he did not believe the cook had ever washed the pots and pans and kettles.

For three days the ship made no progress at all, but stopped and headed into the wind. The interminable steerage card game, which was the main recreation of the men, came to a stop, and everyone sat with grim faces waiting for the end. Water streamed continuously across the deck, and those deer still in the deck pens were drenched for hours on end with no one able to do anything for them. One deer became so upset that he began to attack his stallmates, and in the ensuing fight he was badly injured. Eventually he was butchered as the result of injuries he suffered.[6] Surprisingly, however, the other deer withstood the buffeting and the drenching of the waves amazingly well, though standing for a week almost without food or water.

The Captain was heard by one of the passengers to say that in all of his twenty-five years' experience in ships crossing the Atlantic he had seen only one gale that was the equal of the one of February, 1898. To underline his comment, a wave broke the figurehead off the bow of the ship sometime during the afternoon. It was small comfort for the herders and their families, however, to know that if they were going to drown, at least it had been in a record-breaking hurricane!

When it became time to turn the lights down that night, the passengers realized that the crew were locking the doors and covering all of the air vents to the deck to prevent water from coming into the ship itself. During the night, however, the master of the ship noticed that the barometer was rapidly rising, and the Captain and other officers who had stayed on duty at the bridge almost without break for many hours went to their own quarters for some needed rest, leaving only the watch on the bridge. The passengers did not know this, and when Carl learned of it the following morning he surmised sourly that Captain Braes had surrendered the ship to the whims of the sea, and they might as well forget the whole thing!

The sun broke through that morning, however, the sea became calm, and the air was noticeably warmer. The navigator announced that the ship had made no headway at all for the better part of a week. With the coming of better weather, however, the *Manitoban* began to sail westward once more, though very slowly, for the ancient engines seemed always on the verge of giving up.

Everyone, including the members of the ship's crew, was so pleased to be able to go out on deck in the sunshine that their spirits improved dramatically. The complaints during the week of misery and terror disappeared in an aura of good feeling. By sundown, although no one wanted to go back down to his cramped and filthy quarters, walking around the deck became tiresome. William Kjellmann suggested that to help pass the time until they got to New York, the herders should make large bags to hold reindeer moss so that they could feed the animals while they crossed the United States on the railroad that had been ordered for their transportation.

All went well for the next four days. The ship was still barely crawling across the water, but it was moving toward New York. Sacariasen concentrated his complaints on the quality of the food--soup, beef, frozen potatoes, and sourdough biscuits--meal after meal. Things improved for him, however, when he found a new object for his dislike. Dr. Jackson had improved enough to walk around the deck himself. There he appeared dressed in a huge wolfskin coat, seemingly unconcerned with the peril and discomfort everyone else had suffered. Jackson had told no one of his own problems, and his employees assumed that his quarters were much better than their own. Carl charged in his diary that Jackson had tried to ingratiate himself with the Lapps by taking a tiny baby girl by the hand and walking with the child around the deck. This seemed to Sacariasen to have been a kind of cheap politician's trick.

The Captain ordered that sails should be added to the engines to give the decrepit *Manitoban* more speed, but to Carl's disgust--nearly everything disgusted him now--there were only two sails aboard, and they did not add appreciably to their speed.

On Sunday, the twentieth, Carl was in his bunk "about to take a little afternoon nap,"[7] when he and the other passengers suddenly realized that the ship was absolutely quiet. After having become accustomed to the steady vibration of the engines and the howling of the hurricane, the silence was stunning and almost as frightening as the crash of a loud explosion would have been. Several of the passengers rushed outside to find what had happened. One of the crew members told them that the engines had been stopped to allow the crew to oil and clean them after two weeks of continuous operation. Shortly afterward, one of the more excitable Lapps rushed down to the living quarters yelling that the machinery had exploded and was ruined. The women and children began to scream and cry in panic, and fled to the deck in order to climb into the lifeboats. The annoyed crew admitted that the engines had broken down, and it was more serious than a matter of oiling them, but it would be only a few minutes until the damage would be repaired and they could begin moving again. They vigorously denied that anything had exploded. After about an hour the blown gasket was replaced, and the *Manitoban* resumed its course toward New York.

On the following day Kjellmann told the restless passengers that since they were nearing New York they should begin filling out their customs and immigration declarations for inspection when they reached the harbor. This was certainly stretching the truth, for they were still nearly a thousand miles from the Statue of Liberty, but he needed to give them a psychological lift, and it worked. The people were tremendously cheered to think that soon they would be able to get off the ship.

Their troubles were not over. Fog enveloped the ship when night fell, and their sleep was disturbed by the fog-horn that blew almost continuously throughout the darkness. They were crossing the Newfoundland Banks, and when daylight came they could see nothing. The ship slowed even more than it had been traveling, so that again they were barely making headway. Since there was no schedule to keep no one seemed concerned that they had lost so much time, and the herders revived the marathon card game, and reverted to their old pastimes of complaining about the food, the general messiness of the decks where the deer were kept, and their crowded, unpleasant living area below decks.

Suddenly there was silence once more, as the engines stopped for the second time. This time the steam motor controlling the steering mechanism had broken in some way,[8] and once again they were dead in the water in the midst of an Atlantic sea lane and not able to see anything around them. This time it took about two hours to get the problem solved. Sacariasen noted that the entire vessel was covered with rust, and in some places there were holes in the iron sides of the ship. He wondered how the engines kept turning at all when everything was so loose in the engine room. Once, when he had gone down to look at them, he placed his hand on the moving machinery and it banged so hard in protest to his touch that he was afraid it had come loose.[9]

A few days later the Captain sent word that the herders should clean the deer pens thoroughly preparatory to landing. Carl felt very much put upon when he learned of this order, for he thought cleaning the ship was the job of the crew. Even though nothing in the contract he had signed said that he had to sweep manure overboard, he did it, complaining the entire time. He blamed Dr. Jackson for this new indignity, said he had abused his position and his mistreatment of the herders was disgusting. He suggested that perhaps Captain Braes had given Jackson a few dollars to allow the Captain to order the Norwegians to perform the nasty jobs.[10]

Jackson probably did not even know who Sacariasen was. He may have known that some of the Scandinavians disliked him, but he was so used to personal attacks by his enemies in Alaska that sour looks from the passengers on the *Manitoban* did not disturb either his equanimity nor his relations in subsequent contacts with them.

To the distress of the herders the fog continued, and the cautious Captain of the vessel continued to cruise very slowly through the mist. It took a full week from the time Kjellmann told them to get their baggage ready and to make out their customs declarations before they covered the thousand miles and actually sailed into New York harbor. One entire day of this time was so foggy that their only excitement came when they watched two steamships suddenly emerge from the whiteness, and as quickly disappear into what Carl could only asume was the west. At eight in the evening of February 26 they passed a lightship, though about one hundred miles from land, which cheered everyone. As Sacariasen wrote, "We all knew that nothing could be worse [than the *Manitoban*] no matter where we would go,"[11] and all were excited and delighted that they had reached America at last. They did not even complain when they learned that they had to stop in the New York harbor without going ashore while they stayed for a time in quarantine to find what diseases were aboard.

The passengers accepted the lifting of the fog as a good omen as they approached Long Island. At about ten in the morning, although there was a low bank of mist on the water, they could see a narrow dark strip of land with small hills and trees in the distance. From time to time they could see ships moving back and forth through the rapidly dissipating fog.

Around noon the pilot came on board to take them in to New York harbor, and as they sailed farther down Long Island Sound, in the gathering dusk they saw more and more lights along the coast. As they came into the harbor itself the entire waterfront of New York City seemed "like a sea of fire." Coming from Finnmark, with its sparse population and wide distances between settlements, it must have seemed to them that New York had almost everyone in the world concentrated there to greet them. The lights made a deep impression on everyone. They were amazed when a swarm of reporters came out the next day in a flotilla of small craft, and tried to come aboard to interview the Laplanders. Captain Braes, however, refused to let them aboard because of quarantine restrictions. Apparently the publicity in the press about the reindeer scheme that had been sent all over the country two months before brought a swarm of journalists out searching for a story.

Because Sheldon Jackson had been instructed to get to Alaska as soon as possible to save the miners from starvation, he urged DeVore to rush everyone through immigration and quarantine formalities as quickly as possible. Two trains for the people, relief supplies, and the deer were already waiting at the Pennsylvania Railroad cattle yards when they arrived, and as soon as the ship was cleared they could start west.

At this point the official connection of Dr. Jackson with the expedition was supposed to have come to an end. He left the ship and went to Washington to resume his denominational and educational duties, to make reports and prepare for a new trip to Siberia to buy more deer there. His position as organizer for the herders and deer to go to Dawson was now assumed by William Kjellmann.[12] Nominally the War Department was still in control of the project, and Lieutenant DeVore was temporarily in command, but he readily stepped aside for Kjellmann, who could speak the herders' language.

Alger was not comfortable receiving Jackson's report. He and everyone else knew by this time that there was no starvation at Dawson, and the War Department was being roundly criticized for wasting the taxpayers' money on the kind of scheme that the reindeer expedition represented. The Dawson expedition was certainly unusual, and now the Army had to face critics who denounced it as being inefficient or worse. By the time he received Jackson, however, the two trains had already reached Ohio, and there was no way to stop them, so Alger had to allow the trains to proceed.[13] The Secretary accordingly wired General H.C. Merriam at Vancouver Barracks in Washington State to keep two hundred deer for military purposes and to send the rest of the deer to Dawson to be butchered. The Dawson deer were to use the old Dalton cattle trail from Skagway.[14]

Later the War Department changed its instructions in order to land the deer at Haines.[15] Following this, officials in this department got involved in a wrangle with the Department of the Interior about who should pay expenses if the deer were not to be used for relief at Dawson, but as repayment for those deer taken to Point Barrow two months before.[16] The whole affair began to turn into a bureaucratic shambles.

Meanwhile, DeVore was carrying out his assigned responsibilities with commendable efficiency. Sacariasen did not know what was happening in Washington, but he was impressed by the bustling shoreline and the number of trains he saw "speeding away in all directions." He remarked on the tall buildings with smokestacks that he assumed to be factories. He noted with amazement that no one was using a rowboat anywhere on the harbor, but that all vessels, even the small craft, had steam power and they bustled over the water "whistling and tooting" so that people on board had to speak loudly to be heard over the din.

It is amusing that Carl found the Lapps comical because they seemed so awed by the sights and sounds around them. Obviously he was tremendously impressed himself.

When the immigration inspectors came aboard, Captain Braes raised the anchor and the *Manitoban* moved slowly toward the New Jersey wharves. Carl noted with a shock of recognition that one of the nearby ships was the steamer *Thingvalla*, which he had heard of, for not long before it had collided with a ship, the *Geyser*, off the Newfoundland banks with a heavy loss of life. He remembered a song of mourning that had been composed in Norway at the time of the disaster, for many of *Geyser's* passengers had been Norwegians returning to their homeland.

As the Statue of Liberty appeared, perched on its island about a mile beyond the ship, William Kjellmann came on deck to tell everyone about it. To give them a sense of its size, Kjellmann said that if a grown man could stand on Liberty's teeth he could not reach with his fingertips to the upper part of her cheek. He concluded his little talk with the statement that everyone coming into New York harbor from Europe who had passed the Statue was said to have reached "Freedom."

Kjellmann then turned and pointed to a twenty-two story building on Manhattan Island, one of the taller buildings on the skyline in 1898. Since many of the passengers had never seen anything taller than a two-story house, this created something of a sensation. They were equally impressed by Brooklyn Bridge when someone pointed it out to them.

As soon as the ship tied to the pier on the Jersey shore the deer were driven off. They must have been relieved as much as their human drivers were to get off the ship. Spectators alerted to their coming by the newspapers swarmed to the docks to watch the deer and the exotic visitors who came with them. The animals were docile and responsive to the commands of the drivers, therefore it was only a short while until all were eating contentedly in the stock cars that were waiting for them. Actually, in spite of Carl's grumbling, it appears from the vantage point of time that the logistics of the operation at the dock were quite good. The train was waiting for them when they arrived, there were passenger cars waiting for the people and they had been heated so that the herders and their families could board the train immediately.

Wilhelm Basi (Sacariasen's cousin), Jermias Abrahamsen, and Carl were assigned to one train as cooks, while Hilmar Hansen, Lauritz Stefansen, and John Losvar were on the second train. No one wanted anything to eat, for the excitement had temporarily destroyed their appetites. The cooks didn't want to begin work because of the new sights to be seen, and the swarms of curious people who had come to look at the strangers from Lapland. While some of the crowd could speak Norwegian, most of them knew none and yelled at the herders in English, which the folk on the train could not understand. Those who could communicate asked about the deer, and how many calves had been born on the voyage. Sacariasen thought them fools to ask such a question when the entire cargo consisted of gelded bucks! He assumed that the newspapers that brought the mob out should have informed the Americans about this fact as well.[17]

As night fell some of the men decided they should celebrate their arrival in the United States with some whiskey, which they called "Amerikanskt Brendevin." No sooner had someone suggested this than all trooped off to the nearest saloon. They seemed to have had no trouble communicating with the bartender. The result was entirely predictable, but not serious, for the celebrants "slept it off" and the sleeping quarters were reasonably quiet in consequence.

When they awoke in the morning they went outside to find to their delighted horror that the hundreds of visitors of the previous day had grown to "thousands." A force of policemen was now on the station platforms to help keep order, and they continuously pushed the hordes of spectators back. In turn, Kjellmann told his charges to stay near the trains for he feared that if anyone wandered off this day to get drunk he might become lost, and he would have to be left behind.

Carl noted that what seemed to attract the attention of the curious crowds was the costumes of the Lapps, consisting of a short deerskin coat, tight leggings, felt boots, a four-cornered cap, and a knife thrust prominently into a brightly colored sash. Even the children wore miniature replicas of the clothing worn by their parents.[18] The women wore much the same costume except that they wore lace and a tighter cap on their heads.

These were an attractive and colorful group of fair-skinned people. The citizens of New Jersey had never seen anything like them before. The visitors continued to try to talk to the herders and their families in English, but only Thoralf Kjelsberg and Jafet Lindeberg knew even a few words of that language, and they talked very little. The others could only shake their heads and smile when someone spoke to them.

Carl surmised that they were asking about the reindeer, Norway, and Lapland, but thoughtlessly he tried to speak to them in Norwegian, and it was the turn of the Americans to laugh and shake their heads. All in all it was a kind of picnic, and everyone enjoyed himself immensely.

The reindeer had already been divided into two groups and the people were ready to leave. Shortly after dark, about 6:30 in the evening according to Sacariasen's guess, the first train left the station as the crowds cheered wildly. The send-off they received made a vivid impression on them. Obviously the herders had never heard organized cheering at an athletic contest in America. Carl said he thought the din would blow the trains from the track. As the train picked up speed everyone crowded to the coach windows but could see very little in the dark. In addition, Jersey City was not as large in 1898 as it is now, and very soon they were in the open countryside. Half an hour later the second train followed them.

By Wednesday morning, March second, the train had crossed the better part of Pennsylvania, and stopped for a few minutes in Pittsburgh. As he filled his journal with his impressions, Carl noted the absence of snow in the mountains and wondered at it, for in Norway it was still winter at that time of year. He particularly liked the heavy growth of timber in the Pennsylvania Appalachians, for where he had been born trees are small and grow at considerable distances from each other. Where he could see the farm houses they were so much closer together than in his own land that he wasn't sure whether he was looking at the countryside or at a widely scattered American city.[19]

At Pittsburgh the news of their coming had preceded them, and again the railroad station was crowded with what Carl guessed were several thousand curious people. Since the trains did not have to stop frequently to take on passengers or to let people off, they made considerably better time than a normal passenger train would have done. This very fact made the members of the expedition eager to get off the train and look around. However, whenever anyone climbed down the coach steps he was likely to be beset by the friendly mob. Some spectators climbed on boxes to peep into the sleeping cars. Carl complained, without too much indignation, that the women of the United States were "nervy" and "forward." Some of them tried to seize articles of clothing, especially the Lapp caps with their long tassels. Others pushed calling cards into the hands of the men with their names and addresses printed on them, as much as to say "Don't forget me." Some even tried to cut locks of the blonde hair growing on the Scandinavian heads of the men. Sacariasen does not mention whether the Lapp girls were similarly besieged by the American men. Probably they remained timidly within the cars.

While the men were pleased to be the center of so much attention, they were also frustrated since only two of them understood any English. The American visitors referred to them all as "Laplanders," even though many were not. Somehow the people who were at almost every stopping point across the continent had the idea that Lapps were dark skinned--not the first nor the last time that isolationist Americans thought any immigrant from Europe was black or at least brown! In Carl's case, he let some of the girls hold the Lapp hat he was wearing, but firmly pulled it back again. He also showed them his white deerskin boots of a kind they had never seen. Since his young admirers could talk only English, he was unable to record in his journal what they said to him.

Even after dark, and after the deer people had gone to bed, crowds tried to climb up to look into cars, but Carl said "It was too dark to see anything."[20]

During the night the train crossed Ohio and Indiana. Early the next morning it reached Chicago. They were so early, however, that no one was at the station, nor would Kjellmann let anyone get off for fear they would be left behind. Since there was little going on at that time of morning the people stayed in their places, which was well, for in only a short time they left for Milwaukee.

Here it was a different story. Since they got there later in the morning, once again a large crowd was waiting to see them. These curiosity hunters had waited in the open since breakfast time, and it was cold along the lakeshore. Carl noted this in his diary that the faces of the children appeared to have turned blue. When the train began to move, a member of

37

the crew assured the people standing on the platform that the second section would be along in half an hour. Those watching from the train declared that apparently no one went home, but all continued to stand patiently for the next train to arrive, as though something about it might be different.

On Friday, the fourth, the expedition was on the Great Plains west of St. Paul. On the Minnesota and Dakota prairies, along the route of the Great Northern railroad, more and more of those on the station platforms during their infrequent stops were Norwegian-speaking. The Klondike gold strike was on people's minds, and some of the Norwegian-Americans taunted the herders with the charge that they were not going to Alaska to herd reindeer at all, but were using that only as an excuse to get free transportation to the gold camps. Inadvertently, they were quite correct. There is no doubt that the Dakotans envied those who were going to Alaska, however. They used the word "Klondike" so often that this is possibly the first English word that Carl learned.

As they passed through the North Dakota flatlands they saw country that resembled their own Norwegian landscape more than anything they had yet seen. The immense, treeless land, dropping away to the distant horizon, impressed them even more than the large cities like New York and Chicago had. Here, also, the farm houses were separated from each other by great distances, some of them by miles. Here again they heard mainly English spoken once more.

On Saturday the trains crossed one of the Sioux Indian reservations, the herders found that these people were just like the curious white people farther east. Indian and Lapp looked at one another with astonishment. The Indians had heard from somewhere that these immigrants were just like they were except in language, and they were obviously disappointed that all those on the train were just other white persons. The Lapps knew about the "red Indians" but found they were not red at all, but "sunburned." Each eyed the other's clothing. The colorful Lapp costumes were not at all what the Sioux had expected. To the Norwegians the dress of the Indians appeared drab, for they were wearing nothing more than a ragged bedquilt thrown around their shoulders. Only their dark, "rubber-colored" faces were visible above the garment.[21] Carl also noted that some of the men had painted their faces with red coloring in honor of their visitors who stopped momentarily at the railroad station.

The speed of the train amazed the herders. At one point someone reported that their speed had been over seventy miles an hour. This was not a continuous rate, of course, but even on the vast expanse of Montana the trains stopped only occasionally, and by Sunday they were in the Rocky Mountains.

Unlike the forests in Europe, the trees in the Montana mountains seemed to be very thick--"standing so close together that one could hardly see through the woods for a distance of twenty feet."[22] He judged the evergreens to be several hundred feet tall, which they were not, but they were certainly much taller than his native Norway pine. As the train traveled along the river south of what is today Glacier National Park, they passed through tunnel after tunnel, which made him comment in wonder at the length of them, and what he called "the darkness of the grave."

On the west side of Marias Pass they saw their first snow storm since their miserable days aboard the *Manitoban*. During that night they came out of Montana, crossed Idaho, and by the next afternoon they were climbing the Cascade Range through Stevens Pass.

Looking down the steep slope below the railroad grade they were awed at the distance to the bottom of the canyon. At that time there were switchbacks near the summit of the Pass, and Sacariasen commented on the strange sight of several other trains in plain view moving in the opposite direction from theirs, slowly climbing to the summit, and turning out at some convenient siding while the deer and herders went by. He did little cooking that day, for the scenery was so spectacular that all he wanted to do was look at it. Just as they reached the valley floor along the Tye River a rock rolling down the hillside flew under one of the coaches derailing it, and bringing the whole train to a sudden jolting stop. The train crew put the car back on the track with little damage done to anything, although the locomotive engineer skinned and bloodied his nose when the sudden stop bumped his face against the steel machinery in front of him.

Now in the lower valley leading into Everett the valleys stood warm and green in the early spring sunshine. Trees were beginning to bloom and the vivid contrast between the pink blossoms, green grass, and white mountains in the background to the east made a strong impression on everyone.

Carl did not comment on the lovely approach to Seattle along the shores of Puget Sound at sunset. Perhaps, as is so often the case at this time of year, there was no sunset to be seen and the gray Puget Sound mist kept him from even knowing there was a view to be seen from the railroad. Possibly he had seen so much water in the Norwegian fjords that he was not impressed.

What did impress him, however, was the long trestle just south of Ballard in North Seattle, where the train stopped to spend the night. This was located on what later became the Lake Washington ship canal, and just east of Magnolia Bluff was what is today called Interbay. Sacariasen had never seen anything like it and marveled at the length of the elevated track. While they were sleeping, the second section, which had never been far behind, caught up with them and also stopped on the trestle behind them. In the morning the feeling of suppressed excitement was obvious, for they knew this was their destination on the Pacific Coast, and soon they would be on their way to Alaska.

Instead of unloading directly onto the ship that would take them north, their train was switched to a different line and unloaded at an outlying Seattle suburb called Fremont. This was on the north end of Queen Anne Hill and across the small span bridge from Phinney Ridge. The animals were driven up the spine of the ridge to Woodland Park, which in 1898 was just what its name implied. At that time it was mainly untended grass and trees with little or no formal gardening. It dropped over the hill to Green Lake which would furnish plenty of fresh, clean water for the deer. There was a fence around the park, or at least enough area was fenced (possibly where the present zoo is located) that it served efficiently as a corral for the animals. There was also a large hotel located among the trees where the families could stay until the ship was ready to leave.

Carl himself took a vacation, for each family was supposed to be responsible for its own food while they were at the Woodland Hotel. Kjellmann temporarily released the six cooks from their duties. Some of the single Lapp men pitched tents in the pen along with the deer. The baled reindeer moss was piled on the ground, and the sacks they had filled aboard ship were sent to be stored until they needed it to feed the deer. This led to the first major error by the military command.

Major W.R. Abercrombie was sent by the War Department to assume official command of the expedition when it reached Seattle. He knew nothing about caring for deer, and he did not allow Kjellmann to tell him anything. Since there was grass in the Park he assumed the deer would eat it, and ordered that the herders take them outside the fence to graze. Unfortunately, reindeer did not eat grass, and since they scarcely knew what it was, they ate very little or none at all.[23] This would not have been as bad as it was, except that to add to the problem, Abercrombie had failed to charter a ship ready to go north immediately. This slip-shod bit of logistical failure, combined with the failure to take advice from anyone, enraged Kjellmann so much that he announced that he was quitting the whole operation. He did tell the Secretary of the Interior what a mess Abercrombie was making of the operation. In quick response, Secretary Bliss requested that Jackson stop what else he was doing, go to Seattle, and resume command and control of the operation, while Kjellmann "was standing aloof," as the report put it.[24] Nevertheless, for seven days everything came to a standstill in Seattle as far as going to Alaska was concerned, but not in Woodland Park!

As usual, news that the reindeer and Norwegians were in the Park brought hordes of visitors from downtown Seattle and nearby suburbs such as Ballard or Fremont. Since many Ballard inhabitants were themselves of Norwegian descent, the language barrier that had hampered conversation in the towns and cities farther east was no longer a problem. One of the men who seemed able to talk both Norwegian and Finnish, which the Lapps could also speak, was an expatriate and former neighbor of Sacariasen from Lapland named Hedly Redmyer.[25] He was also Kjellmann's cousin.

Redmyer had already been in America for twelve years, and had a good command of English, though he spoke it with a pronounced accent. He had once applied for a position in the Reindeer Service and Jackson hired him, assuming they could get the army out of the way, and asked whether he would like to go with the herders as interpreter for the expedition until they reached Dawson. Redmyer agreed to go and soon became a visible and highly valuable member of the group. He remained with them for well over

41

a year. While they were waiting for something to happen, the Lapps were given time off to visit downtown Seattle. The first thing they did when they got away from Kjellmann was to buy some liquor which they brought to the Park and consumed speedily. As the night went on their celebration grew in volume and enthusiasm. So many had their sleep disturbed that Kjellmann confined all of the participants to quarters the following night.

Sacariasen and Wilhelm Basi had not been part of the guilty contingent, nor had they participated in the party that followed. Since they were entirely sober they were given permission to go to the city by themselves the following evening. Seattle was a small city of about sixty-thousand permanent residents in 1898, and most of them lived on the hills above Elliott Bay and to the south of Queen Anne Hill. This small city was still surrounded by forest land on Capitol Hill, though these trees were rapidly being cut down to make room for the large homes being built by the more prosperous merchants. In far away Brooklyn there were four buildings deep in the woods that marked the site of the state university that had been moved from the center of Seattle. The Norwegian herders had neither knowledge nor concern for the university, however, and Carl did not mention it in any way during his days in Seattle.

Because they knew no English, Sacariasen and Basi asked Redmyer to go with them as spokesman, which he agreed to do. They walked down the hill from Woodland Park to Fremont where they boarded a streetcar for the city center. (It cost them 5 cents for transportation each way!) In the business section, composed of stone and brick buildings, some of which were five or six stories high, the three men tried to look at everything at once. They walked through department stores that seemed huge to the cousins. It seemed to them that everything for sale was designed for the Alaska trade-- sled dogs, pick axes, gold pans, bedding, warm clothing--everything a well-equipped prospector would need in the Yukon.

The streets and dock area were jammed with milling people. Carl guessed that there might have been 100,000 people in the few downtown blocks, but this was far more than the number that could possibly have been there. Nevertheless, the city was packed with transients trying to get tickets to the north.

When they grew tired of walking Redmyer found a Fremont car and after a while they were back in the familiar surroundings of Phinney Ridge, where a short hike took them back to Woodland Park.

On Friday those Lapps who swore repentance were once again given leave to go to town. While they were gone, more visitors came to the Park to picnic, hike, or gawk at the immigrants and the reindeer. Since there were many Swedes and Danes as well as Norwegians living in Seattle, and some of these could talk to the herders, everyone had a fine time. Carl lumped all those who could speak only English as a mongrel group he called simply, "other people."[26]

In the evening the "repentant" Lapps returned, and by the noise they made it became quickly evident that they had once again "fallen off the wagon." "Drunk and crazy," was Carl's diagnosis. One of the Lapps, Samuel Balto, the Arctic explorer, put on a marine cap and pinned a large star to his shirt. He walked around the camp, careful not to let any of the drunken men see his face and saying nothing to anyone. The drunken men were bleary-eyed enough not to be able to make out who he was, and others announced that he was a Seattle policeman who had come to quiet the celebration. The noise subsided as the herders tried to avoid arrest, and the camp got some sleep.

Saturday came and went. Not many visitors bothered them that day, and had Abercrombie been able to decide what to do, it might have been a good time to get something done toward shipping the reindeer, but he did nothing and another precious day was wasted. The deer were not properly fed, and no one knew what to do. The military seemed totally disorganized, and Kjellmann disappeared from sight for the time being.

Sunday was a wild day. *The Seattle Times* described it under the headline, "A Day For Reindeer And Dears That Reign." The newspaper reported that eight thousand picnickers came to Woodland Park to pry into the lives and habits of the strange people living with their strange animals. Carl complained that the "stylish ladies were a little too forward." They kissed the Lapp men until one youth seized one woman and kissed her in return. Everyone roared with laughter, and Sacariasen's sense of propriety was shocked that the girl herself laughed, utterly unembarrassed. Soon everyone was drinking again, and the Seattle people shared freely with the immigrants. Even the women and children drank, not only in the park, but in the nearby saloons. Obviously there were no Sunday closing hour, or "No One Admitted Under 21" signs posted in the wide-open city that Seattle was at the turn of the century. The *Times* claimed that the herders not only accepted "treats" but were also seen "filling their pockets and blouses with suspicious-looking bottles for future use."[27] Those who came from across the city became totally irresponsible, and fed the deer all kinds of indigestible food. As a result, twelve deer died in the park partly from eating the indigestible grass, and partly from what they had been fed by the mob. The *Times* complained that so many people crowded onto the streetcars that the overloaded electrical lines created a power shortage in other parts of Seattle.[28]

At long last a boat was ready to take them to Alaska. Even while he was speeding west, Jackson had started using whatever pressure he could to get the Army to do something about his expedition. Today we know how dreadfully incompetent the Army was at the time of the Spanish-American War.[29] The herders had a different image of American military efficiency, however, and they were shocked to discover the appalling blunders Abercrombie made.

Now Jackson was in Seattle. He wired the Secretary of the Interior that he had arrived, but there were no orders for him.[30] However, it did not take him long to get Kjellmann over his peeve, and back on the job with his customary efficiency. Carl dismissed both Abercrombie and DeVore succinctly by stating that neither knew "in or out about anything."[31] Jackson, who knew how to bluff, used his War Department appropriation to push ahead without worrying about ruffled feelings. He chartered a three-masted bark, the *Seminole*, to take the deer and the herders to Dyea, Alaska. He appeared in the Park, to the surprise of everyone, and told them what he had done and that they would be ready to leave immediately.

So many of the herders had hangovers from the afternoon spree that it took them the better part of a day to get back to normal. Meanwhile, several stock cars came to Fremont to transport the deer to the ship at the dock.

On Tuesday, the fifteenth of March, the men and the hungry deer left the park, walked to the railroad and went aboard. It took well over half a day before they could finish their job. While they were putting the last of the deer in the cars, one of the children in the hotel died.[32] Carl noted that he had been ill ever since they left Norway, but his condition may have been complicated by what he ate or drank during the saturnalia two days before.

By evening the deer were aboard the ship, four in a stall, and with Kjellmann's help, the loading was done efficiently and quickly.

The tiny ship was far too small to hold five hundred deer and all the people who were supposed to look after them. Because it was so small, most of the little bit of reindeer moss that had been saved back for the animals to eat after they reached Alaska was thrown away. Abercrombie loaded the ship with a few bales of hay which cows might have eaten, but deer could not. Neither Jackson nor Kjellmann saw what the officers had done.

Jackson did see that the overloaded ship would not accommodate all the women and children at the same time as the deer and the men. A quick exchange of telegrams resulted in the Brigadier-General at Fort Vancouver ordering the *Seminole* to stop at Fort Townsend in order to leave the women and children there,[33] along with any of the men who were ill. They would wait there until other transportation could be found to take them to the northern reindeer stations.

Jackson also changed Redmyer's assignment from that of interpreter to being in charge of the overland expedition to Dawson. In this way Kjellmann could return to his main assignment of teaching the Eskimo apprentices how to become self-sufficient. He was to go along to Alaska, however, until the deer could be started toward the Yukon valley.

During the night the *Seminole* was towed out into the Sound, and by morning it had arrived at the army post on the east side of the Olympic Peninsula. Those assigned to stay at the fort were taken ashore, and their baggage unloaded. This took more time. By mid-morning, however, the men remaining on board were told that they were headed for Haines instead of Dyea,[34] and that they would drive the deer over the mountains to the Klondike, either to be butchered for food or to act as a freight service inland to the miners. Once again the War Department was indecisive, though it had already directed Jackson and Kjellmann to drive 337 deer to Dawson, and the balance of the animals should be sent to pay for the deer borrowed for the relief of the whalers.[35]

45

When they resumed the trip north, the *Seminole* did not hoist its sails or start its engines. Instead, the tug *Sea Lion* continued to tow them out into the Strait of Juan de Fuca.

By noon the men were prowling about the ship to see how it compared with the *Manitoban* on which they had crossed the Atlantic. Since Sacariasen was a cook, he naturally went to the galley to see what the facilities were like that would be used to prepare food for the men and the ship's crew. To his horror he found the two men at the cooking range to be non-white. One man was black, and the other was of Japanese ancestry. One of the myths of white-black relations is that white prejudices against non-Caucasian people have been the result of careful indoctrination by parents and peers. But in Carl's case he probably had never seen a black man nor an Asian before he came to America, yet he was enraged at even the thought of two men of a different race cooking his meals. No one had taught him to dislike them. He just reacted emotionally to a different kind of human person from himself.

He peered into the two large kettles filled with stew, potatoes and meat simmering together--not an unusual combination in the United States. He didn't like the appearance of the food but more importantly, as he explained it in his own words:

> I could see only a little white in the Negro's eyes. Otherwise, he was so black that one could not tell when his skin was clean or dirty. There was essentially no difference in the two cooks, since they were both so dark.[56]

He complained about the dark skins of the cooks throughout the entire trip to Haines Mission.

There were several good things about the ship in his mind, however. One was that they were using the "Inside Passage" to Alaska which was much smoother than the Atlantic had been, and they had neither heavy storms nor high seas. As they worked their way between Vancouver Island and the British Columbia mainland they were sailing against the tide, and during those hours their speed did not exceed five knots. As Carl noted dryly, "they had a great deal of time to watch the beauties of nature along the forest-covered shore." Just the same, this was faster than the old *Manitoban* had moved for many days on their voyage to New York, and it was a pleasant trip as compared with the February voyage.

The following day the complaints of the herders that they didn't like the appearance of the cooks showed that Sacariasen was not the only man who had prejudices against non-whites. The long-suffering Kjellmann once more had to intervene, and he suggested tactfully that if two of the Norwegians were detailed to work with the cooks the men would know that the food was prepared carefully. This seemed like an intelligent move to the men, and the Superintendent assigned Wilhelm Basi and Jermias Abrahamsen to help the cooks, although Carl remarked sourly that the added help made no marked change in the poor service. Obviously he didn't want to be appeased.

A strong north wind blowing across their bow through Johnstone Strait stopped the *Sea Lion* on Saturday, the 19th, which naturally stopped the *Seminole* as well. They took refuge in a sheltered bay to wait until the wind died down. This came about after only one day, so on they went. No visible human inhabitants or signs of recent habitation could be seen from the ship, but rather mile after mile of beaches and driftwood, sand and surf. Overhead were scudding clouds from some kind of weather disturbance in the Gulf of Alaska. In his journal Carl noted the increasing crispness of the air as they approached the 55th parallel, as well as the greater snow cover on the coastal mountains.

On Monday, four days after leaving Seattle, the *Seminole* and the tug that was towing it reached the open water of Queen Charlotte Sound. The wind had now died to the point that no one became seasick as sometimes happens in these waters. After their Atlantic experience, this bit of the Pacific seemed quite mild. After only a few hours, the ships once more entered a passage between islands, and in a few instances the passengers noted with delight that one could almost jump ashore on either side. Soon the weather became warmer and a light rain began to fall.

On Thursday the rain turned to snow, and a heavy fog obscured their passage. The masters of the two vessels decided to anchor in shelter once more until they could see where they were going. On Friday, the 24th, visibility improved and as they crossed the open water at Dixon Entrance it was another beautiful day. Before nightfall they had left Canadian waters and stopped to clear Alaskan customs.

That night the herders, though cold sober, reverted to childishness and broke into the supply room to steal a pail of butter. Their excuse was that "the big fat supply officer" and the two dark-skinned cooks rationed them so closely on butter than they were underfed. They now actually had too much butter, so they fed the remainder to the Lapp dogs. The delighted pranksters recorded that neither the supply officer nor the cooks even noticed that a pail was gone.

While they were enjoying their private joke a steamship sailing under its own power passed the sailing vessel and its tugboat power. It was the *Queen*. The men on board recognized the stubby figure of Dr. Jackson on the bridge waving to them, and though Carl had never liked him from their first contact, he admitted that it was good to see him again. At Kjellmann's suggestion the herders on deck gathered closely together and gave a unison cheer directed toward Jackson. The other passengers on the *Queen* did not know whom the men were cheering for, and they responded with loud shouts in response as the swifter *Queen* passed the *Seminole* and soon left it behind.[37]

After Jackson had left the herders at Port Townsend he had been ordered to go to Vancouver Barracks to consult with General Merriam. He spent the night on the train to Portland, met the General at 9 a.m., and by 5 that evening was back to Seattle. Merriam told him that they had changed their minds about what to do. Two hundred deer and 25 drivers were to stay with the War Department. One hundred deer were to be taken to Circle City. One hundred were to be saved back for a small mail service that was planned by P.C. Richardson to carry letters between St. Michael on the Bering seacoast, and Dawson.[38] Any other deer could be used to replenish the herds from which animals had been taken for the relief of the whalers. Jackson started for Haines immediately, accompanied by a Captain Robinson, in order to relay the new orders to Kjellmann and Redmyer when they got there.

He need not have hurried. The next day another snowstorm blotted out the passage between the islands, and the *Sea Lion's* captain decided they had better stop again until better weather allowed them to move. As frequently happens in these northern waters at this time of year, after only one day the good weather returned, calm and sunny, vindicating the judgment of the officer. They were at the entrance of Lynn Canal, and it was no problem entering into this splendid fjord.

By four in the afternoon they had anchored offshore from Haines, which was where the War Department finally decided to start them for their various assignments.

Haines was an Indian winter town, where Jackson had established a Presbyterian mission a decade earlier, and it was also an outpost of the United States Army. Each of the three groups had quarters especially designed for its particular needs. The herders noted the flat peninsula coming down from the mountains in the background, and the three-foot depth of snow on the ground. They saw that most of the soldiers were living in white tents on the beach. Farther to the west, at the base of the mountains, were the huts of the Tlingit Indians who stayed here until they could move inland to the mountain valleys. Between the Indian village and the army camp was a large red building which was the mission school. Next to it was another wooden structure used as the mission headquarters, and a small hotel to accommodate overnight travelers. Behind it was a large barn.

Although Merriam had sent orders to the commanding officer at Dyea to have barges and tents waiting at Haines for the men and animals, there was nothing there when they arrived.

Characteristically, Kjellmann set about to remedy the situation, and he induced Captain Bernard of the Haines post to go from Haines to Dyea to bring barges to unload the deer. The commanding officer at Dyea professed astonishment at the request, saying that not only did he not know they were coming, but that he had received no orders of any kind to furnish anybody with anything. Considering the inefficiency of the army at that time, it is possible that he was correct. In any event the barges did arrive after another day's delay and the deer were taken ashore.[39] When Kjellmann saw that everything was safely ashore he put four men on guard in shifts to protect the deer around the clock against attacks by the dogs in the Indian camp. These deer had been dehorned in Norway and their natural protection was gone, so they had to be protected by the herders.

49

To Kjellmann's consternation he learned that all of the reindeer moss had been used on the leisurely trip north, and now what was left for feed was the bales of alfalfa that Abercrombie had put on the ship. It was Monday, the 28th of March. The long drive to Dawson had not even begun, and already they were out of digestible feed for the deer.

Immediately the resourceful Kjellmann sent four men under the command of Redmyer, though nominally commanded by an army officer who insisted that he was in charge, to climb the mountains of the Indian village to try to gather enough moss to keep the animals alive. Thus far, the reindeer had proved amazingly healthy. Only seventeen of the original 538 deer had died since they left Norway on February 2, and most of these had perished as a result of junkfood that had been fed to them by the Seattle visitors in Woodland Park. Five hundred and twenty-one deer were taken ashore at Haines.

Their luck ran out that same night. Delays caused by weather and the inability of the army officers to make quick decisions finally caught up with them, for on the 29th of March the spring thaw began. There was no way to take the animals over the river ice to the head of the Thleheena, a tributary of the Chilkat River, which they had planned to use to get to Dawson.[40] In the mountains along the rivers there was plenty of food for the deer, but they were not in the mountains. The local army commander could think of nothing to do about the disaster, and referred the matter to his superior officer at Dyea. That person quickly decided to do nothing. He sent word to Kjellmann that he was to hold the deer where they were until someone could tell him what to do.[41]

The herders were brought ashore from the *Seminole* to wait for action from Dyea, and placed in the barn near the mission. Carl had seen the small guest house, and hoped that they would be allowed to occupy that, but how he expected to get several dozen men into that small building he did not say. General Merriam had sent word to Alaska to provide the herders with tents as well as barges to unload the *Seminole*, but since the authorities denied ever receiving such orders, nothing was ready. When Kjellmann showed the men where they were to wait until tents arrived, Sacariasen was enraged once more by the injustice of life. He wrote of his resentment at being quartered with cows and horses, but did realize that it could have been worse, for they might have been compelled to sleep in the open with no tents provided.

The shed used as a mess hall was almost half a mile distant from the barn, and was so tiny that a stove didn't fit inside. Accordingly, the black cook from the ship had to prepare meals out of doors. Carl continued to show his distaste for the hike between their barn and the cook-shack, which he took out by fuming over the inefficiency and the "ugly" features of the cook. Truly he was not in a happy mood, and neither were many of the other herders.

As the thaw continued, the warmer weather brought torrents of rain. The reindeer had to stand in the open inside a pen without adequate food. Some baled hay was thrown over the fence, but it was so bad that even the cows refused to eat it. The reindeer didn't even know what it was, so let it lie on the ground while they went hungry.

The rain lasted for the next nine days. It is easy to understand that in conditions like these the weaker deer began to get sick, and on March 31 the first of them was found dead in the stockade. Since no further orders came from the military, the men and animals remained in forced inaction. At least the men could leave the barn, but there was very little for them to do while they waited.

Carl went to the river and watched the Indians maneuvering their dugout canoes in the rushing stream, commenting about the skill the Indians showed as they paddled "the long white boats built out of whole trees without boards or nails, but simply carved out of the timber."[42] He had never seen anything like the fishing gear the native peoples were using. He described it as being made mostly of wood at the end of which were fastened a number of three-inch nails. He commented also on the carved decoration on the fishing poles, which appeared to him to be stylized fishlike figures. With this type of equipment the Indians were able to snag large halibut which ended in their cooking fires.

Since the men had nothing to do at night but guard the miserable deer from marauding dogs, and four armed men could do that, they decided the only excitement available was a prayer meeting the missionary was conducting for the Indians at the parsonage. Since he preached in English, which most of them could not understand, they listened politely but obviously without any personal benefit from his efforts. The Norwegians were as handicapped as the Indians, for they understood no English either. However, the Indians received a translation paraphrased by a young Indian girl who had learned a little English at the mission school. Since he was young, Sacariasen grumblingly admitted that he was favorably impressed by the pleasant good looks of the Indian translator. He got nothing from the sermon, however.

The Norwegians woke from their beds in the haymow the next morning and were thunderstruck when they saw the missionary approaching the barn with a pail in his hand. They were even more amazed when they watched him seat himself beside a cow and begin to milk her. In Norway "parsons" did not do menial tasks of this sort, but had servants to wait on them. Instead of approving, they felt an uneasy sense of culture shock at this apparent breach of decorum.

Dr. Jackson was still in Alaska and he visited Haines to find how things were going. Since nothing was happening and deer were beginning to die, in his characteristic manner he announced plans to return to Port Townsend, bring the women and children to one of the missions on the Bering Coast, and move the deer to Circle City down the Yukon River and to leave the ones needed for Dawson. It was evident that the famine in Dawson had not happened, but he was still under orders to distribute the animals to various agencies in the Interior of Alaska, even if they were not to be used for food. He told the herders, with Kjellmann's help as interpreter, how pleased he was with them and with what they had done. Then he turned to the Indians who had also gathered at the mission where his remarks were translated by the attractive young interpreter Carl had noticed on the previous evening. At the end of his remarks, he invited the Norwegians to sing a song in Norwegian, which they were pleased to do. They sang a hymn that they all knew, "Hvor salig er den lille flok," which may be freely translated, "How Blessed is the Little Flock."[43]

The young Indian girl and the Tlingit children then sang a song in their own language, and Carl noted with approval that she had an "especially good singing voice." After the Indians were done Dr. Jackson closed the meeting with a short prayer, and they all hiked back to the drafty barn for a night's rest.

In a few days the men detailed to climb the nearby hills to find moss returned without any food at all. Immediately Jackson and Kjellmann started another group of herders to look for food farther away, to be able to take the deer to the food, since it was evident that none was forthcoming from anything the supply officers of the army had to offer. The two men in charge were Hedley Redmyer and Jafet Lindeberg. They did find food, but it was well over fifty miles away from Haines, a distance much too far for hungry and weakened reindeer to walk without losing many of them.

Jafet Lindeberg has not played a consequential role in Sacariasen's diary to this point. Wilhelm Basi had mentioned him in his own diary, and described him as a huge man, six feet four inches tall, a natural leader, and the only member of the expedition with any personal finances. More and more as time passed he emerged as the strongest person that Kjellmann had brought from Finnmark. Because Kjellmann had heard that some member of his family was ill in Wisconsin he asked to be relieved of his duties as soon as possible, but until Lindeberg or someone else was able to take over he agreed to stay for a time. His own health was not too good, but he stuck to his assignment, and without him there is little doubt that it would have been a complete fiasco.

While Lindeberg and Redmyer were gone the men set out to amuse themselves in other ways. They took up a collection among themselves on April Fools' Day, and after they had raised 36 ore they bought a bottle of whiskey, which they donated to the cook. It did not take him long to become drunk, and then they offered the balance of the funds they had collected to anyone who would kiss the black man. A young Lapp boy, Klemmet Nilsen from Karasjok, agreed to do this if they would pay him. He was rewarded with the money. Carl asserted that *none* of the Norwegians would have done such a dreadful deed, even if someone had offered a reward of ten American dollars!

Another day went by. Still no decisions were reached in Dyea, and more and more deer weakened and lay down on the wet ground, still alive but unless help came soon they would not be living very long.

That night Jackson sent word to the barn that the men were to come once more to the mission house where he would talk to them. Again Kjellmann acted as interpreter. Faithfully, Sacariasen recorded what he had heard which was a kind of sermon-pep talk. Jackson's remarks contained admonitions to lead God-fearing lives, and coupled this theme with the idea that most white men there were a disreputable lot. The natives of Alaska, where they would be living for the next months, needed examples they could look up to, and it was the task of the herders to show what Christianity and civilization was like. He told the men he was returning to Seattle.

In only a little more than a month the General Assembly of the Presbyterian Church was holding its annual meeting, and as the chief officer of this religious body, Jackson was expected to preside. He had been involved with so many activities during the year of his serving the church that he was able to do very little in this role. Now he had to put on his ecclesiastical hat for a few weeks.

Sacariasen did not know about this, but reverted to his normal opinion of Jackson, complaining that he was deserting them when things looked blackest because he wanted to enjoy himself in Seattle. He did not know, either, that Jackson's efforts to move everyone from Haines and Port Townsend to the Unalakleet River on the Bering Sea had finally been approved, or that the Army had at long last told him they would approve moving the deer to the reindeer moss if Redmyer and Lindeberg and their companions were able to find some.[44]

On Sunday, April third, things changed for the better. The post at Dyea finally issued protective clothing for them--boots, coats, rubber hats, and other covering for their constantly wet clothing. They had no tents yet, but at least they could keep warm and moderately dry during the constant drenching from the rain. Lindeberg returned this day also, claiming that the men had traveled almost one hundred miles before they found a good patch of moss. However, there was a small patch on a hillside about twelve miles from the mission that they could use during the emergency, and then they could start the animals toward better supplies.

By now, however, the deer had been eating only inadequate food for seventeen days. Nevertheless, during the next two days the herders were instructed to put packs on the animals and start for the mountains. What would have been easy for them a few days earlier was now impossible. The Chilkat River was broad at Haines, and the herders finally got some of the weakened beasts on the trail to the river, but some simply lay down and died, and others stopped even trying to eat the wilted rotten grass that the thaw had uncovered, for there was no nourishment in it for them.

Kjellmann saw at once what was happening. He directed several men to stay with the herd, to try to get the living animals on their feet, and to protect them from predators. The rest he directed to go upstream to gather moss to bring to the valley where perhaps the deer could be fed. It was easy to see that there was not a single deer that was strong enough to carry a pack, so they were unloaded and the men divided their supplies into twenty-five pound packs to help them get to the moss that Redmyer and Lindeberg had found.

This was not a simple task. It was exhausting and slow. The men were divided into groups, and they dragged loads on Lapp sleds that were not designed to be dragged on bare ground. Others started hiking along the river carrying enough equipment to allow them to survive, but little more. Kjellmann hired several Indians to carry other gear upstream in canoes, and detailed some of the herders to meet the natives at the river's edge to load the craft. Everything depended on the men who traveled without heavy loads moving as rapidly as possible to get the moss back in time. Unless some of the deer could regain their strength, the expedition was at an end. Even the army officers saw that there was no chance of using the animals for carrying freight.

On Good Friday Kjellmann had twelve of the men at the river's edge before two o'clock in the morning. He thought that the change in tide would aid the Indians in getting a good start before they were slowed by the current. The Indians felt no sense of urgency, however, and sent word that they did not plan to start work before noon. Accordingly, the miserable herders waited for nearly ten hours in the rain beside the river, huddled around a large fire built among the trees, which kept them marginally warm, but without any other comfort. Their breakfast was coffee, and their lunch consisted of four pounds of meat divided twelve ways, and some crackers. While these twelve ate the uninspiring lunch, Carl, who was with them, boiled some water in a tin can and made coffee once more. Their regular coffee pot was packed in the loads waiting for the Indians, and he did not want to unpack to find it.

Finally the Indians arrived when they said they would. In only a few minutes the herders loaded the largest canoe with seven hundred pounds of food, tents, and camping equipment to help them get to the Yukon. Similar, but smaller amounts were packed into the smaller canoes. The Indians, aided by four of the herders, started upstream without benefit of the tide, towing and poling the canoes. The rest of the drivers not involved in protecting the herd were sent upstream carrying packs on their backs. Because it was still raining Kjellmann told everyone to put on his rain clothes.

He led by example. He scrambled over the most hazardous cliffs and ledges, and forced his way through the dense underbrush with the other men following closely behind him. From time to time they would walk into a marshy spot, which they had either to cross or make a wide detour to avoid. If any one of the men dropped behind to rest the others plodding slowly along soon lost sight of him because of poor visibility along the river bank. So the day passed. Since the nights were still long and darkness came early they were forced to make camp to avoid an accident in the darkness along the unknown trail. No one had had much to eat for the entire day, and all were exhausted from their strenuous scrambling through the forest. They were thoroughly depressed. Some men complained of thorns in their hands, others had ripped their protective clothing and were wet, and some had nasty scratches on their cheeks from whipping brush they had pushed through. Some had fallen in the muddy spots, and they complained of muscle strains, though no one had broken bones, or even sprained an ankle.

Those with the Indian boatmen were no better off, for the Chilkat River was so shallow in places at that time of year that the loaded canoes would get stuck on gravel bars, and the men would have to jump out, push or pull the dugouts over the obstruction, and try to keep dry. Once or twice a canoe had to be partially unloaded to allow the men to lift the barges over a log or other more serious obstruction. On the other side of the barrier everything would have to be put back while the men stood knee deep or even up to their hips in cold water. It took them most of the afternoon to go only ten miles. Both groups camped near each other.

In Sacariasen's party their demands for coffee were so urgent that he did unpack the cooking utensils and get out the coffee pot. For a more substantial meal he got some pork out of another load and boiled it, then added flour and salt to the mixture to make a kind of unappetizing soup or gravy. Since soup and coffee were the entire menu, after their skimpy meal the men curled up to try to get some rest. Most of them had been awake for almost twenty hours, and still had many miles of packing and hiking to go. Kjellmann shared the primitive camp with his men. Now, however, he became the next object of Carl's suspicious nature. For the first time he began to have second thoughts about Kjellmann. He could not see what the supervisor had to gain by sharing hardships with his men. While he acknowledged that his leadership had been superb, he surmised that he did what he did only to assure himself of a better government appointment when the expedition was over![45]

Early the following morning they resumed their way upstream, but the route seemed worse than it had been the day before. The canoe carrying the food became separated from the hikers, and for the second day they ate little or nothing. There was plenty of water, however!

The canyon grew ever narrower, and the mountains now came down to the edge of the river in the form of sheer cliffs. Whenever this happened the packers were forced into the river itself and had to wade in the shallows along the banks. To keep their clothes as dry as possible, they would undress partially, taking off their boots and pants, then dress again when they reached a place where they could walk along the shore of the stream. Men slipped on the rocks and to their supreme discomfort their boots filled with water. Jermias Abrahamsen thought of putting dry grass in his boots, but the little that was available did not help.

The previous night they had learned that there was an Indian village only a few miles beyond their camping place, where they could find shelter and buy some food. It took until four in the afternoon before they covered the fifteen miles that brought them to the Indian town. The best that the herders could make out was that the place was called "Klokwong." This appears on modern maps as Klukwan, so they were not very far off. The efficient Kjellmann got the Indians to loan them two houses where the men could dry their clothes and remain under a roof for the night.

About an hour after they arrived the canoes with their food reached the town also, and the cooks started immediately to get a meal for the famished party. This time Carl cooked hotcakes in addition to the pork and flour soup and coffee. This was not a very well balanced meal, but to the hungry crew it probably tasted like a Roman banquet. That night Carl cooked for the Lapps, Jermias Abrahamsen cooked for the Norwegians, and John Losvar waited to cook for those coming from Haines with deer if anyone got there. They did not because the deer refused to move from the woods along the river where they had been left two days before.

Now, with a meal under their belts, the men could take notice of less important things about their housing. First, Carl wrote of Indian building design:

> They were built of some sort of planks or wide thick boards held together with ropes made of twisted roots in place of nails. The roof rested on poles, and on the ridgepole along the center. In the center of the roof was a hole for the smoke to escape from the fireplace in the middle of the floor. In the inner wall, in each corner, stood a great carved housepost of wood, painted in several colors. On a platform behind the images were piled chests of all descriptions and colors, old and new.[46]

One man lifted the lid from a chest in the room and to his horror found that he was looking at the badly decomposed corpse of a human being. He quickly slammed the lid down, and they realized that they had been quartered in an Indian mausoleum. They sat in gloomy silence, now highly conscious of the odor of carrion.

Before they went to sleep they were visited by some of the local Indians. They were especially interested in the Lapp caps, and tried to indicate their willingness to buy the knives the men had stuck in their belts.

Easter Sunday in the gloomy charnel house was a day of rest, and they needed it. There was no one there who could conduct a religious service, and no one really cared. Instead, Jafet Lindeberg persuaded some of the Indians to stage a dance in honor of their visit. Whether they wore their ceremonial costumes or not Sacariasen did not say. He was no anthropologist, and moreover he carried his antipathy toward blacks and orientals over to the Indians. No Edward Curtis or Ruth Benedict he! Instead, he described their dancing as "horrible as they twisted and bent their bodies in all directions while rolling their eyes and singing in a manner terrible to hear." He had a bad case of culture shock, indeed!

Now it was the turn of the Norwegians to show their hosts how they danced. Lindeberg and Ole Rapp went through the steps of a Norse dance similar to a schottishe, called a "ringlender."

After the dancing was over and the Indians and whites had gone their separate ways the homesick herders decided this was quite the worst Easter Sunday celebration that they had ever spent anywhere. It dragged as though it had been ten days long, Carl noted.

On Monday morning they left Klukwan, and worked their way along the river until eventually they reached a spot they estimated to be fifty-two miles beyond Haines. Here they established a base camp at the foot of the mountain where Lindeberg had found the moss, and left the packs and equipment beside the river. Fifteen men stayed to carry the packs up the mountain, while the others went with the Indians back to the mission. They could then tell the herders that everything was ready if they could get any deer up to the food. The men would have to pull reindeer sleds for there was no possibility that the animals would have energy enough to pull them. After only a few hours the lightened canoes were back to Haines, and the men who had returned were once more in their dismal barn, which looked good to them after the house in Klukwan, or camping in the open.

Now, at last, they were ready to try to get the deer to follow the trail they had broken. It had been so many days since the animals had had the right kind of nourishment that it seems almost a miracle that any were alive at all. Kjellmann, who had returned with Carl and the others, sent a message to those staying with the deer on the little peninsula at the river's mouth, to start the animals upstream on Tuesday. The herders there were glad to start, for their only shelter had been an Indian shack in such deplorable condition that the roof had leaked badly. To keep dry the men had used their wet coats and rain slickers to cover themselves, but whenever the wind blew, which was frequently, it howled through cracks in the walls, thoroughly chilling everyone inside. Two of the men had caught bad colds as a result of their exposure during the week of waiting.

For breakfast Kjellmann sent five men with food to the spot where the herders were gathering the deer for the drive upstream. Since they planned to leave at once, these herders had packed all their gear as soon as they got up, preparing to send it by canoe to the camp fifty miles away. They had not had time to eat, and when Carl arrived with the food and set about cooking it he guessed by their actions that the men were hungry enough to eat him! He and John Losvar prepared the usual meal of hotcakes, soup, and coffee. Everyone was on such short rations by this time that the men did not complain about the quality of the food, only that they had not had enough. They must have had good appetites, however, to make such a complaint, for Sacariasen cooked enough to give each man ten pancakes to take with him for lunch, as well as a small piece of salt pork to gnaw on during the morning.

By April 15, they had found three hundred animals, but the rest of the deer refused to leave the scanty food they had found on the spit and stampeded over the whole forest, a woods about twenty miles long and several miles wide. The men knew the starving animals would not get far, so they went out into the forest to find the others and try to get them moving toward the main herd. The wet brush and soggy snow hampered them, and even though the Lapps picked up some deer and carried them bodily into the camp they lost another day waiting for the others. The stragglers were driven along, two or three from one place, and even small herds of a dozen or more located a few yards beyond. Otto Greiner, Peder Johannesen, and Samuel Josefsen, all from Lakselv, were the most successful, bringing in a "sizable herd."

That night, as they reached Haines, several men from the barn came out to work with them to get past the village where there were many dogs that might attack the weakened herd. Ten men were still on the spit looking for lost deer, including Jafet Lindeberg. He had become visible enough that he was put in charge of this final sweep looking for living deer, and told to come on with whatever he could find and leave the rest. He could search for only another twenty-four hours, Kjellmann said, then he must go upstream.

It took most of those twenty-four hours to get the animals the eight miles to the river bank and the mission. Their progress was painfully slow, and the drivers picked the narrowest spot in the river they could find to swim them across. At Haines itself the Chilkat River is very wide, being more an inlet of the sea than a flowing stream. But as slowly as they moved, they still had to abandon some exhausted reindeer, for to wait would have ended any chance of getting the rest to food and safety. By nightfall of the following day Lindeberg had about fifty animals still alive, and had lost about the same number during the eight mile drive.

Although the river was only about a hundred yards wide at the narrow point they had chosen to have them swim, a number of the deer had been too weak to hold their heads out of the water even for this short distance and had drowned. If the herd had been in good condition this would have been scarcely good exercise for them. After driving them only seven miles every deer had fallen down, and there was no point in trying to go farther that day. "Neither dog, nor man, nor anything else would have been able to move them another step."[47] As far back as the men could see there were dead or sleeping reindeer. Before dark some had rested enough to awaken and join the main herd, but those farthest back died where they lay.

The next day, the herders climbed the nearby hill where Redmyer had found the small patch of moss near Haines. They picked up handfuls of the gray and unappetizing appearing stuff that was life itself to the deer. Each man gathered a small armload of food and took it back to the living animals, putting it in their mouths. When the deer felt a little better from the good food they got to their feet and browsed on the marsh grass, but it had such low nutritional value that it did little good. The men watching them felt almost as hungry as the deer, for all they had to eat that day was one bowl of the usual flour and pork soup.

Kjellmann went back to the mission to get some more food, and the men spent the next day scrambling over the hillside trying to scrape enough moss from the rocks to distribute to the deer. This time they had sacks that they stuffed full of nourishment, and those animals strong enough to stand, ate it and improved at once. The herders pushed them upstream another five miles so that Kjellmann could easily find them when he returned.

Another day went by, and Kjellmann had not come with the food. The men tied each deer to a bush or small tree, allowing it enough rope to graze on the sprouting grass. Almost no one stayed with them, but for the third day everyone combed the woods looking for moss. The supply had not been great at any time, and by now almost all of it had been gathered, so they were able to bring back only about a mouthful apiece for each animal, but the deer devoured the food greedily.

No Kjellmann. No dinner. Their rations were entirely gone, and for breakfast and lunch they had eaten only the last of the terrible soup, lacking flavor and like the grass the deer tried to eat, almost without nourishment. When darkness came they sat around their campfires, watching the river intently. From time to time someone would shout, "There he is!" only to find it was an illusion. Later, well after eleven o'clock, the watchman's cry proved to be true, and even though it was close to midnight by the time Carl had food ready, the men gathered closely to watch him work. The diet of soup, hotcakes and coffee was the usual poor fare, but to the glittering eyes of the ravenous herders it looked good. They ate their fill, and their dispositions improved markedly. They were then able to sleep in some comfort on beds of pine and spruce boughs. Their roof was described as having an "open skylight."

Each day the deer traveled a little farther up the river, but since there was no more moss and the grass was not satisfactory, accordingly each day a few more died. By Thursday they finally reached Klukwan where they had to rest the deer again, for they were barely now able to stagger only a few steps at a time. There wasn't even grass in the Indian village. The men themselves needed rest, for some of them had almost carried deer along. Two men went on to the main camp at Rainy Hollow to try to bring back some of the herders who were waiting there. Kjellmann gave the others a day to rest, and planned to have fresh herders relieve them so that they could regain their own strength. This plan was a good one, for the new herders took over the deer while the weary men who had come up from the river's mouth returned to get their own belongings. These had been piled on the Lapp sleds, boatlike contrivances known as "pulks" or "pulkas." Normally these would have been hauled by the deer, but none was capable of pulling anything so they had been temporarily abandoned.

On their way back to the stored pulks they met Lindeberg with the last of the deer from Haines that he had stubbornly refused to abandon. Amazingly, he had found another sixty deer in the woods, which brought the number of living beasts to the three hundred number once more. This meant, however, that by now almost half the cargo brought on the *Manitoban* had died of starvation, drowning or exhaustion. Lindeberg's crew had two or three pulks with them, but they could not bring the rest. He went on to try to join the main herd while the others finished their return trip to Haines and the sleds with their belongings.

On Sunday Carl went with another group of men to take food to some of the herders who had not yet left for Haines, and found them again staying in the Indian funeral house. A storm struck just as he got there. Everyone crowded inside. As he remembered the experience when he recorded it, Sacariasen complained again of the rain, the wind, and the odor of decaying corpses. Added to that were smells of decomposing salmon, bird bones, and other debris thrown on the floor by others who like themselves had sought shelter in this unpleasant place.

When they got their pulks, the only way they could think to take them upriver again was to use them as boats, so they waded in the river pulling the loaded sleds behind them. Since there was always a risk of capsizing the pulks no one wanted to put his bedding on the load, so they left that behind, planning to return to pick up their sleeping bags and bed rolls later. That night they had to sleep on the ground, the storm returned, and they had no protection. No one slept well and some of the men went completely sleepless.

A short distance beyond Klukwan they caught up with what was left of the herd, and once again they were moving, for the drivers had found a small patch of marsh grass where they let the deer feed for the following two days. Poor as it was, it was better than letting them all die.

Next, they reached Redmyer's camp at the base of the hill below Rainy Hollow. They immediately started the deer up the mountain and the pass above where they knew there was ample moss. It was still early enough in the year that after climbing only a few hundred feet they got out of the slush and once again were walking on snow and ice. Men from northern Europe were not intimidated by winter, however, and they found that pulling the loaded pulks over the crust was far easier than towing them through the river. Late in the afternoon, after the sunlight reached the snow, a mild thaw turned the crust to slush, so they stopped in order to get an early start in the morning when it would be hard once more. Carl noted that Kjellmann, who had been shuttling back and forth between camps, herds, and crews of men, pulled a sled with a full load and slept on the ground as uncomfortably as the humblest Lapp herdsman.

The following morning they climbed rapidly. They knew they would have a hard time getting up to the pass if the weather turned warm so they had their morning meal and were on their way by four a.m. Sometime during the late morning the sun touched the snow again, and they stopped for a needed rest. By now there was a total of twenty-six men pulling loaded pulks up the steep ravine. This was the same route that Jack Dalton had once used to take cattle into the Yukon, and is still referred to as the Dalton Trail.

Slush or no slush, they had to go on; seemingly at the end of their endurance, they found strength to get up and start pulling the sleds again. Since there were neither tents nor bedding for anyone, they were afraid the night would find them caught once more in a downpour of rain. They took turns breaking trail through the mushlike snow, but finally gave up and took shelter under the branches of a grove of convenient spruce trees, where they drank some coffee and laid themselves on the ground for another night of little rest. As they suspected, the drizzle soon became a downpour. Just before Johannes Ravna went to bed he saw reindeer moss in the rocks a few yards away, and gave the welcome news to the herders. It was too dark to go back with him to where he saw it, but each proposed to check the moss supply the next day as soon as it was light.

The last day of April turned out to be one of pleasant work and sport. As Ravna had predicted, there was plenty of moss handy so each man unloaded his pulk, dragged it to the moss, filled it to the top, then sat on the load to hold it in place, took it to the snow, and coasted all the way back down the mountain to the river, guiding the sled with his feet on either side. Here they dumped the moss into a pile, and started climbing the mountain once more. Since the pulks were not loaded this time they were able to climb over the trail quickly. One could hear their whoops of pleasure as like children they slid down to the river bank.

Now Kjellmann sent one messenger to Lindeberg who was in charge of the herd telling him that there was plenty of food if he could get the deer to the mountain. While they waited for him, Redmyer's troop relayed provisions and freight to the pass above the camp, and for the first time it appeared that they might be able to salvage something from the disaster.

At the end of the third day Kjellmann judged that they had stored enough moss at the river's edge, and the herders dragged full sleds of moss downstream to meet the herd that needed the food so badly. Seven miles from the supply they met Redmyer's men, and left the moss with these herders.

For their return trip they filled the sleds with supplies but found little food in these packs, so once again the men were put on short rations. Since they had not expected to hike back the seven miles with loads, they had brought no camping paraphernalia with them, for they expected to be back at their base before night. The loads slowed them down, however, and finally they had to crawl beside their pulks, or unload them, turn them over and sleep beneath their sleds. Though they piled limbs and brush at the sides of the sleds there was no bedding for covering, and they had nothing to keep them warm in the chilly winds that blew down the canyon.

They knew that it would not be until the end of the next day that they could finally get back to their destination where they could find adequate food and shelter. They were normal men, and disliked a constant diet of salt pork roasted on a stick over a fire for breakfast, and pork plus a piece of bread for lunch. Neither were they enthusiastic over the evening meal. Sacariasen as cook made some more of the unpalatable pork and flour soup which the grumbling men had to eat or go hungry. Now Kjellmann's leadership began to pay dividends for, while the herders were uncomfortable, tired and dissatisfied with the monotonous food, almost no one criticized his leader since he shared the hardships with them uncomplainingly.

Finally, on May 4, they reached the camp at the top of the mountain and at last had a good meal. As they rested on the ground under the trees they heard the welcome sound of walking reindeer, and found the diminished herd had recuperated enough so that the stronger deer had caught up with them. They knew the food they had carried down to them had saved many of the animals who seemed able to recuperate quickly with proper food. Apparently the deer could smell the odor of fresh moss, however, and took off toward the piles of moss. Since it was dark and the brush under the trees was heavy no one wanted to round up the beasts for fear of injury to themselves. As Kjellmann saw the animals disappearing into the gathering darkness he shook his head in dismay and scratched his ear, which was about the only way he showed frustration or anger. He told the men to make themselves as comfortable as they could for the night, and they would find the deer in the morning. They had bedding at the base camp so they wrapped themselves in blankets, huddled by their fires to keep warm, and dozed fitfully as they waiting for daybreak.

Lindeberg told Kjellmann within the hearing of the wakeful men by the fire that he had had to leave some deer on the icy slopes below, and there was no moss there. A few of the men were detailed to search for them as soon as morning dawned.

Sacariasen was one of these. While others fanned through the woods trying to round up the feeding deer, the men looking for the dying animals on the hill below carried moss with them. When they got to the deer, they tried hand-feeding them, then stopped and cooked their own breakfast. Ravna and Carl tried to get the deer on their feet, while others went farther to see if there were any more that they had missed.

This part of the herd had finally given up. They were too far gone to save. As Carl lifted an animal bodily to its feet, he wrote later, the deer would take a few steps, then would lie down again, ready to die. Not one of these deer survived this ordeal. One by one they would fall, be seized by a cramp, and die, even while the two men tried to revive them. This discouraging scene was repeated over and over again that day and when night fell they camped once more on the bare hillside without food, but did have enough fuel to heat a little coffee--enough for one serving for each man. They ranged back and forth gathering enough firewood to keep warm and again spent a miserable night.

When daylight came again, they found four stronger deer farther up the mountain, and still alive. They dragged these to their feet urging and helping them along until they came to Camp Pleasant, as they now called their rendezvous.[48] Only these four deer arrived out of the forty head that Lindeberg had been forced to abandon two days before. It was a small return on the labor of half a dozen men for two days, but it is a marvel that even these four lived.

It is also astonishing that as many as did were able to endure the lack of good food for the seven weeks that had elapsed since they landed at Haines in March. Their resilience was proof enough that Jackson's original scheme had been a sound one.

The animals that had fled to the feeding grounds beyond Camp Pleasant were satisfied, and allowed the yelling herders to drive them back into a herd again without any trouble. Yet when Kjellmann counted all surviving deer, he found that only 185 head remained out of the original 521.

Everyone rested in camp for the next few days while the deer grazed on abundant moss, and visibly gained strength in the process. Soon there would be no reason why the survivors could not be driven over the trail to the Yukon and down to Circle City as their orders now called for. Kjellmann decided that the depleted herd would need no more than fifteen men to drive through to northern Alaska, and Redmyer was given a crew and put in charge. The rest of the men were told to go back to the mission and await further orders. Since they had been living on a drab diet of hotcakes, pork, flour soup, and coffee, Samuelson and Sacariasen tried to buy some different food from some passing prospectors camping on the river below them. The men were heading for Dawson, and didn't want to sell any food, but gave them a few rolls of bread. Even this was a welcome change from what the herders had been eating.

Now they had neither canoes nor boats to help them carry their gear, so they walked the fifty miles back to Haines. Their packs were light, but those who had bedding found a bedroll to be a clumsy thing. Sleeping bags were not in common use then, so each man was top-heavy with his load. Everyone tried to pick the smoothest trail along the river, and some tried other routes than the ones they had taken going upstream. They crossed, then recrossed the river, getting their feet wet as the water covered their rubber boots, and eventually everyone was soaked from head to toe as some of the men would lose their balance and fall into the stream with a loud splash. Others who did not fall were drenched by the dashing wavelets around the rocks.

Peder Berg and Jermias Abrahamsen decided to build a raft and float downstream. Hans Samuelsen, Jafet Lindeberg, and Samuel Josefson found an abandoned Indian canoe, and tried to make it seaworthy. The rest continued hiking.

Since by now they knew the best camping spots, they had agreed in the morning that they would all meet that night in one of these places. Wilhelm Basi, Carl, and Otto Greiner stayed together, and were the first to reach the designated camp. This was just above Klukwan, so they had hiked close to twenty-five miles that day. Since the weather was improved and they did not want to spend another night sleeping among the corpses in the charnel house, they stopped in the woods. The men in the canoe joined them and the six built a huge fire which helped dry their clothes, and made them feel much better. Lindeberg was standing in front of it almost mother-naked, drying his clothes and admitting ruefully that he was not skilled in working a dugout canoe. Consequently, as they rushed through the rapids, he had capsized the craft. Two of them had clung to the upturned boat until they got to quiet water, but Lindeberg was a powerful man, and he had swum to shore. Probably, however, they were no more soaked than those who had walked the entire way.

During the night the rest of the men drifted into camp, two or three at a time, and all ravenously hungry, wet, and very tired. In the morning Balto and some of the other Lapps decided to build rafts and this spread the various groups along the river. Kjellmann stayed behind with the slowest hikers, and they did not reach that night's camp but had to stay in a small clearing upstream from the main body of men. No one had food, however, for they had eaten all of their rations during the day, expecting to join the main group that night. Some tried to take meat from the dead reindeer along the river, but these had been dead too long and the meat had gone bad. Another man reported finding some dried beans that one of the prospectors had spilled, which he gathered carefully and ate.

The following day the hiking men came to another prospectors' camp on the river bank and took up a $5 collection to try to buy something from them. When these people heard that the Norwegians were hungry they assumed they were starving and generously sent food to them, refusing to take any money for it. Thus, the next meal Carl cooked had rice to mix with the pork. Kjellmann, behind with the slower men, refused to buy food for himself and he would not beg, so the evening meal in his camp "was none too elaborate."

After sunup the two rafts with their crews poling them came into camp. Both crews had had a bad time of it, and both rafts had capsized. The men who built them were not only soaked from their dunking, but their packs, clothing, and bedding were all dumped into the water as well, for they had not lashed them to the logs. Berg went back to try to salvage something for he had lost his possessions in the darkness. Abrahamsen gave up, stumbling along with the others with no pack and all of his personal possessions somewhere at the bottom of the river.

The herders must have been in good physical condition, however, for in spite of their strenuous efforts they were back at Haines on the third from Camp Pleasant. Sacariasen's group were back in the barn at dusk, although others did not make it until well after dark.

On Sunday, the 8th of May, almost two months after they had reached Haines the first time, they rested at the mission where Kjellmann issued enough food to give them their fill. Some of the men became ill from overeating as a consequence. They were cheered to find that the weather had become mild enough by this time of year that they could move out of the barn into tents. Late that evening Peder Berg finally came in, triumphant because he had found his pack along the riverbank.

Soon everyone went to work making a cache where anything they had to leave behind at Haines could be stored until they returned or could send for it when they reached some new assignment. For this, they made a storage platform of some of the pulks that they had not been able to take to Pleasant Camp, putting them into trees after they had been filled with the surplus supplies. Their own personal belongings as well as their packs and bedrolls were made ready to be shipped back to Puget Sound. Kjellmann told them they could either return to Port Townsend to join their families or go on to Seattle if they wished to take leave there. He left them to go to Dyea himself to buy passage for his men between Haines and Seattle. This was not difficult, for while all ships were heavily loaded coming north, all were virtually empty on the return trip.

The following Wednesday the soldiers who had been in their encampment at Haines received news that war had been declared on Spain, that Dewey had fought the Battle of Manila Bay, and that they had been ordered to leave immediately for war in the Philippines. The herders were not much concerned with a war between the United States and Spain but were excited to hear the roars of noncommissioned officers, the shrill tones of bugle calls and the general uproar of an army camp yanked from its lethargy by the call to duty. Surprisingly, the army was able to get things started promptly and before the afternoon was over the men had boarded a ship and left for San Francisco. The Norwegians did not mind, for they had made friends with neither officers nor men the entire time they had been there. Since their feet were sore from their long hike in their watersoaked boots, the men could only walk along the beach for short strolls, or go visiting the Indians living nearby. Since they didn't like Indians either, they did not find this very exciting. Most of the men stayed in their tents.

Saturday, May 14, Kjellmann sent word from Dyea that their transportation was ready, and would be at Haines at eight o'clock the following morning. It arrived on schedule and they found the steamer *Syntiof* to be clean, and the crew efficient and courteous. Basi described the accommodations as "luxurious."[49] Sacariasen was more restrained in his approval, but did say he was surprised that they were "permitted to eat seated in the saloon with the Americans."[50] He could still understand no English, for he had had little chance to learn any, but he enjoyed observing the disappointed gold hunters who had turned back from Dyea or Skagway, and noting how many different kinds of people were on the ship.

In the afternoon they paused briefly at Juneau where the mine at Douglas across the waterway was shown to the men as "the world's richest gold mine."

On Monday, to their delight, the herders found that some of the passengers were Norwegian-speaking. These told them of the conditions in Skagway. They reported drunkenness and gambling there, with murders and robbery commonplace. Little efforts were made to apprehend the thieves. Men short of money found few opportunities to earn any more. The Norwegians who talked to the herders said the criminals were known, and pointed out several passengers who had robbed or killed, but were still at large. Carl noted that the accused felons appeared to be well-mannered and well dressed, but he claimed that their actions aboard would have identified them as "riff-raff" anywhere. He did not say what actions had betrayed them.

The *Syntiof* stopped the next day in Wrangell long enough to permit the passengers to go ashore if they wanted to. They were warned that they had only two hours for sight-seeing. The village was very small, however, and the only things to see were a fish cannery and a church beside the Indian village that looked like other Indian towns they had already seen. The men found little entertainment in the sights, and returned to the ship long before the two hours had gone by.

They continued south, spending the 17th of May in the inland passage. This was Norwegian Constitution Day, commemorating the Fundamental Laws granted by the monarchy in 1814. Sacariasen did not seem to be filled with much patriotic sentiment for either the United States or Norway, but he and his fellows did complain that they had not yet been paid for their three and a half months service, so they had no money to buy liquor to help them celebrate the Day properly. On this sorry note Carl crawled into his bunk.

By the following day they awoke in Victoria, British Columbia. Port Townsend where the Lapp women and children were staying was just across the Strait of Juan de Fuca and a few miles to the east. Although they were allowed three hours ashore in Victoria they wanted to be sure to get to their families and friends as quickly as possible, so did not go far from the ship.

Although Sacariasen did not know it so did not record it in his journal, Jackson had received orders to send the men to St. Michael on the Alaskan Coast, to consolidate the reindeer herds there or at some of the other stations between St. Michael and the Seward Peninsula, and to prepare to start a freight and mail service up the Yukon valley. Now that his official duties with the Presbyterian church were ended he could spend more time on his Alaskan affairs.

Meanwhile, the deer they had left at Pleasant Camp in the mountains above the Chilkat River were fairly well recovered, and Redmyer decided to begin to move them. He selected Anders A. Baer, Peter J. Hatta, Klemet P. Boino, Hans A. Siri, Per Nilsen Siri, and Emil Kjelsberg to start with him toward Circle City on the morning of June 1.

The route Redmyer expected to follow was the Dalton Trail to Dawson, then to follow the river past Fortymile to Circle City. The route was not difficult and fairly well marked, so there was little likelihood of their getting lost. They placed their equipment on the reindeer sleds, harnessed the deer, and soon felt the familiar rush of wind past their faces as the now healthy reindeer swiftly pulled the sleds across the snow. The surviving animals were familiar with sleds, and seemed to enjoy being at work again.[51]

As though the Fates were still against them, they found that the snow had been thawed to the bare earth after they had gone only about forty miles.

It seemed impossible to Redmyer that here, one hundred miles north of Haines, the climate was warmer than it had been on the river, but there was no use complaining. All of the sleds had to be unpacked and were then abandoned along with the harnesses. Everything not absolutely essential was piled in a heap along the trail for anyone to take who might have need of it. Two packs of twenty-five pounds weight each were placed on the backs of the reindeer, and the men carried their own supplies on their backs as well. The deer had not minded pulling the sleds, but they did not like acting as pack animals, and objected. Some tried to run away, and others made every effort to get rid of the objectionable loads. The herders were forced to stop long enough to accustom the beasts to carrying the packs, and wasted several days, though by now it didn't matter. Even after that, however, the deer might decide they had had enough of acting as mules, and would run through the woods, scraping their packs under the branches in hopes of ridding themselves of their burdens. This would compel their herdsmen to tramp for hours through the brush before they could bring the animals back to the trail.

By the end of July they were far behind any schedule they might have been trying to keep. Redmyer thought that there must be a faster and easier trail to Dawson than the one they were following, so he turned east to strike the Yukon. They never did find a good trail this way, so reluctantly came back to the Dalton route near the Mendenhall River. Through the rest of the summer and early fall the herd drifted northward without major problems, though they did not move very fast. It was a good thing the Dawson miners had not been starving as the alarmists had predicted, or they would have all been dead had they depended on the deer to feed them.

By November, with the onset of winter once more, they were committed to the Dawson route, but had not reached the mines yet. When the snow began to fall and became deep enough, the men stopped and built pulks out of material from the nearby forests. Harnesses were a greater problem, but in Lapland they had always made their own gear so it was only a matter of time. In about two weeks they had finished the sleds and harness, loaded them, and again were able to travel northward and now much more rapidly. Not many days afterward, Kjelsberg suffered the first accident when he was caught in the open during an especially cold day and suffered severe frostbite. The herders immediately put him in a tent and tried to save his life. They succeeded, but he was badly weakened and his recovery was slow, and delayed them further.

Finally, on January 27, 1899, they reached Dawson. The miners knew about them, and tried to buy the whole herd for fresh meat. Once they had expected to sell them but now the government officials wanted them for other things, so they had to refuse the miners' offer. Even when the hungry prospectors offered $300 apiece they had to say "no." Had they been allowed to sell the animals to a local butcher shop they could have recovered between forty and fifty thousand dollars for the surviving reindeer, which would have gone a long way toward repaying the expenses of the ill-starred adventure, but this was not to be. Since these deer were not breeding animals, about all they would have been for was to eat, though Jackson as well as military and postal officials hoped they could be used as draft animals.

For the next ten months Redmyer, his six herders, and the deer traveled slowly down the Yukon, from Dawson to Circle City. He had to be careful with his animals and his men for it was winter, and he wanted no more experiences like the one at Haines, or during Kjelsberg's recuperation from freezing. The deer could look after themselves if there was plenty of food and if they were not put in pens. Since the various missions had loaned deer from their herds to the relief expedition to the Point Barrow whalers in 1897, Redmyer was supposed to deliver these nine dozen deer to several of the inland missions as partial repayment for their loan to the government.

He tried to divide the herd as evenly as possible and, finally with all of them disposed of, Redmyer resigned from the reindeer service in October, 1899,[52] and returned to Seattle.

After a few months, he returned to Alaska, and opened a saloon in Cross River. By 1904 he was back with the Reindeer Service, and drove a herd of 300 deer to Iliamna Lake. He stayed with them as Superintendent of the Station for another four years. In 1908 he returned to Washington State, married, and lived at Bow, Washington until 1916. After his divorce from his wife, Mareth, in 1916, he lived for a brief time in Minneapolis, then returned to Seattle where he built boats for a living. He died in 1953.[53]

Most of the six herders who took the Norwegian herd to Circle City and beyond, rejoined the other herders on the shore of Norton Sound and at

Golovnin Bay during the fall of 1899. Some continued working for the Reindeer service. Others resigned and began their search for gold.

NOTES

[1]*R.i.A.,* p. 17.

[2]Lazell. *Alaskan Apostle.* p. 169; *R.i.A.,* p. 17-18.

[3]Lazell, pp. 169-170; Stewart, *Sheldon Jackson,* p. 445.

[4]*R.i.A.,* p. 19.

[5]55 Cong., 3 Sess., *House Document #5, Jackson Report:* "Commission to Lapland." p. 1791.

[6]55. Cong., 3 Sess., *House Doc. #5.* Jackson Report, *Op. Cit.,* p. 1791.

[7]*R.i.A.,* p. 25.

[8]Basi, *Diary,* February 23, 1898.

[9]*R. i. A.,* p. 26.

[10]*R. i.A., loc. cit.*

[11]*R. i. A.,* p. 27.

[12]Telegram, Interior to War Department, March 1, 1898. IDTP:AK roll 5.

[13]Morgan, Edward E.P., and Woods, Henry F. *God's Loaded Dice, Alaska, 1897-1930,* Caldwell, Idaho: The Caxton Printers, Ltd., 1948, pp. 141-165.

[14]Telegrams, R. A. Alger to Merriam, March 5, 1898. IDTP:AK roll 5.

[15]Telegram, Assistant Secretary of War to Merriam, March 11, 1898. *Ibid.*

[16]Telegram, A.C. Corbin to Merriam, March 16, 1898. *Ibid.*

[17]*R. i. A.,* p. 31.

[18]56 Cong., 1 Sess., *Senate Document #245,* "9th Report on Reindeer in Alaska," F.H. Gambell, M.D., *Resident Physician's Report,* p. 69.

[19]*R. i. A.,* p. 33.

[20]*R. i. A.,* p. 34.

[21]*R. i. A..,* p. 36.

[22]*Ibid., loc. cit.*

[23]Andrews, Clarence L., "Reindeer in Alaska," *Washington Historical Quarterly*, 10:3, July 1919, pp. 171-186.

[24]Letter, Jackson to Harris, March 21, 1898. IDTP:AK reel 5.

[25] There are spelling problems again with this name. Helen White (*The Tale of the Comet*, p. 200-201) cites the U.S. Census for the spelling used here, though Sacariasen used the Norwegian spelling, Redmyre. For more information, see White, Helen M., *The Tale of A Comet and Other Stories*, Minnesota Historical Society Press, St. Paul, 1984. pp. 200-210.

[26]*R. i. A.*, p. 39.

[27]*Seattle Times*, March 14, 1898.

[28]*Seattle Times*, March 16, 1898.

[29]Freidel, Frank, *The Splendid Little War*, New York: Dell Publishing Company, Inc., 1962. pp. 13, 33-34, 48, 88-89, 128-129, 178, 209 ff.

[30]Telegram, Jackson to Interior, March 16, 1898, IDTP:AK, Reel 5.

[31]*R. i. A.*, p. 42.

[32]Report, Jackson to Harris, March 21, 1898. IDTP:AK, Reel 5.

[33]Telegram, A.C. Corbin to Brig. Gen. Merriam, March 16, 1898. IDTP:AK, Reel 5.

[34]Telegram, G.D. Meiklejohn (Assistant Secretary of War) to Merriam, March 11, 1898. IDTP:AK, Reel 5.

[35]Telegram, Meikeljohn to Merriam, March 12, 1898. *Loc. Cit.*

[36]*R. i. A.*, p. 43.

[37]*R. i. A.*, p. 45.

[38]Letter, Jackson to Harris, March 21, 1898, IDTP:AK reel 5; Andrews, Clarence LeRoy, "Driving Reindeer in Alaska," *Pacific Northwest Quarterly*, 26:2, April 1935, pp. 90-93.

[39]55 Cong., 3 Sess., *House Doc. #5,* Jackson Report, "Commission to Lapland," p. 1792.

[40]55 Cong., 3 Sess., *House Doc. #5*, Jackson Report, "Commission to Lapland," p. 1793.

[41]Lazell, p. 48; *R. i. A.*

[42]*R. i. A.*, p. 48.

[43] *R. i. A.,* p. 50.

[44]Arestad, Sverre, "Reindeer in Alaska," (citing Chicago SKANDINAVEN, July 31, 1899,) *Pacific Northwest Quarterly*, 42:3, July 1951, p. 215.

[45]*R. i. A.,* p. 56.

[46] *R. i. A.,* pp. 56-57.

[47] *R. i. A.,* p. 61.

[48] *R. i. A.,* p. 69.

[49]Basi, *Diary*, March 15, 1898.

[50] *R. i. A.,* p. 74.

[51] Arestad, *Op. cit.*

[52] Jackson report to Interior, March 19, 1900 IDTP:AK, Reel 6.

[53]White, *The Tale of the Comet*, p. 210; f.n. 62, 62, p. 261.

Chapter Three

INTERLUDE AT FORT TOWNSEND

As soon as the herders had reached Port Townsend, Kjellmann hired a steam tug to take them across the Bay to the army fort where their women and children were housed. By the time they reached the bluff where the fort was located it was so late that everyone had gone to bed. The routine of those who had been left behind when the deer were shipped north in March was well established by now, and it did not include much night life. Consequently, although it was only ten o'clock it was dark, and that meant that they were supposed to be in bed. Regnor Dahl, whom Kjellmann had hired to be in charge of the families, was a person who took his position seriously, and expected to have his authority recognized.

The captain of the tug blew his whistle in the darkness and silence of the waterfront, since there seemed absolutely no sign of life ashore. The first time he got no response of any kind. Twice more he let the sound of his whistle reverberate through the trees until finally a light in one of the cabins came on, which showed that someone on shore was awake. Soon the eager herders saw a dark figure come down to the dock carrying a lantern and calling to the tug to find out what the disturbance was about. It was Dahl.

He had been employed largely because he knew both Norwegian and some of the Lapp language as well as English. Since he was one of the few people in Port Townsend who could talk to the Lapp women and children, his linguistic ability qualified him to govern the camp. His other talents were less conspicuous.

When he saw who was in the tugboat he welcomed them formally and they all went ashore where he showed them a building where they could sleep that night. Since they had not eaten anything since they left Victoria, Dahl roused some of the sleepy women, and after they were dressed told them that their men had returned. How they could have missed the commotion Sacariasen did not say. At any rate they prepared a meal for the hungry men, and Sacariasen, the cook, did not have to work at the stove.

The next morning they looked out over the water of Puget Sound to see where they were. In June the weather here is lovely, and this was one of the days that Chambers of Commerce liked to talk about. Fort Townsend was located about five miles south of the town, and the site was a well-chosen one. Even the dour Sacariasen found it to be "very attractive."[1] It had been built during the Indian Wars of the 1850s, but although by now the War Department had decided that the Indians were no longer a threat, nevertheless naval powers of European nations might be. Accordingly, defense installations needed to protect Puget Sound from hostile warships were built to use artillery on the highlands at a point northeast of town, rather than at the infantry post in the forest south of Port Townsend. Local Indians were not hostile, and the raiding parties of Alaskan and British Columbia Indians had not come down looking for slaves, or heads to take home, for many years. The smallpox epidemic of 1862 had killed so many northern Indians that no fort was needed to control them. The survivors were miserable and destitute, and their fierce reputation earned in an earlier time was only a memory. Politics being what they were, however, the Fort stayed on as a local example of pork-barrel politics. No soldiers were stationed there any more but appropriations still came from Congress.

Actually, of course, the Spanish navy was so far away and so ineffectual in June, 1898 that building Forts Flagler and Worden at Port Townsend or Fort Casey at Admiralty Head on Whidbey Island was equally useless, but in wartime this kind of activity is expected. On the bluffs beyond the small city one could see construction everywhere. Since the old army post was virtually abandoned, and since it belonged to the War Department which needed some place to house the herders, it was a logical decision to use the buildings for the Lapps.

These weeks at Fort Townsend became a vacation time for the Norwegians--a break for rest and relaxation. They were not restricted to camp. They could go into the American town any time they wanted to; however, the language barrier between them and the English-speaking citizens usually kept them at the Fort. It took only a little over an hour to walk through the forest around the waterfront, and it was an easy hike. Dahl had built a ten-by-eighteen-foot square-sterned boat which he used to haul freight and supplies to the Fort, but it had to be rowed and it was a very slow moving craft. It took longer and more effort to use the boat than to make the hike, so the scow was not used often.

Kjellmann left orders for Dahl to buy food and issue new clothes for the men who had worn out what they had taken from Seattle in March. When he left, he chose the two men who seemed to have the greatest leadership, Magnus Kjelsberg and Jafet Lindeberg, to be the policemen in the camp while he was gone. Since Carl was a Norwegian and looked down on the Lapps he noted that he approved of the choices, who would be needed "if the Lapps should get drunk." Later, after he grew more mellow, he admitted that the Norwegians were as prone to drunkenness as the Lapps, but he was not yet willing to make such a concession. The military jail was only a few yards from the barracks, and Dahl had it unlocked and prepared for any malefactors that might appear.

After he had made these appointments, Kjellmann left for his home in Wisconsin to visit his wife and children. He told the men and women as he left that he could return just as soon as the ice was thawed on the Bering Sea. Actually, however, he returned much sooner than that.

After the terrible weather on Lynn Canal, the pleasant climate of a Puget Sound May was too hot for the men, but they basked in the sun, soaking up the heat in sensuous relaxation. They refused to do more than minimal work on the grounds that they were exhausted from the heat. Carl admitted that they walked around and enjoyed themselves most of the time, "for either way, our pay was the same."[2]

For about five days the weather stayed warm, and the camp was peaceful. One of the Norwegians returned to the Fort from the town one morning after being gone all night and told a wild tale of an encounter with a strange American. He had hitched a ride with a teamster who was bringing supplies to the Fort, and planned to return that same night. In the afternoon he struck up an acquaintance with a stranger whom he probably could not talk to, and stayed with him for several hours. Carl did not say, but probably they had spent their time in a saloon. After a time these temporary acquaintances decided to leave and walk to the Indian village west of town. Apparently by now he had learned a little English for he told his friends at the Fort that his "friend" had communicated with him in some way that he was going to have some "fun." The horrified Norwegian saw him draw a revolver from his clothes, take aim at an Indian child, and fire. His bullet struck the leg of the little boy, who fell screaming to the ground. At once there was confusion in the camp and shouts of rage and alarm from the people there. The Indians sent at once for both a doctor and the town police. Meanwhile, the adult men began searching for the gunman. When the police arrived it was obvious that the crying child was not dead, nor was he seriously injured, and they were little concerned in any event with anything that happened in the Indian town. The Indian men continued looking for the whites, however, and the two drunken men fled into the forest where they hid for the rest of the afternoon and through the night. The thoroughly frightened herder said he had no idea why the American had shot the boy. To him the only justification for someone to shoot another was in self defense or to gain revenge, and this shooting was totally uncalled-for. Drunken Americans seemed incomprehensible!

The weather stayed warm and sunny, and the main excitement came from lying on the grass near the forest and listening to the garter snakes crawling through the rustling underbrush. Since they had worked so hard on the Dalton Trail only a month before, no one really minded that they were accomplishing absolutely nothing. Two weeks passed in the same pleasant way. Only one trivial and amusing incident seemed worth recording in Sacariasen's journal.

Several of the Norwegians had bought whiskey in one of the town's saloons and had returned with two bottles unopened. The people at the Fort quickly remedied this oversight, and a young Lapp named Johan Rist got out of control very quickly. He was visiting in the quarters of Jakob Hatta, there was a fight, and Rist broke one of the windows in the room with his fist. In his befuddled state he tried to run into the room of Johan Tornensis, but found the door locked. He banged on the door so loudly that Dahl heard the disturbance and called for his two policemen to do something about it. The three men together subdued young Rist and put him triumphantly into the nearby jail to sleep it off.

Now everyone woke the next day with high anticipation, for Dahl decreed that there should be a trial to demonstrate American court procedure to the Lapps and other herders. Since everyone wanted to attend, he held court in the large general area of the barracks where the Norwegians lived. He had benches placed around the wall, while a long table in the middle of the room was used for the actual court. Regnor Dahl sat at the table along with Ole Berg, Lauritz Larsen, Ole Krogh, and Per Prosanger, who served as jury. An American employee of the Fort was appointed to serve as adviser to Dahl to give an appearance of legality to the proceedings. No one took the affair seriously, however, and everyone there thought of the "trial" as just a lark and a welcome break in the monotony.

At a signal from Dahl, the policemen brought in the now sober and repentant Rist, who had spent the night in discomfort. He was instructed to sit on a bench near the table while Dahl read the charges against him. The statement charged that he had been cruel to Hatta, had been drunk and disorderly, and had damaged property by breaking a window. The witnesses agreed that Rist had been drunk all right, and that he had indeed tried to break into Tornensis's room. Inga Balto was called to the stand, and she contradicted some of the witnesses on the property damage charge, which caused a wrangle on the spot between her and the men she contradicted. Finally she was shown to have perjured herself because she was sympathetic toward the accused man. The next witness rejected Balto's testimony, but said the first witnesses weren't telling the truth either. Dahl added to the farce by reading the American law about a man being secure in his own habitation. Without consulting the jury, Regnor Dahl then announced the verdict! Rist was guilty of drunkenness but not of property damage. Who broke the window, Dahl did not say. After this profound bit of wisdom, Dahl finally instructed the jury to retire to reach a verdict, and ordered the policemen to clear the courtroom of all spectators. Rist was not allowed to take the stand on his own defense, he had no defense attorney, and the judge had already announced his decision. The spectators must have been puzzled about American jurisprudence, if this were an example of it.

As might be surmised, since there was no real doubt that Rist had been drunk, the jury ratified Dahl's judgment, everyone was called back into the courtroom, and the magistrate sentenced the culprit to two days in jail on bread and water. The prisoner was then taken back to his cell. This escort turned into a procession since everyone followed the policemen. The Lapp women, including Rist's wife, wept openly and loudly at the fate of the unfortunate Johan.

The ludicrous affair had a happy ending, however, for that night Dahl's own wife kept him awake as she scolded him for his role in jailing the poor fellow. After a fountain of tears and continuous nagging she succeeded in convincing her husband that he would have no peace until he turned the Lapp offender loose, and he gave in. Once again a procession marched to the jail, the two policemen and Dahl unlocked the door, took Rist out, turned him over to his wife, and everyone who was watching made appropriate approving noises at their leader's mercy.

For five additional days the men played catch on the beach, cleaned their quarters, washed their clothes, or walked to town to pick up mail from Norway. Some went out to look at the farms in the countryside beyond the Indian town to see what American agriculture was like.

Late in the week Dahl informed everyone that Dr. Jackson was coming to visit them. After the weeks of doing very little this seemed an opportunity to celebrate something, so the Lapps dressed in the brightest clothing and even Dahl, who was not a flashy dresser, "spruced up" his appearance, as Carl expressed it. He had not read his message carefully, however, for three days passed and Jackson did not arrive.

Finally, on Tuesday, June 7, a small white steamboat was seen approaching their little harbor, which tied to the dock below the Fort. The people on shore could recognize the figure of Dr. Jackson waving to them from the deck of the steamer. Dahl approached the vessel to welcome the man who had brought the herders to America. The observers saw an army officer approach Dahl, take him to Dahl's house where Jackson joined them, while everyone milled outside wondering at what was happening. Finally Regnor emerged and called loudly that all should gather around to hear what their Leader should say.

Everyone then crowded closely together and Jackson came out, standing on the porch where he spoke slowly to them in English as Dahl interpreted. His announcement might be paraphrased:

> I have chartered a large sailing ship which will carry us to St. Michael's Mission, and as soon as it is thoroughly inspected for safety it will leave the Seattle drydock to pick everyone up.

> I am sure it is safe enough, for it is only
> three years old. We should be ready to leave
> Port Townsend on June 19.[5]

He had chartered the sailing vessel *Louise J. Kenney*, and had agreed to pay the owners thirty dollars apiece for the passage of sixty-two adults and fourteen children to their destination.[4] He was asked why he did not charter a steamship for them, and strangely he did not admit it would have been too costly and that all steamers were already overbooked for passage to Alaska. Instead, he chose to dissemble by assuring them they would be more comfortable on the *Louise J. Kenney* than they would be on any steam-powered ship. This was possibly true, given the terrible conditions under which the gold-seekers sailed north and the decrepit state of some of the ships that sailed from Seattle that year. When he told them they would reach St. Michael sooner on a sailing ship than on a steamer, however, it was so manifestly untrue that the skeptical Norwegians and Lapps almost hooted in scorn. Jackson not only destroyed his own credibility but was so obviously ruffled by this vocal skepticism that he offered two men a trip to Seattle to check on the *Kenney* and see that it was actually as comfortable as he claimed it was. The two policemen, Kjelsberg and Lindeberg, were chosen by the herders to go with Jackson. By now Lindeberg is clearly emerging as the leader among the group, and his name appears in Sacariasen's and Basi's accounts more and more frequently.

Jackson next had a more unpleasant task to perform. He had to tell Johan Oleson Pulk that he must take his family and return to Norway. His children had all caught measles and, while they had recovered, the Immigration Service had decreed that no one with communicable diseases could remain in the United States. Only one of Pulk's older sons was exempted from deportation. He asked to be allowed to go to Alaska with the others. Both Jackson and the immigration authorities agreed, and he was put on the payroll of the Reindeer Service as soon as they reached St. Michael. Dahl was told to pay the elder Pulk for his services from February 1 to June 30, and for all deer and equipment he had sold to the Service before he left Lapland. The Pulk family boarded the paddlewheel steamer with Jackson, Kjelsberg, and Lindeberg for Seattle, and then he and his family proceeded on to Norway.

On Sunday the two-man inspection committee returned from Seattle with their report. They agreed with Jackson that the *Kenney* was almost new and well built, but complained that it was much too small to carry seventy-six passengers in comfort. Some food or baggage might have to be left behind in consequence.

Nevertheless, all prepared to leave for St. Michael and Norton Sound as soon as the ship arrived. Those who had money decided to spend it on whiskey, for it might be a long time before they would get another chance to buy any. In anticipation of a severe drought when they left port, most of the men left for town that evening. By now these strange Laplanders had been there so often they created very little comment. By the time they got home that night, however, even Regnor Dahl and Lindeberg were tipsy.

Dahl announced that since Lindeberg was drunk he should be arrested and put in jail but, since Lindeberg was the policeman and Kjelsberg was not available, Dahl tried to put him in jail by himself. He was unable to coordinate his own movements, and Lindeberg was so much bigger and stronger that the two drunken men struggled with one another to Dahl's chagrin, and Jafet's pleasure, for he enjoyed "resisting an officer."

Since Lindeberg was a six-foot four-inch giant, and heavy in proportion, while Dahl stood at least six inches shorter, this was strictly a "no contest" affair.[5] Clearly, Dahl's courage was greater than his common sense, though it was obviously bolstered by the alcohol he had consumed.

Now in a drunken rage, Dahl staggered to the jail bawling for policemen to come to his assistance, to help him throw the erring Jafet into the lockup. Since the only policeman in sight was Lindeberg himself, two mellow Norwegians joined Dahl and the three men managed to subdue the roaring Jafet and throw him into the same cell that had been occupied by Johan Rist a few days earlier. Not long after the noise had subsided another commotion in a different part of the Fort aroused everyone once more. A woman began to scream, and a crowd quickly gathered to see what was wrong. They discovered that Anders Balti was thrashing his wife and even threatening her with a knife. Dahl immediately arrested him too, and with the help of others they pushed Balti toward the jail where he was supposed to spend the night beside the now snoring Lindeberg. Balti was not so drunk that he could not break loose from his captors, however, and he tore free from his tipsy captors and ran down a high clay bank into the woods. Dahl and others then hid nearby waiting for him to come home, for they knew he would not want to spend the night in the forest. No one saw anything of him, the hours passed, and the men began to fall asleep. Finally Dahl roused them and they went to check to see whether his wife was all right. To their chagrin they found Balti snoring beside her in bed, with all forgiven. Dahl charged inside, yanked the sleepy man outside, and put him into jail because of all the trouble he had caused them.

Unlike the Rist affair, there was no trial for everyone was sober again, and they needed all the time they had to get ready to go to Alaska. Both Lindeberg and Balti were released the next morning. Lindeberg testily demanded a trial, but Dahl refused to grant anyone the time off a trial would take. Carl Sacariasen did not like Dahl much better than he did Jackson, and said that everyone would have sided with Lindeberg so there was no point in holding a trial. Balti admitted his guilt but was not given any punishment, so the whole affair blew over.

The following day Dr. Jackson came back from Seattle to tell them of his final arrangements. He planned to go to Siberia, and to stop at St. Lawrence Island on his return trip. He had to buy more deer to replace those sent to Point Barrow, and the deer from Norway who had survived the starvation time were not numerous enough to repay the loans from Antisarlook and the mission herds. He asked Dahl to appoint four men to help him and to leave one man to work with the Eskimo herders on St. Lawrence. Dahl appointed Rolf Wiig and Lindeberg without a moment's hesitation, along with Ole Krogh and Johannes Ravna. Since both Lindeberg and Wiig had quarreled with Dahl, Carl Sacariasen surmised that his choice was conditioned by his dislike for the two men. What he had against Ravna and Krogh, Carl did not say. When Jackson left for Seattle, all four men went with him.

The males on the expedition wanted to be sure when they got to Alaska that they would be eligible to take land or mining claims, but to do this they had to be American citizens or to have made a declaration of intent to do so. They knew that in Alaska it would be difficult to find attorneys or judges to help them, so Dahl took those who wanted to take out "first papers" to Port Townsend that afternoon, where they could be placed under oath by the immigration authorities. In a short time a considerable number left for this office.

Thus, one day before they left Washington State, they foreswore their allegiance to King Oscar II of Sweden and Norway, and under oath declared their new-found allegiance to the government and constitution of the United States. Most of them had only the haziest idea of what was going on, for the American magistrate had them raise their hands while he read from a book in English. Dahl did not bother to interpret, but told them when to lower their hands. After the ceremony ended each man received a certificate noting that in due time he would become a citizen of the United States and be eligible to own land.

When they returned to the Fort, they had little to do except wait for the schooner which arrived the next day. To their consternation, they found thirty-seven strange passengers from Seattle already aboard. Demand for passage to the gold fields was so great that extraordinary sums had been offered to the captain of the *Louise J. Kenney* by those trying to find their fortune in the Klondike. He sold tickets on his tiny sailing vessel far beyond its capacity. In spite of the fact that he had chartered the entire ship to Jackson and the United States government to carry the herders and their families, the owners took the passage money and put the people on board. The captain conveniently "forgot" to tell Jackson what he had done, and the Norwegians, already thinking Jackson to be a liar, began to believe that they had uncovered more of the Commissioner's skullduggery.

It didn't take Jackson long to find what had happened, however. He immediately chartered another ship, the *Navarro*, to carry thirty-five of the adults and six children originally scheduled to sail on the *Kenney*. The Norwegians had not heard from him, and quite properly refused to go aboard the schooner until all the strangers had been removed. By now the captain was in too far to do this, for he would have faced personal violence had he tried to refuse them passage after taking their money and getting down the Sound as far as the Fort. He began to talk earnestly to Dahl in English, so that the herders did not know what they were saying. According to Sacariasen, Dahl received money to try to convince everyone to go aboard. Dahl must have been eloquent, for all but five Norwegians agreed to try it, crowded though it might be. Carl himself went aboard. The five hold-outs were Thorolf Kjelsberg, Ole Rapp, Lauritz Stefanson, Peder Berg (the cook who had tried to float down the Chilkat River on a raft), and Jermias Abrahamsen. These men simply walked away from the ship and started for Port Townsend to see what they could do. Later they said they planned to enlist in the United States Army for service in the Philippines rather than be taken to Alaska on the overcrowded schooner. They had no money, but since Kjelsberg by now spoke English and they were young, they had no fear for the present, and no worries about the future.

The captain tried to frighten them back aboard by conspicuously raising the sails, and appeared to be raising anchor as well. He did not actually get underway, however. He remained in Port Townsend harbor and told the others he would stay until only ten o'clock the next morning whether the five truants were aboard or not. During the evening the herders discussed what they should do to keep the captain from abandoning their friends in a strange land, but after much talk they reached no conclusions, and went to bed to await further developments in the morning.

During the afternoon, the five men who refused to board the boat had gone to the local newspaper to tell the publisher how the wily captain had tried to cheat them. The paper printed it that night, and the Norwegian consul in Port Townsend read the story. He immediately wired Jackson in Seattle to come at once to help resolve the problem.

When the next morning came, the passengers came out on the deck to find another pleasant day with bright sunshine and a fair breeze for sailing, but nothing happened. The captain paced the deck, but gave no orders to move. The ten o'clock deadline came and went, and the *Kenney* continued to lie at anchor.

Not long afterward, Carl and his companions noticed a small white government steamboat leaving the dock and coming toward their ship. When it reached them, it turned toward their schooner and tied alongside. Three federal officials came on board, including a customs officer and the health inspector. In addition, the Norwegian consul came out to check on the welfare of his countrymen. After the health inspector introduced himself to the commander, the officials took out a tape measure and walked around the ship, making notations in a book. When they had finished, they told the captain not to make any attempt to leave but to remain in port until Sheldon Jackson got there.

The herders were almost besides themselves with curiosity over what was going to happen. They were tremendously pleased when someone told them the rebellious five had gone to the newspaper. Jackson was probably not as pleased, for the Seattle newspapers had picked up the story, and he read it there just before he received the telegram from the Norwegian consul.

Now the fat was really in the fire, and Regnor Dahl, who had induced the Norwegians to go aboard the impossible vessel, now tried to convince everyone that it was he who had alerted Jackson to the problems of overcrowding. The herders simply did not believe him, for by now they were convinced that it had been a mistake for Kjellmann to hire him as their leader in the first place.

By two that afternoon, the harrassed Jackson was at Port Townsend. Fortunately, William Kjellmann was with him, safely back from his visit with his family. Always in their earlier activities, Kjellmann had brought organization whenever there was a problem, and they hoped he could resolve the overcrowding on the ship.

The two men wasted no time. They asked the captain to go with them to his cabin, and after only a short time they came out and started calling the names of those who were to get off the ship. Almost half were told to go ashore, and even after they were gone Carl stated that the *Kenney* was still overcrowded. Meanwhile, Kjellmann went to look at the food supplies aboard. It didn't take long because the ship's owners had left considerable amounts in Seattle to make more room for passengers. Had they crammed everyone aboard, there would be soon been an acute shortage of food, and some genuine suffering especially among the small children. Kjellmann was highly displeased, but in his usual efficient manner he went ashore, ordered food enough for everyone, and had it delivered to the schooner. Then, and not until then, he permitted the captain to raise his anchor and set sail for the north.

Those of the herders who had been taken off the sailing ship were sent back to Seattle with Jackson and Kjellmann, to the wooden steamship *Navarro* which Jackson had chartered after he read the newspaper. It was four in the afternoon before they left Port Townsend, but it had been a very full day.

On the leisurely trip back to Seattle, Kjellmann talked to the Norwegians and told them he had heard from Redmyer who was now on his way to Dawson. Because so many deer had died, he had taken only six of his men while the rest of the herders were waiting in Seattle to go to Norton Sound with the others. Olai Paulsen, who had brought Redmyer's report, had told Kjellmann that when they were on their way down the mountain as they returned to Haines for the last time, they had run out of food and went hungry for three days. At Klukwan village, they had bought an Indian canoe, and were then able to reach the mission quickly and safely. When he met Jackson in Seattle, Paulsen asked for leave to visit relatives in Denver, and Dr. Jackson gave him permission to make the trip. Since all were technically still under contract to the United States War Department, Paulsen was told he must return to Alaska as soon as possible, and he agreed. The herders were pleased that Redmyer's group had saved as many deer as they had, and that the living animals were not only recovered but sleek and fat. These particular reindeer must have been tough beasts.

On June 23rd, after an all-night voyage, they reached Seattle again. They put their things aboard the *Navarro* and gave their quarters a quick inspection. Characteristically, Carl complained that it was not better than the *Kenney*. Even as he recorded his grumblings in his journal, however, he resigned himself almost philosophically for he had complained so much already that he felt he probably would not get much of a hearing from the leaders if he were too loud this time. He was chiefly disgusted because, as usual, several American miners had managed to buy tickets and were already aboard. Sacariasen predicted more discomfort, poor food, and overcrowding.

Rolf Wiig did not want to spend the winter on St. Lawrence Island or in Siberia buying deer, and asked Kjellmann to let him go with the others. Kjellmann said he would talk to Jackson, and after a short consultation they announced that Jermias Abrahamsen had been substituted for Wiig. Abrahamsen was not pleased to have to live for many months on that barren island, but agreed to go.

The *Navarro* did not sail that night, nor for the following four nights. Since they had little to do, the men decided once again to see the sights of

Seattle which they had not visited since March. For most of them this meant finding a saloon as quickly as possible.

The next morning they climbed into a small side-wheeled steamer that served as a kind of water taxi to the boats moored away from the docks in Elliott Bay. Though the herders had all visited the small city briefly when they were at Woodland Park, they wandered through the area now known as Pioneer Square District, but then the center of Seattle, looking at the sights and hearing the sounds of the gold-crazed city. They were amazed and delighted at the excitement. The streets were jammed with hurrying men and a few women trying to buy "outfits" to take north. The stores still seemed huge to them. Before they crossed the Atlantic in February, they had seen only the small shops in their home villages. While, as noted earlier, Seattle probably had only a few more than sixty thousand permanent inhabitants in this summer of 1898, there were many other transients passing through. Hundreds and even thousands of people poured into the dock area trying to book passage on anything that floated, and seemed likely to get to Alaska. The merchants of Seattle were overwhelmed with demands for what they had to sell. Their profits, in consequence, were extraordinary. The Depression of 1893 had hit Seattle very hard, and the merchants basked in the warm glow of their balance sheets. For them the Depression was over. They sent large orders to their eastern supply houses. In other parts of the United States the Depression was still hurting business, and news of "good times" in this far western outpost traveled fast. The supply wholesalers eagerly filled the Seattle orders, and so much arrived all at once that there was not enough warehouse space to store the merchandise until it was needed. Day and night the horse-drawn delivery wagons brought boxes of goods to the stores, where they were left at the front doors on the sidewalks. Eventually, as more and more goods piled up, the boxes were pushed out into the streets themselves, and stacked there. Every day was a "sidewalk sale" in Seattle during that lively summer.

Nine years before, Seattle had had a severe fire that had destroyed much of the downtown business district. This was a collection of false-fronted wooden shacks and ramshackle store buildings, built in some cases along plank-covered, narrow streets. When the city was rebuilt it was changed to one of brick and stone, and the structures put up during pioneer days were gone. When Carl and his friends saw it, Seattle was a handsome new city, though quite compact, for no one dreamed that the Alaska-Yukon gold rush would turn their economic world upside down. Everywhere at the edge of the business district to the north, new construction was going on as fast as material could be collected and men could be hired, to build new stores and office buildings. South of town land removal on Beacon Hill resulted in more than a hundred acres of tideflats being filled for industrial uses.[6]

To the people from distant Lapland this city was wonderland. Sacariasen rather smugly recorded that the Lapps had an inordinate craving for whiskey, and wrote that they literally sold some of the bright clothes off their backs for only a few cents which would buy them enough liquor for them to get drunk. The expansive Americans on their way to hoped-for riches in the Yukon frequently "treated" the Lapps, because when they got drunk, their behavior provided cheap amusement for the men in the saloons.

The herders had been warned against allowing strangers to buy whiskey for them, and they had heard lurid tales of persons who had been enticed into disreputable spots where in their drunken state they would be robbed of everything they had. Worse, this was a seaport town, and they might be given whiskey loaded with "knockout drops" of chloral hydrate, which would put them to sleep almost instantly. When these unfortunate people awoke they might then find themselves aboard some ship bound for the Orient as an unpaid member of the crew. Gangs of desperados were known to specialize in furnishing crews of "Shanghaied" sailors for captains who asked no questions as to how the recruits were obtained. One of the Lapp boys reported later that he had had such a narrow escape while he was in Seattle. He was still conscious when he heard several men coming down the hall toward his room. He started to open the door and found it locked from the outside. Quickly he tried the window, which was unlocked, and climbed out on the ledge. Fortunately, Seattle was such a small city that there were no high-rise rooming houses, and he was on only the second floor. He heard the men, who had paused outside his door, turning the key in the lock, and after a momentary glance in the empty room they rushed to the open window and saw him standing a few feet away. One started crawling out to seize him, and although he was a good dozen feet from the sidewalk the terrified lad thought a broken leg was better than months at sea taking an unwanted voyage to China, so he leaped to the ground. He was not hurt, but when he returned to the *Navarro* he was still badly shaken by his narrow escape. He enjoyed being the center of attention, however, as he told and retold the story of his misadventure. Carl was told that even old and experienced men were sometimes kidnapped for labor on nondescript freighters on the Pacific runs, and legends of such happenings are still told in histories of the Puget Sound ports.

On Friday, the 25th of June, another steamer, the *Del Norte*, left Seattle for St. Michael, Unalakleet, Golovnin Bay, and Siberia. It carried provisions for the Bering Sea towns to get them through the following winter, and passengers heading for the gold fields beyond Skagway. Lindeberg, Ole Krogh and Ravna, were ticketed for Siberia. Jermias Abrahamsen was booked along with a missionary to St. Lawrence Island. After the herders saw their companions off, they went to their quarters on the *Navarro*, hoping to leave the next morning.

They did not. Cargo was still arriving, and the crew of the ship kept busy stowing everything aboard. This particular day was a Norwegian holy day. It was known there as St. Hanschlegan, or St. John's Day. The men were curious to see how it would be celebrated in America, for at the turn of the century it was a very special day in Scandinavian countries. The origins of this feast day seem to have been lost among the myths of mid-summer celebrations of the longest day of the year. It probably had religious overtones that might have been added by Germanic missionaries to pagan festivals hundreds of years ago. They soon found out how Americans celebrated. No one in Seattle seemed aware that this was a holiday, for they treated it no differently from any ordinary Saturday.

Sunday, as usual, was another quiet day, and Sacariasen wrote a short entry in his journal grumbling that while they were waiting on their poor excuse of a passenger steamer Jackson and Kjellmann were leaving for Alaska "on one of the finest Alaska steamers."[7] He needn't have been upset. There were really no "finest" ships on the Alaska runs, and even the best were only in the "fair to good" category.

Since Jackson had not thought it worth his while to keep the herders informed about his negotiations with the War Department, they did not know that the military authorities had directed Jackson to arrange for a reindeer-mail service from the Bering Coast to the interior of Alaska on a semi-regular basis during the coming fall and winter. The reindeer mail was expected to connect St. Michael to the mouth of the Tanana River, and would provide revenue to repay the government for its expenses in the aborted "relief expedition" for the miners at Dawson. It would also provide some employment for the herders until their year-long contracts expired the following February.

NOTES

[1] *R. i. A.*, p. 79.
[2] *R. i. A.*, p. 79.
[3] *R. i. A.*, p. 84.
[4] 55 Cong., 3 Sess., *House Document #5*, "Commission to Lapland," p. 1794.
[5] Basi, *Diary*, September 20, 23, 1898.
[6] Hynding, Alan, *The Public Life of Eugene Semple: Promoter and Politician of the Pacific Northwest*, Seattle: University of Washington Press, 1973. pp. 156-157.
[7] *R. i. A.*, p. 95.

Chapter Four

GOLD!

Monday noon, the *Navarro*'s whistle sounded loudly across the waters of Elliott Bay, warning everyone of some important events to come. The passengers who were milling around the docks and streets of Seattle already knew that when the ship's whistle blew they were to board the ship at once. Now these people hurried to the dock to go to their ship, and soon all of the people who had bought tickets for Alaska on this vessel were ready to sail.

The young bachelors among the herders were amused to see how much kissing went on in America between the men headed north and the women who were there to see them off. Carl noted that even some of the men kissed each other, which was certainly not in accord with his own standards of conduct!

Twice more the ship's whistle blew as a final warning, and as no one else appeared the Captain gave orders to cast off, and once again the Norwegians left the Seattle waterfront. People on the slowly receding shore waved handkerchiefs to their friends aboard, until faces could not be distinguished because of the growing distance between them.

By evening, June 28, *Navarro* had passed Port Townsend, and turned northwest through the Strait of Juan de Fuca, where they had not gone before. It traveled slowly, for it was pulling a large scow loaded with goods for sale in Alaska, and freight belonging to the passengers. This barge had once been used by James J. Hill's venture in trans-Pacific passenger service, and had been called the *Minneapolis*. Now it was attached to the powered *Navarro* by a tow rope. Some of the passengers had been allowed to buy tickets to ride on the uncomfortable and barely seaworthy *Minneapolis*, and she was almost as packed with boxes and humanity as the *Navarro* was. As was the case with so much of the traffic between Seattle and Alaska in 1898, the scow seemed in imminent danger of springing a leak at any moment.

All was well until they reached the open Pacific beyond Cape Flattery. There they encountered a stiff breeze which caused the steamer to rock violently in the swells off Vancouver Island. The barge did worse than that. Although the seas were not exceptional, the *Minneapolis* did spring a leak shortly after she moved out into the open ocean, and the towing *Navarro* had to stop and turn about in the heavy sea. The passengers aboard the towed vessel were taken off and placed on the steamer along with the injured commander of the *Minneapolis* who had hurt his hand while trying to repair the leak in the dark. One of the male passengers broke his leg while transferring from the tow to the *Navarro*, so the two ships re-entered the Strait and anchored about seventy miles west of Port Townsend in order that the two casualties could receive proper medical attention.

It was expected that the damage to the *Minneapolis* could be repaired in the quiet waters where they were anchored, but this proved impossible. In the morning both ships and passengers steamed back to Port Townsend where skilled shipwrights took only a few hours to get the leak stopped and the water pumped out.

The master of the *Navarro* judged that it would be far too dangerous to try to go through the Strait again; therefore he changed course so that their voyage took them through the inside passage between Vancouver Island and the mainland of British Columbia. This had been the route taken by the reindeer expedition in March. He now needed a pilot to take him through Canadian waters, and this caused a further delay until he could arrange for one, and the man could come aboard. The reindeer herders did not mind, however, even though they knew that the delay would mean they would arrive at their destination at least four days behind schedule. They had seen how difficult it was for the *Navarro* to pull the scow in the Pacific winds, and they knew that in a three thousand mile voyage they were almost certain to encounter a storm that might be even worse than they had met at Cape Flattery. Since the two vessels made only three knots in calm seas, a storm would stop their progress entirely, and they had had enough of that in the north Atlantic on the *Manitoban* in February. As Sacariasen noted, however, there was no hurry, for "their pay was the same" whether on board or ashore.

Since their earlier voyage to Haines had also followed the same Inside Passage for the first thousand miles, Carl and his companions recognized some of the landmarks along the coast, as they passed through Johnstone Strait and into Queen Charlotte Sound. They attended a church service that first Sunday conducted by an Alaskan-bound missionary. They didn't understand many words of the sermon, but they enjoyed the songs that the English-speaking passengers sang without knowing what the words meant. Carl's mastery of the English language had barely begun.

During the pleasant days on the ship, Carl reported that the passengers were in good humor and satisfied with life, "because we were able to steal through the narrow passages between the high and low forest-covered hills without feeling any waves, and because the weather every day was warm and sunny." Of course early July in these waters is the ideal time to make a sea voyage to Alaska, as any modern travel agent knows. The main event of the first few days was the Fourth of July, their first Independence Day in North America. The missionary who had preached the previous Sunday read an address from a Seattle newspaper, and when he had finished the fifty American passengers aboard clapped and cheered. After this they sang several patriotic songs, which Carl referred to as their "national songs." Those who could interpret for them explained to the curious herders that this was the greatest of all days in America, and was celebrated with many kinds of festivities. The Norwegians observed proceedings soberly, and quietly recorded what happened.

Twelve days after they left Seattle, they reached Juneau. No one cared much. The weather had been beautiful while the scenery, then as now, had been unbelievably spectacular. They were allowed two hours to visit the little city, but that did not take the full time, for Juneau did not have much to offer in the way of tourist attractions in 1898. The *Navarro* filled its tanks with fresh drinking water, sent its Canadian pilot ashore, and headed once more out to sea by way of Cape Spencer. It was impossible, even for a steamer as tiny as the *Navarro*, to sail directly north from Juneau because of shallow water at the end of the inlet. Midway across the Sound they were suddenly surrounded by a heavy fog, and they turned back to Juneau, still towing the *Minneapolis*.

The fog soon cleared, and they resumed their voyage across the Gulf of Alaska. It took a week to cross it, but even at that they sailed faster than they had through the Passage. When a breeze came up, the Captain ordered his crew to set sails to aid the engines. With this auxiliary power their speed, while still not great, increased noticeably. The weather stayed calm and fair, and all of the passengers were thoroughly contented, including Carl.

They passed Kodiak Island without stopping, for they were already behind schedule, and they needed nothing by way of provisions. Another bank of fog rolled down from the island, and they saw very little of it. No one wanted to go ashore, for there they knew they would be wet and miserable.

Finally, while still at sea, they lost their good weather, but by this time they had almost reached the Aleutian chain. They expected since they were so close to shelter that they would not encounter much more bad weather. However, the Gulf of Alaska is the place where most storms affecting the north Pacific coast first develop, so it is not surprising that a small one struck them that very afternoon.

By evening the breeze had become a violent squall. Carl noted that the crew was busy putting cross braces under the deck to keep the deck crane from toppling and perhaps tearing some of the deck planking with it if it went down. There was no accident, and though the storm continued all night, it gradually eased until by morning skies were blue again. "It was everybody's good fortune that all went well," wrote Carl.

The day of July 17 was highlighted by the sight of a volcano in eruption, which was a new experience for most of the passengers. They crowded the deck rails and watched it for several hours as they passed it. As darkness came again the fog began to form once more, and they realized that they were far enough north to have cold weather, even in July. The erupting mountain disappeared from their sight. They could still see the shoreline in the gathering twilight, and they noted the almost total absence of trees on the bare hillsides of the Islands. This Aleutian landscape was different even from Norway, where the trees though stunted grow on the hillsides of Lapland.

On Monday, July 18, they reached Akutan Pass and Dutch Harbor. By noon the *Navarro* stopped, and anchored beside the village. Sacariasen judged that this was the most beautiful spot he had yet seen on the coast of Alaska. While mid-July is mid-summer in more temperate zones, this far north it is late spring, and everything on the island was green from the water's edge to the tops of the mountains. In the absence of timber, the green cover gave a soft pastel tint to the entire landscape, which delighted the eyes. The headlands were not precipitous, there were no rocky cliffs to be seen, but the hills were all softly rounded and covered with the lush green grass. Here and there patches of wild flowers added to the charm of the place.

Once again the *Navarro*'s tanks were filled so that they could cross the Bering Sea to St. Michael with no more stops. The passengers were permitted to visit Dutch Harbor, but told to return in a few hours, though there was no urgency about their orders, for they were close to their destination.

They walked along the crooked streets of the town of Dutch Harbor and Carl noted the different kinds of peoples who lived there. He did not seem to be aware that Aleuts are somewhat different from either Indians or Eskimo, but referred to them as a "mixed population of Eskimo, Russian, and American"--Caucasian. These mixed blood people were listed in government reports as "Creoles." While this is an ambiguous term traditionally used to refer to various mixtures of Spanish or French and indigenous people in Louisiana or the Caribbean islands, it was used in Alaska to describe a different ethnic mix. How the term got transplanted to Alaska is hard to say.

Even though the town was small, there were two churches--one Russian Orthodox and the other American Protestant. The third major structure there was the warehouse of the Alaska Commercial Company, where coal was stored for the passing ships, and water could be furnished for those that carried passengers.

The men finished their brief sightseeing excursion, and began to climb the mountain back of Dutch Harbor. The grass was pleasant to walk through, and when they heard the ship's whistle they picked handfuls of wild flowers and trooped down the hill to their quarters sniffing their fragrant bouquets like children, weary, happy, and at peace with the world.

Early on Tuesday morning, the *Navarro* with the *Minneapolis* in tow left Unalaska Island, and went through the passage into the Bering Sea. It would be at least a week before the *Navarro* reached St. Michael, but now the herders were impatient to get there to see what lay in store for them. The wind was fair, the sea was calm, though it rained intermittently during the next four days, and from time to time they would lose sight of everything in a fog. Fortunately their engines were sturdy, and though they couldn't raise any sails to help their speed, they traveled northward steadily.

The day before they should have reached St. Michael, a sudden headwind stopped them almost entirely. Since they had trouble with the *Minneapolis* off Cape Flattery early in the voyage, they did not push their luck but slowed to a stop and waited for the storm to pass. The scow was all right in the lea of the steamer, but it was not seaworthy enough to stand being pulled directly into the teeth of the heavy gale that was blowing.

On the 25th of July they finally reached St. Michael, with the *Minneapolis* still at the end of the tow line and on top of the water, though somewhat worse for the experience. Dr. Jackson had reached the harbor with thirty-five of the herders and their families before they arrived, and he was at the dock to meet them. Regnor Dahl was there too. Jackson had hired him to take charge of the reindeer mail service that the War Department planned to operate that fall in connection with P. C. Richardson who held the contract for mail delivery through the entire Yukon Valley.[1] Since Dahl could speak to the Lapps in their own language and the Americans could not, he would presumably be a valuable addition to the crew. Seeing these two men together, Sacariasen could indulge in his favorite pastime of writing things in his journal about them. He disliked both almost to the same extent.

Although Alaskan towns in 1898 were small and facilities for tourists or immigrants were virtually non-existent, Carl's main complaint against Jackson this time was that they had to stay in uncomfortable quarters wherever he billeted them.[2] This time was no exception. They were told to stay in a "little old outbuilding" which had "no stove or anything else in which to keep a fire to warm ourselves." They were soaked by the falling rain and, as they looked around, they saw that there were no beds of any kind to raise them off the hard floor. They made themselves as comfortable as they could on bare boards which were only a few inches above the marshy ground below. Carl admitted that he had not expected Dr. Jackson to house them in a hotel, but he had been comfortable aboard the *Navarro*, and had been warm as well. Now he was thoroughly disgruntled, and imagined the worst of motives on the part of Jackson.

The men asked about their evening meal, and when it came it consisted only of hardtack and canned beef. This was quite a change from the steamer's menu, and they did not like it. Carl described the "crackers" as "moldy" and no one was accustomed to eating what they called "canned ox meat." He asserted that all felt as he did, and sat huddled together, sulking in the darkness, at what they had found in this bleak village so far from their homes in northern Lapland. Eventually, however, they began to grow sleepy, and they unrolled their sleeping bags, crawled into them, and soon fell asleep, even though they were not furnished mattresses or any kind of stove.

In mid-July, even here, it should have been warm enough to do without a fire, but they were wet and depressed, and they wanted warmth.

The next morning the herders were no more cheerful, though they had had a night of rest. Carl referred to St. Michael as "this so-called town" as he took the morning off to see the sights of the place. Since he had never seen an Eskimo before, he went out to look at these strange people. The town had two stores--one more than Dutch Harbor. There was the establishment of the ever present Alaska Commercial Company, and that of its competitor, the North American Transportation and Trading Company. There were several American style dwellings for the employees of the stores, and the winter huts of the Eskimo. The summer housing for these people consisted of tents, and the huts were empty. In addition, there was a considerable number of temporary shelters for prospectors headed up the river to the gold fields farther inland. Not far away from town was a tiny army camp, which represented the law and order for nearly everything north of the Yukon River. Sacariasen wrote that in 1898 it was almost entirely a collection of tents and wooden buildings where the transient inhabitants tried to wring as much profit for themselves or their companies as they could before they returned to the "Outside," which usually meant Seattle.

As Carl walked around the village his curiosity took precedence over his prejudices, and he watched the townspeople carefully. He was particularly interested in the Eskimo kayaks, with their sealskin covering stretched over a slender inner frame. He noted that when the operator was seated inside he appeared to be sitting in the water, for the tiny craft was barely above the water line. All one could see of the person paddling the kayak was his head and arms, and the paddle he used to propel it. As the day was fair again this morning, and the wind had died down, he marveled at the speed the Eskimo maintained in their tiny canoes. He estimated that they could cross a considerable body of water in an hour or two.

As he got closer to the Eskimo tents he looked to see what they were eating for their morning meal. Once again his normal reaction to strangeness overwhelmed him, for he was repelled by the strong odor coming from the food they were eating. He reported their menu to be dried seal meat which they dipped into seal oil before each bite. They washed their food down with gulps of hot tea. He did not try to join them, nor did they invite him. He wrote that evening that over the entire scene was a "pestlike stink." Perhaps his "canned meat" would have been equally distasteful to the Eskimo had they watched him eating that.

Later in the evening after his visit to St. Michael was ended, Sacariasen added comments to his Journal and made anthropological observations about Eskimo that he could not possibly have picked up in a two-hour visit to their camp. Whether he learned it before he got there or added it to his journal later, he never said. For this first year after he came to North America, his impatience and intolerance toward whatever differed from the Scandinavian way of doing things showed in almost everything he wrote. He was no trained observer of human culture, nor did he care to become one. His opinions were those of a highly provincial emigrant, and sometimes might have been based on myths told by prospectors in Seattle, on the ship, or even later, about Indians or Eskimo and their customs. There are inaccuracies in his comments about the marital customs of the Eskimo, and the impression he gives from time to time about food and housing patterns that he had seen or heard about have some of the same kinds of inaccuracies. Before he left Alaska, however, he saw much more of Eskimo life, and grew to understand it better. The main value of what he wrote when he got back to his journal lies in the fact that he has allowed us to see what impressions northern Europeans had of Eskimo or Indian mores when they observed them for the first time.

He wrote in his journal, for example, that he could tell Eskimo from Indians because they were not as dark in appearance as Indians. Eskimo were more ruddy, and always smiled when he met them, he stated.

Their clothing was made chiefly of skins at that time. Sealskin was favored for summer wear, and deerskin for the colder seasons. For protection against rain they put bear and seal intestines together, sewing them into a slipover coat with an attached hood to cover their heads. These were transparent, but according to Carl's observation they were not very effective. However, he said if one commented that they were not keeping their wearers dry, the Eskimo would not agree, but would say "Nak gorak" which he translated as "Good." They said this even though they were soaked.

The *Del Norte* arrived safely at St. Michael the day after Sacariasen and the others on the *Navarro* did. Now all the Norwegians and Lapps were together again. Their supplies had been sent on to Unalakleet, and there was not enough food ashore for the herders and their families in the hostel where all were housed. Carl attacked Dr. Jackson once more for his apparent lack of concern about their welfare. The forty new people who came to the warehouse where they were sleeping were issued two pounds of sugar, two pounds of butter, and some roasted coffee, but no flour. Other than the same "moldy crackers" left over from their previous day's ration, they had nothing else from the supplies. Instead, they were told that they could spend the day gathering "cloud berries," which grew in profusion through the bog surrounding them. They spread out to harvest the ripening fruit, and supplemented their uninteresting and ill-balanced meal with plenty of berries. The following day they did it again.

On the evening of July 27, Dr. Jackson came to the warehouse and made signs to the scattered pickers that they were to come to him. When all had gathered around him, he told them that they would leave for Unalakleet the following morning. He told them that he was aware of the poor food they were eating and that they were discontented, but the supplies were waiting, there would be plenty of food when they arrived, and they should be ready to leave as early as possible to get a good meal. Carl was glum about this, for he reasoned that Jackson could have bought food at the Alaska Commercial Company's store. He did not know the way of bureaucracies and government auditors, however. He did not realize what a commotion would have occurred in some accounting office had Jackson bought food when he had already received enough supplies for several months before the expedition left Seattle. The auditors held Jackson responsible for every dime of appropriations that had been made for the expedition, and anything they disapproved, he had to pay for out of his own pocket. Indeed, Jackson's enemies, who were numerous, already were accusing him of frittering away the money for his own benefit, and over-indulging the herders with extravagant luxuries.

To Jackson's distress, he could not even buy food for a sick woman who was traveling with them for a short distance. She was the wife of Otto Leinan, a Swede, and was on her way with her husband to St. Lawrence Island. There was no way he could use government money to buy food for her, and he had to refuse Leinan's request for aid, though he did send him out into the bog to pick berries with the herders.

Carl's grimmest predictions came true when the ship to carry them to their food did not arrive. By now the berries were almost all picked, and Jackson did manage to rustle up enough food for their morning meal, though where he got it neither his own reports nor Carl's journal stated. Magnus and Thoralf Kjelsberg spoke for the herders in saying that their supplies for that many people were simply not enough, and Jackson would have to give them more. Sacariasen must have been hungry, or he had difficulty in filling his daily entry, for he listed the food sent to them in detail--ten pounds of rice, two pounds of butter, two pounds of sugar, twelve pounds of meat and another case of the moldy hardtack which no one liked. Since forty-eight people had to share his food, it certainly appears that no one over-ate. His record of the number involved leads one to wonder what the other seventy herders ate, since there were well over a hundred different individuals.

Finally on Saturday morning, the *Del Norte* sent small boats ashore to pick up the herders. When the last man and woman went aboard, the ship immediately got underway. There were many other passengers than the herders already aboard, for by now the summer gold rush up the Yukon was in full swing, and the easiest route to the great river was up the Unalakleet, where they were going. No one on the deck got much rest, for the boat was so crowded that it was difficult to find enough space to stretch out.

On Sunday morning they reached their destination and anchored off shore, since there were neither docks nor enough depth of water to allow their ship to get closer. Jackson overlooked his custom of taking Sunday off from work so that he could get his people ashore, housed, and given food.

He also directed that any baggage to be landed should be unloaded at the same time for, although the day was warm and beautiful, at this latitude no one knew what the weather would be like the next day.

As their small boats came ashore, they were delighted to find William Kjellmann on the beach to greet them. He was ready to resume his responsibilities with them. Beside him stood Dr. Francis Gambell who was to be their doctor and schoolteacher. Also Regnor Dahl was there, ready to take over the mail service when and if it were initiated. These men had reached Unalakleet two days previously on the *Louisa J. Kenney*.

The beach where they piled the boxes being unloaded was about two miles from the mission in the village, but near the herd of Siberian reindeer that had been concentrated from various small herds to the north. Since they had come to Alaska in the first place to care for deer, it made sense to stop there. Two Lapp families, those of Johan Tornensis and Mikkel Nakkila, who had come to Alaska four years earlier with the first group of teachers, were herding the animals by themselves until the rest arrived. They had taken most of the summer moving their animals from Port Clarence to Unalakleet, which Kjellmann had given them instructions to do before he left for Norway the previous December.

Not long afterward, Frederik Larsen, also one of the original herders, and Dr. A.N. Kittilsen came down to see what was going on. Larsen, the eighteen-year-old Roman Catholic Lapp that Kjellmann had hired to squelch complaints that the Protestants were monopolizing the reindeer business, was now twenty-two and a veteran of the reindeer service. A few months before he had married a young Eskimo girl, and said he had no intention of going back to Norway, but would live out his days on the shores of the Bering Sea, which is exactly what he did. Kjellmann had not known of the romance before he left for Norway, but he did not oppose it now that he found out about Larsen's marriage.

Sacariasen was so curious about the young woman that he asked all kinds of questions about Eskimo customs. Apparently his informants had told him some pretty wild stories. Perhaps the people talking to him believed what they were saying, and perhaps they were just filling Carl full of tall tales to see whether he was gullible enough to accept them. In any event he seemed to be completely credulous.[3]

Sacariasen did not understand the Eskimo customs, and dismissed most of their activities as "vulgar heathenish customs" which had changed little since the coming of the missionaries, but he also denounced those whites who discarded their native companions when they tired of them.

He soon had his mind turned to other subjects, however, for as Tornensis, Nakkila, and Larsen talked with the newly arrived herders busily piling their goods on the beach, they reported matter of factly that there were reports of gold discoveries in and around Golovnin Bay to the north of Unalakleet, and some people had taken claims there. Each of them had also filed on gold claims. When Jafet Lindeberg heard this news of gold only a few miles away, he announced loudly that under no circumstances was he going to Siberia to buy deer, and Dr. Jackson might as well know it then and there.

Carl reported that Lindeberg and Jackson stood on the beach beside the piled equipment yelling at each other. Both soon calmed down, and Jackson suggested that if he wanted to go gold prospecting, Lindeberg should resign from the reindeer service and take a settlement of his wages. Lindeberg accepted this reasonable offer with alacrity. It did not take him long to gather up his own baggage and go back on board the *Del Norte* to try his fortune at looking for gold. Since there was another mission at Golovnin Bay, the *Del Norte* had scheduled at stop there to unload supplies, and Lindeberg could go ashore there, where he could search for gold to his heart's content. Golovnin Bay is a considerable body of water, and gold could have been found anywhere along the streams emptying into it, but Lindeberg was willing to start searching. For the men who stayed on with Jackson, there was to be no prospecting but rather building houses and shelter for herders and animals at a new reindeer station that would be located a few miles inland from the village.

Kjellmann had earlier located a spot on the Unalakleet River between the river bank and the low mountains to the north, which was named the Eaton Reindeer Station. Officially now, Kjellmann again assumed his position as Superintendent and matters were back to the situation in March when everything seemed to go right as long as he was in charge.

Immediately the decisive Kjellmann told the herders his plans. He divided them into groups of fourteen. Three tents were assigned to each group for their shelter and for storing their personal belongings. Each married man was given a tent for himself and his wife and their children, if they had any. If there were no buildings built, everyone would have to stay in the tents, even though the weather should grow cold. Kjellmann systematized the issuing of food rations, giving each person a diet of pork, butter, coffee, brown sugar, milk, canned meat, baking soda, and yeast. It may be noted that there were no green vegetables of any kind in these supplies, not even of the canned variety, and a balanced diet depended on the whims of the cooks, who decided on the menus for each day with no interference from the Superintendent. For this reason, it is not surprising that one of the problems traditionally associated with living in the northern latitudes at the turn of the century was scurvy, which even as late as 1898 was a somewhat mysterious disease to the people of Alaska. The herders were no more immune than anyone else. After a while scurvy appeared among them too.

Apparently Kjellmann divided the squads of men somewhat by nationality for, because of his experience, Carl was made cook for the "Norwegian Division." Peder Johannesen cooked for Division Two which was Lapp, and Amund Hansen for Division Three. These three men were also charged with the responsibility to see that the rations divided for the feeding of the crews were used in such a way that there would be something left for any emergencies at the end of every month.

Unalakleet itself was a small village with about thirty Eskimo huts and a trading post operated by a Norwegian named Englestad, who was not connected in any way with either the herders or the missionaries working nearby. The local Swedish Mission consisted of a schoolhouse, a combination dining hall, dormitory and chapel for the mission personnel.

As usual, Carl walked around the town, as he had done in other places he had visited. He judged the tiny hamlet to be in a lovely location with a view of both the ocean and the mountains and valleys behind it. Food was plentiful and easy to obtain, with salmon running up the river throughout most of the summer in quantities hard to realize today, and wild game abounding in the forests on the mountains. The ocean did not exactly "teem" with seal, but there were enough for Eskimo needs for clothing and meat. These people avoided scurvy because long ago they had learned that if they supplemented their meat diet with oil and wild berries--cloudberries, cranberries, and huckleberries--they would not suffer dietary problems. Men were the hunters and fishermen while the women gathered the berries and dried the meat their men brought home for use through the long winter. Carl noted that they ate a kind of frozen dessert made from dried cloudberries and salmon eggs, which they allowed to freeze as soon as it grew cold enough. These were stored, and when they were taken out the native peoples sucked on the frozen blobs of food.

His sensibilities were affronted, however, when he saw that the Eskimo also ate any rodents they could catch, leaving them uncleaned, but hung them up to freeze and then dipped them in seal oil and ate them without any cooking. He marvelled at the obviously strong constitutions of the native peoples, and gave his opinion that they could eat and digest anything they could chew. He even saw that they ate kelp, which he thought to be totally inedible.

These Eskimo had taken well to the Christianity taught by the Swedish clergyman, Axel J. Karlson. He had come to Unalakleet alone in 1887, the first missionary in this part of Alaska. While he was not overwhelmingly successful in getting the Eskimo to join his church in any official way, they would attend his worship services, and also send their children to the mission school. He seemed to be respected by the local people. During the following twelve years at the village he had seen his mission grow from a sod hut built with the help of the friendly local people, to the two frame buildings standing there when the herders arrived. As his energy, time, and funds permitted, he added to the buildings. He was to play a continuing role in the future of the reindeer project. He eventually married, and he also had two young women school teachers working there--a native woman known to the herders at first only as "Alice," and Malvina Johnson, who had come up from the United States where she had been educated in a denominational college near Chicago. Interestingly, Karlson preached in Norwegian, even though it was a Swedish Mission.[4]

On August 5, after a delay of several days because of a storm, the men hiked upstream to the location of the future Eaton Station. The Eskimo of

Unalakleet paddled kayaks upstream carrying light loads of tents, provisions, and some of them carried passengers. Fifteen of the men, including Kjellmann, as well as Regnor and Alex Dahl, went with them. In addition to these, a Norwegian who had been at Haines Mission in March and had followed the Finnmark herders back to Seattle after the spring disaster, was now at Unalakleet. His name was Alex Jorness, and he was one of the first to get to Eaton where Kjellmann put him on the payroll. Sacariasen believed that he was related in some way to the Superintendent, but he was not sure. Originally Jorness had planned to go to Skagway, but had changed his mind, and was now living far to the west in an entirely different vocation. He had Americanized his name to Jones while he was in Seattle.

Of those who went by kayak to Eaton, Kjellmann was first to arrive, for either his canoe was lighter than the others, or his Eskimo boatman was stronger. By the time the hikers arrived, he had climbed to the top of a nearby spruce tree and raised an American flag to its summit. As soon as the necessary supplies were unloaded on the river bank everyone sat down, and the new Station was christened with a whiskey bottle from which everyone drank. When someone proposed that they add to the ceremony by raising a cheer, the men shouted "Hurrah!" or its Norwegian equivalent. All they needed to do now was to pitch their tents and build an entirely new set of buildings in the wilderness.[5]

Regnor Dahl returned with the Eskimo to Unalakleet. Why he came at all when he was there for such a short time, neither Kjellmann nor Sacariasen said. Dahl returned later, however, found that the mail service was delayed, took a job as foreman at Eaton for a time, then went to the Seward Peninsula to look for gold.

The Superintendent knew how to get the best service from the men, and they did not mind working for him, though there was the usual grumbling that one might expect. He took time after everyone was settled into his tent to explain to a general meeting that he had chosen this site because the nearby hills were covered with stunted spruce trees that could be worked into logs and planks as the need arose. There was plenty of pasture for the herds, and as soon as they could get to them, they must build nine structures on the hillside before the long Arctic night set in. Six of these buildings were to be cabins twenty feet by sixteen feet,[6] to house the workers and their families.

There was to be a two-story headquarters building with five rooms on each floor. A warehouse for storage was planned for the river bank to make unloading of supplies easier. Between the river and the six houses a workshop was also in the plans. Kjellmann's idea was that everything should be built from whipsawed lumber.

After the difficult work and celebration of the Friday they arrived, Kjellmann told the men they could take Saturday morning for rest or pleasure. Carl noted the profusion of moss as he wandered out into the nearby forest, and could not help comparing this site with the miserable camp and food supply they had experienced on the Chilkat River by Haines a few months before.

In the afternoon the Superintendent called the men back to work and they were assigned the job of clearing the scrub brush from the actual site of the foundations for the buildings which would be laid on Monday.

Sunday morning Dahl returned, bringing the men of "Division Two" which now put the work crew at twenty-five men. Kjellmann gave each person his assignment for the next day, and then let them take the rest of the time off. Since he was not one to allow the days to go by without anything to show for them, as the army leaders had done when they were in command, and because of the ten-hour shifts they worked during the long Arctic summer days, the crews could show considerable accomplishment after each day. As soon as breakfast was over Monday morning, some began to cut trees, and pull the brush into piles, while others tended fires to burn the brush that was cleared. This preliminary work took four days.

On Friday Dahl went down to Unalakleet once again, and told the Third Division to get ready to move. It is unlikely that anyone objected, even though most of them disliked Dahl for the way he had acted at Port Townsend. Monday this third group came up to Eaton.

By Tuesday, everyone was there except for Jakob Hatta, his wife and his children, who had been sent north to Cape Prince of Wales to help the Eskimo herders there take care of their herds. Here, at the Teller Station, was where the surviving deer from the relief expedition of the previous winter were to be brought back from Point Barrow. Some of them were returned, though there continued to be a considerable herd at Point Barrow for many years. Eventually the Teller herd numbered more than five hundred animals--descendants from the Siberian deer that Jackson had been buying during most of the decade.

Several other herders went to the Point Clarence Station as well to receive the deer that Dr. Jackson planned to buy in 1899. For the time being he had to put on another hat and serve as Superintendent of Alaskan Education, for he had not done much along this line since he went to Norway in January.

As far as the herders were concerned, they did not know where Jackson was or what his plans or duties were. They were kept busy at Eaton. On Tuesday they built a saw platform, and dug a pit beneath it. The first logs were brought in from the woods that same day, and were hoisted to the frame to be sawed. The boards could be put in place as soon as the foundations were finished. Eventually four sawpits operated, and three-man crews taking turns at the arduous task occupied the time of twelve men.[7] Dahl was assigned a small crew to move the supplies still sitting on the riverbank into the camp to be put under cover. The Lapp women were sent out to gather dried grass and to cut green hay to be cured for the lining of the Lapp boots so that the men could be sure their feet were in good condition. Other women sewed new boots or made moccasins. A different squad of men dragged logs from the forest to be squared for the foundations instead of being sawed into planks.

Carl was able to avoid much of the heavy labor, but he was kept busy filling the stomachs of the workmen and their women. To vary the diet, he asked Kjellmann whether he could have several men to catch some of the salmon that were running in tremendous numbers up the river to spawn. Kjellmann gave his permission, and after the noon meal Magnus and Thoralf Kjelsberg, Otto Greiner, and Hilmar Hansen took a net to the stream. In less than an hour they had pulled one hundred forty-five large salmon ashore. Carl put as many as he could into a huge kettle for a fish dinner. The hungry men found this a welcome change, for it was both more appetizing and more nourishing than cornmeal mush, which had been a large part of their monotonous previous diet.

Nothing stopped the progress, and the men worked hard. The delighted Kjellmann ran from one crew to another checking on each bit of activity, praising those who were doing well, and mentally taking note of how everything was working together. Since some of the deer were already at the Station, he had to send several of the construction workers out to move with the deer, mainly to protect them from predators. J.S. Tornensis and Mikkel Nakkila were taken off herding duty and put to carrying logs, while J.I. Tornensis and Aslak A. Gaup took their places with the herds. Two Eskimo in the apprentice program named Donnak and Martin went with them to see how it was done. After a few more days, Kjellmann detached two of the teen-age Lapp boys to work with the other four, and sent a Lapp girl to cook for all seven of them. With these preparations complete, he sent word to Unalakleet to bring the rest of the herd up to Eaton so that everyone could be together. By night there were 750 reindeer in the field which had been fenced to receive them. These were watched by the six men and one girl.

Before the week was over everyone had settled into his or her routine, but the weather remained so pleasant that it was more like a picnic than work. The labor was heavy, and Kjellmann felt a sense of urgency that the others did not, for he was in charge and he knew it would not be long until the days would grow much shorter. As a result the temperatures would drop sharply at night, and they had to have permanent shelter before the river froze. If they did not have it, there would be real suffering and sickness among the people in the camp. Nevertheless, he allowed Carl to send some of the older children to the river almost every day to catch fish for the main meal in the evening. So many were brought in on Friday of this week that Carl could not cook them all, but had to salt some for preservation and storage for use during the coming winter. Probably it was no coincidence that when the first building was finished, it was the combined cook shack and storage facility for food. Carl could now prepare his meals under shelter.

The sun was so warm in this month that the men caught a belated case of "spring fever." It was only with difficulty that the Superintendent was able to get much work out of them. By Saturday four buildings were marked off, the foundation stones put in place, and for the first time the potential cabins could be visualized with a little imagination. They were located about one hundred yards apart, probably for protection against fire. That same day, some of the Lapps began building frames for reindeer sleds to be stored until snow came when they could haul goods with the deer. No one knew how soon it would begin to snow, but everyone knew it would not be many weeks away.[8]

Since the next day was Sunday, and as was the custom no work was done, everyone was happy to rest. It had been a successful week, and there was no complaining about the hard jobs they were put to doing. They had enough to eat, they were warm, and reasonably housed for the time of year. They could see that their efforts were accomplishing something, everyone was in good health, and the weather was glorious. Morale was high.

The week following was much like the one before. Everything went well, and the weather stayed warm and pleasant, although now and then there might be a short rain shower. On Thursday, however, Kjellmann found a short letter from Sheldon Jackson when the mail was delivered from Unalakleet. Jackson had taken time off from his educational duties to make a flying trip on the *Del Norte* to the Siberian coast to check the number of deer that were waiting to be brought to Alaska the next year. Now, eighteen days later, he was back in Alaska with bad news. He wanted to discuss his problem with Kjellmann.

When he arrived in Siberia he found that the man in charge of the purchasing had deserted his post, allowing all of the deer to run away to the former herds. Many of the supplies he left at the post had been ruined by lack of care, and some were entirely absent because of looting. The head man of the local Eskimo village had taken equipment which he could not use, but would cost at least $20,000 to replace. Jackson spent most of his short visit to Siberia trying to recover the purchased animals and reclaim the equipment, but was unable to do much.

This meant that the next year's deer purchase would be measurably reduced, and he was forced to give up all thought of repaying the natives and missions that had loaned deer for the Point Barrow relief the winter before. The few deer he reclaimed were left at Point Clarence. He brought Ole Krogh and Johannes Ravna back with him to Unalakleet, since there was no need for them any longer at Point Clarence. If Lindeberg had not already resigned, there would have been no need for him to go to Asia either.

Another reason Jackson wanted to see Kjellmann was that he wanted to break the news to him that his father, Torvald Kjellmann, had died the previous May 27 at Point Clarence and had been buried there. No one had written about it because the people at the reindeer station there were not sure where William Kjellmann was, and there were not enough people there who knew how to write who could have told him.

In spite of such sad news, Kjellmann continued to urge the men to greater efforts as soon as he returned. Always before him was the spectre of the great Arctic cold that would soon be upon them. The fishing responsibility was given almost entirely to the older children to release their parents to work on construction. This gave these young people a sense of pride in the contribution they were making to the winter food supply, as well as to the daily menu. It was a rare day thaat they did not net a hundred salmon, and Carl spent much of his time preserving the fish for later use. The older men felt a sense of accomplishment as well, for each day they could see considerable progress on the housing. Everywhere if a person stopped working for only a few moments he could hear the sound of chopping, sawing, and shaping the whipsawed logs for supports for the walls. In the distance, the women sat in front of their tents working at making skin clothing as they talked with one another. Pleasant odors blew toward everyone as the cooks prepared the meals for the day, and preserved foods for the winter.

One small crew went upstream to search for larger logs that could be used for special supports, and could be floated down the river to the Station. As with everything else, they were successful, and the record of the passing days was that of one achievement after another. No one stopped working. The weather remained beautiful as well.

As they took their Sunday rest at the beginning of the third week, Carl wondered in his journal why they had bothered to take the day off when there was still so much work to be done, especially since there was no formal religious activity at the station. He decided that it was to make an impression on the Eskimos living nearby, even though their station was in no way a religious establishment like the mission at Unalakleet. Dr. Jackson was a clergyman and a missionary, however, and it was probably through his influence that they took the day off, for to him Sunday was a day for only minimal work. Except in times of emergency Kjellmann followed the custom.

When the next work week began, Dahl took a crew up the river to roll the larger logs to the river so that they could be floated downstream. By midweek the walls on the first four cabins were finished, and the door and window frames were installed. The roof-trees were hoisted into place ceremoniously. Kjellmann allowed the stores to be tapped for another bottle of whiskey, and when the supports were all in place everyone close stopped work and celebrated with a swallow from the community bottle. The roofs themselves were not put on, and no one could move into the structures as rain could pour freely into the rooms. The lack of doors and windows to keep out the weather made it impossible in any event.

Preparing food for the changing labor crews kept Sacariasen so busy for the next ten days that he did not have time to make a daily entry in his journal. Instead, he gave a general summary of the week in a single paragraph or two and continued this practice for the balance of the month.

The first thing the carpenters had to do, of course, was to get the roofs in place, then to build partitions, making a kind of duplex out of each cabin with a separate family living on each side. Each would have a tiny area sixteen by ten feet for the whole family, not much by modern standards, but as large as their Lapp tents at home, or the huts they had lived in during the winter times in Norway. While the builders constructed the partitions and put on the roof, the glass for the windows arrived and was placed in the window frames. Floors were laid at the last, and a cookstove was put in each room for warmth. By the beginning of the next week, the foundation for the headquarters building was completed, and immediately other men were sent to the riverbank to begin to put up the warehouse. A kind of deck was built on the riverside so that this would extend out into the current, and could serve as a docking area as well as storage. The inner sill of this building was on shore, and since there was no tidal action there was little danger of the structure being washed away. Dahl had returned from getting the big logs, and each day he and his crew went to Unalakleet with boats to bring up more supplies to the reindeer station. Long before the warehouse was ready, the material brought upstream and piled on the riverbank had grown to a huge heap of boxes and bags. For awhile they had tried to protect this pile with a tent, but this was now too small, and the boxes had to be left outside. As summer gave way to fall, increasing amounts of rain fell every day.

114

Kjellmann found it easy to impress on his builders that the storage warehouse had to be finished as quickly as possible if their supplies were not going to be ruined.

When Jackson met Kjellmann in Unalakleet in mid-August, he told his Superintendent that the War Department had not yet given up the idea of a reindeer mail service, so Kjellmann had to detach thirty men--almost half of his work force--from building to training animals to haul sleds for the expected project. Since the War Department had furnished the funds that had brought them from Norway in the first place, there was little chance of arguing with their instructions. As in any situation where orders came from four thousand miles away, the conditions were totally unrealistic. Kjellmann had to have the animals and men ready within a month. The projected mail line would operate from St. Michael and up the Yukon to Dawson. From there it would go to lower states by way of Haines, and outside by steamer.

Now that it was after the first of September, the days were growing noticeably shorter and the rain fell continuously. Regnor Dahl, who was working on the river and was consequently wet most of the time, was stricken with an acute case of arthritis and had to be put to bed. Carl did not say who replaced him as foreman.

It is interesting to note that the same day that Dahl went to bed was the day that Hedley Redmyer reached Lake Kukshu with the 144 surviving deer that had landed at Haines the previous March.

When mail came from Unalakleet this week there was a letter included from Jafet Lindeberg who had not been heard from for a month. His communication was full of good news. He had found considerable amounts of gold near Council City nor far from Cape Nome, and believed that it would not be long until there would be a major gold strike on the Seward Peninsula. The herders became excited, and spent much of their evening time talking and planning ways to resign from the Service and go to the peninsula across Norton Sound where they could make their fortunes prospecting for themselves or working for Lindeberg. For the time being, however, there was no chance of doing this, for they were under contract with the War Department until the following February, and they had to get the reindeer mail ready and finish the buildings at Eaton.

Every day now prospectors from St. Michael and Unalakleet came up the river and stopped at the station. They brought news of gold discoveries everywhere, but most of these were mere rumors. They sufficed to keep the herders in a state of continuous excitement, and those who had learned to talk in English to their visitors spent the nights regaling the Norwegian speakers with what they had heard.

One story that intrigued Sacariasen enough to record was a tale of three prospectors who lived in the same camp. One of the men claimed to have made a spectacular find, and offered to guide the other two to the place where they could all stake their claims. They did not know one another particularly well, but in their excitement they did not check on character. The three stopped to camp the first night, and the "discoverer" who had found no gold, but thought this would be a good way to restock his dwindling supplies of food, tried to steal all the provisions while the other two slept, leaving them to die in the wilderness. His companions woke for some reason and finding him missing did a quick check, and saw that he had stolen their possessions. They feared at first that he had become confused and had wandered off into the barren wasteland and had been lost. After searching for him briefly, they returned to camp and found that he had circled back and was stealing the rest of their things. At first their reaction was to kill him on the spot, but since they still believed his story of the gold strike and thought he was the only one who knew where they could find the gold, they would spare his life if he would guide them to where he had found it. When light came, they started together again, but he started to run, making a break for freedom since he knew that there was no gold where they were. He probably thought they would kill him anyway when they discovered that he was not only a thief but a liar. As he started to run his companions raced after him, overtook him, beat him with their fists, stripped off his clothing, then chased him out of camp naked and foodless to an almost certain death. This kind of morality story showed not only what gold fever would do to people, but the need to impress that grim retribution was sure to be the payment for the dreadful crime of stealing supplies in a place where lack of food or shelter was an invitation to doom.

Early in September the men again waited eagerly for the mail to arrive to find whether there was anything more about the gold discoveries or the evil deeds of discoverers. The Superintendent noted with satisfaction in his own log that one cabin was finished, that another three would soon be done, and that a fifth was being built outside the camp in the forest to be disassembled and moved to Eaton with the other four. Because of this visible progress, he took some of the remaining men and started them building the main structure on September 5th. His plans, sketched on a piece of rough paper, called for a two and a half story frame building of logs and whipsawed planks, sixty feet long and twenty feet wide.

This was far more pretentious than the cabins. Neither Kjellmann nor Sacariasen recorded whether Dahl had recovered enough to take over the position of foreman, but the loggers and sawyers busily cut logs into studs and rafters 2 x 8 feet in size, which was considerably stouter than would probably have been necessary. There were plenty of raw materials available, however, and Kjellmann wanted a sturdy building. Within the next two weeks, logs and studs poured into the Station faster than they could be put into place. While the skies turned to sunny again, the air had a bite to it and the summer warmth was definitely gone. Everyone felt good, according to Carl.

Dr. Francis H. Gambell, the physician and school teacher at the Station, was now authorized by Kjellmann to move into one of the cabins temporarily, and to use it as a school, a doctor's office, and a first aid station. The families continued to live in their tents, but they did not resent this apparent favoritism, for they recognized their own vulnerability to accidents or sickness if there was no medical attention available. Thus far they had been singularly fortunate, and neither in the journal nor in official reports is there any notation of a serious accident. Dr. Gambell told the people that he would try to teach them English at night if they cared to come to his office, and that he would hold classes five nights a week. There was so much interest that he began his school for them on the first Monday after his announcement.

Very probably a mere thirst for learning was not the primary force that motivated the Norwegians and Lapps. Gold was nearby, and they needed English to be able to cope with the English-speaking society surrounding them. Regnor Dahl, who could speak English, resigned from the service because he was too crippled to continue, he said, and Kjellmann accepted his resignation. Immediately, he recovered and induced three of

117

the herders to desert. They announced as they prepared to leave that they were going north to Golovnin Bay to join Lindeberg and become rich. It is ironic that Lindeberg and Dahl detested each other in Port Townsend but, with the possibility of wealth, Dahl decided that Lindeberg was a far better person than he had at first believed.

Most of the herders disliked Dahl as much as Lindeberg did, for they said he talked too much and didn't work as hard as the others. However, he was an American citizen, so they all crowded around him and thrust pieces of paper into his hands, giving him power-of-attorney to locate gold claims ("guildklaime" Carl wrote it),[9] for them if he found signs of the valuable stuff. These authorizations were to create an interesting legal problem which plagued the Nome area for the next several years. Could a power of attorney given to an American by another person who had made only a declaration of intent to become a citizen be valid in an American mining camp, and would it be upheld in American courts if someone challenged it?

Dahl did not leave for Nome until Wednesday. Kjellmann talked the three men who wanted to go with him into coming back after a three-week absence, so everyone parted on good terms. Wilhelm Basi, Magnus Kjeldsberg, and Ole Krogh were the men who went with Dahl.[10] Two other men, the original 1894 herders Johan S. Tornensis and Mikkel Nakkila, went with them but they promised they would return. They felt that they needed to do some "assessment work" on their own claims. They would come back, they promised, when the snow became deep enough for them to come back with sleds. The custom at that time was that if a claimant did $100 worth of work on a mining claim in a year, he could hold it against all others. Theoretically no one else could legally "jump" the claim, but if he failed to do his assessment work, anyone could move in. Actually, "jumping" claims was very common all over Alaska and the Yukon Territory, especially where one of the claims holders was not an American citizen. Where the courts were not active, only miners' associations enforced the rule against claim jumping, and in the part of Alaska where the reindeer were kept, courts were held quite infrequently.

Kjellmann was able to impress his urgency on the people working with him when he told them that if they had mail for Norway they would have to get it ready by September fifteenth if they were to catch the last boat outside for 1898. Any ship that stayed in the Bering Sea that far north after that date ran a risk of being frozen in for the winter, and all of the captains were eager to get away as quickly as possible. The weather remained clear, but it was growing very cold now, and it would not be long until ice would begin to form on the river and even along the saltwater beaches.

After that, it was rush, rush, rush to beat the storms that would come in a few days. The warehouse building got its roof by September 16, and Otto Leinen, the man who had been hired by Kjellmann for his skill as a stonemason, began getting loads of rocks from the nearby hillsides to strengthen the foundation of the main building. Kjellmann kept after his crews to increase their output, and finally some of them began to complain that he was overworking them. They tried to get Dr. Gambell to prescribe bed rest for them and to tell Kjellmann that they were too ill to work. They got little sympathy from either man, and the older and wiser people who had lived in this part of Alaska for some time knew that there was little time left for them to get finished, and out of their tents into decent shelter.

In the midst of these feverish activities, Kjellmann learned that the plans for the Arctic mail route for reindeer had gone awry. Richardson, the American who had been proposed to employ the surplus drivers for light express and mail service, had decided to abandon the project. This meant that the Station was no longer short of workmen, but was actually overstaffed for the winter, and since there were too many men there to work, just as soon as the buildings were finished, Kjellmann would have a problem stretching the supplies to take care of the needs or wants of over a hundred people. He put in a kind of rationing system immediately. Rolf Wiig, who had gone to St. Lawrence Island after all, was appointed storekeeper and, although the men and heads of families were allowed to draw their rations at any time of the month, he was to keep close check to see that no one received more than his share. This caused more grumbling of course. Now, if anyone drew supplies beyond what Kjellmann decided was equal to the rest, he had to pay for these "luxuries" in cash, and at $22 a month wages, they did not have much for extras. Basic supplies could be charged against the future earnings of the workers, but if anyone resigned he had to settle what he owed before he could leave. To solve this problem, Kjellmann said that anyone who did

119

not owe money and wanted to resign before his contract was ended could do so by giving sufficient notice of his intention to do so.

Although September 18th was a Sunday and supposedly a day of rest, the Superintendent sent two men with a boat down to Unalakleet to carry some supplies up to the Station, then to take them up river another seventy miles to sell them at a gold camp there. On their way back from the coast, they stopped to leave some fresh vegetables harvested from Missionary Axel Karlson's garden. The growing season that far north is very short, and the seeds must be planted late in the spring or in the early summer or they won't germinate. Yet the yields are good if they are of a variety that will mature in a few weeks. The hours of summer sunshine per day at that latitude mean that the growth rate is almost explosive, and the size of some of the vegetables is amazing.

On Monday, Kjellmann urged everyone to make up for the Sunday of no work. It was still dark when he called for the men to get out of bed. Some of them refused to budge, complaining that they were ill. Kjellmann would thunder at them "Where do you hurt?" A Lapp might answer, "Mos lä selki bachi," which is to say "I have a pain in my back." Unless the man was visibly ill, and few were, they were ordered outside. The result was that Leinan finished the foundation in two additional days, and the best carpenters were put to work placing the planks in piles for the siding and the roof. The prefabricated cabin was brought in one log at a time from the forest, and reassembled in its permanent location. It worked together beautifully, and seemed to show how some time could be saved.

That night the weather turned bad. A thick fog settled over the camp and the cold that seemed to penetrate everything chilled the tents where the people were sleeping. During the following day it began to snow. These men so familiar with snow in their northern European home, found no childlike excitement in watching the falling flakes, but knew that their long, long winter had at last begun. Although the sky cleared that afternoon and the pale sun melted this snowfall, as soon as the sun went down, which was about four o'clock in the afternoon, once more it became very cold.

Kjellmann continued to exhort his workers to greater efforts. He shortened the noon rest period to half an hour, and since the days were growing so much shorter, he made up for it by letting the men stop work in the late afternoon by the same half an hour. This was a kind of Bering Sea daylight savings time. Everyone knew from experience that soon there would be very little daylight at all.

The wisdom of the Superintendent's decisions became amply evident during the following week, for while the weather became somewhat warmer, moisture fell as a cold rain instead of snow. Each evening it became very cold, and those who kept the temperature records noted readings lower each successive night. Now, with the carpenters racing to finish the headquarters building and the winter supplies finally in the riverside warehouse, the Superintendent had the sixth and last cabin brought into the camp and assembled during the following week. Kjellmann seemed unperturbed by the reluctance of some of the men to do their share of the work, but he became short tempered with those who chronically tried to convince him that they had back trouble. He said that anyone who was too injured to lift timbers could climb the nearby hills and gather reindeer moss to store for winter use. This order brought the expected result and some of them recovered immediately.

Apparently the men actually were very tired, however, after two months of strenuous work, for Dr. Gambell's English class dwindled until only two boys appeared for instruction. Everyone else climbed into his bed almost as soon as he had finished eating his evening meal. Time passed quickly in Alaska for the men, though. Their days were filled with work, and they wasted little time talking with one another until they had eaten. They didn't even talk about the gold they hoped to find to the north of Eaton. Carl noted on Michaelmas Eve that at the churches in Norway there were lights, food, excitement, and girls, while in "this lonely Alaskan outpost" there was only monotony and loneliness.[11]

It was now October. They had been gone from Norway exactly nine months. On the second of the month Basi, Krogh, and Magnus Kjelsberg returned from Cape Nome with the boat they had taken to help Dahl move his prospecting supplies to Lindeberg's camp. They had not found any gold for themselves, but reported that they heard that Lindeberg had been successful, though they could not locate him. They did stake eleven claims, including one each for Kjelsberg, Rapp, Sacariasen, Larsen, and Kjellmann, but admitted these were located at places no one else wanted. Winter had almost caught them at the Swedish Mission with their boat frozen for the cold season,[12] which would have forced them to wait until the spring of 1899 to return and try again to find their fortune in the gold fields that they hoped to find in the beds of the sluggish streams coming out of the interior. Lindeberg's claims were rumored to be of high quality, though he had not taken any measurable amount of treasure from any of them. They reported hearing that he had been influential in calling a meeting of all claim holders to organize the Cape Nome Mining District and that this might bring some order to affairs there.[13]

Since it was Sunday, the men did not go directly to bed, but spent the evening trying to get all the information they could from the men who had been on the grounds. Again and again the three travelers told what they had seen and done in Council City. Even Carl was caught up in the excitement of this night. All of the younger men declared that they would quit the Service just as soon as they could in the spring, and go to the new village of Anvil City which was emerging from the tundra west of Council City. There they believed they could find work that would pay them much more than the Reindeer Service was paying them, and in their spare time they could search for gold.

Olai Paulsen also came from Nome and joined in telling stories. He had returned from Colorado after he had visited his home, and Jackson saw that he had tickets for boat passage from Seattle to St. Michael. Since there was no direct connection between St. Michael and Unalakleet, he had gone on to the Swedish mission above Golovnin Bay, and come to Eaton with Basi and the others on October 2. Even he had staked a claim while waiting for some way to get over to the Station.

Although the talk was of gold on the following workday, there was no break in the usual routine of hard work from sunup until dark. There was much finishing work to do on the headquarters building before it could be used as a dwelling. The weather continued clear for a few days, but the nights were growing colder and colder. Kjellmann had some of the men dig a grade for a dirt road to run along the slope in front of the row of cabins, for the digging had to be finished before the ground froze solid.

After the day's work, a delegation approached the Superintendent and gave him notice that they were going to quit just as soon as he would let them go. He acknowledged their right to leave any time they wanted to, but cautioned them against leaving in the winter when living conditions for those without adequate shelter on the barren wastes of the Seward Peninsula would be the most harsh of any time of the year. His calm good sense appealed to them, and they agreed that finding provisions and an outfit good enough to protect them from the climate was going to be out of the question for awhile, so decided to stay for several more weeks.

During the month of October, Klemmet Nilsen, one of the Lapps from Karasjok, who had been complaining constantly of his poor health, was finally pronounced genuinely ill by Dr. Gambell. He was allowed to stay in bed in his tent. The unfortunate young man never did regain his health. Although he rallied from time to time, and even worked for a few days, he grew progressively weaker for the next three months. He died far from his home and friends on Christmas Eve.

Because the sun was so bright during the brief hours of daylight, the other men found that, cold as it was, they could make good progress finishing the interior of the headquarters. Kjellmann told them they could move out of their tents into the cabins or the main building just as soon as the big structure was finished, and this prodded them to increase their efforts. Though the Lapps had always lived in tents in their own land, the canvas structures were not as sturdy as their skin structures at home, and no one wanted to live indefinitely in what the Service provided. Their only recreation, day in and day out, was to dream aloud of the wealth they were going to find, or to be sent out of camp to go on an errand for the Station. Several such trips were provided to the Golovnin mission to bring back a few deer that were still being cared for there. Now that winter was almost on them, the animals had to be herded where they could be properly protected until spring.

By mid-month the sixth cabin was finished, and the roof trusses were in place on top of the second story of the headquarters building. That morning Sacariasen found ice in his cooking water when he went to make breakfast, and the river was filled with floating chunks of ice. Even though the weather was still clear, the sun was no longer warm enough in a whole day to melt the ice that had formed along the shoreline during the previous night, and each day the ice extended farther and farther into the river itself.

Now the men had to work with mittens on their hands, and they almost longed for the warm days of summer which had inspired so many complaints at the time. They had to work hard just to keep warm in the brisk, cold wind. The night of October 17, the river froze from bank to bank, and though it was a long way from the solstice, in this harsh land it was winter once more.

The Lapps with families pressed Kjellmann to allow their wives and children to move into the finished cabins, but he told the men that they would quit working as hard as they had been if he yielded to their wishes. He was aware of their needs, however, and made up his mind to relax his rules when it became cold enough to endanger anyone's safety.

For the single men, there was no relief. They continued to live in their tents as usual. The next day after the freeze the weather was somewhat milder, and the Superintendent knew there was still no danger, even though there was some discomfort.

One night Peder Berg forgot to put his warming stove outside his tent when he went outside to gather fuel for the cooking fires. Somehow, a tent flap touched the side of the stove inside the tent and in an instant everything was flaming. He lost all of his clothing and personal belongings, except for a suitcase which he was able to salvage by reaching through the burning material and jerking it from the fire. Fortunately the wind had died down enough that none of the other tents caught fire.

On October 21, the ridgepole of the headquarters building was finally lifted into place, and Olai Paulsen began to build stone fireplaces in the various downstairs rooms of the main building. The men working on the roof complained of their great discomfort, for the wind was both strong and bitterly cold in their exposed position.

Even though everyone wanted to finish the job as quickly as he could, the Station took Sunday afternoon off as was their custom. Carl never commented about the lack of religious services, but usually mentioned it when they had one. More than ever he emphasized their need to rest after their six days of hard labor. This Sunday the men skated on the ice of the river in the afternoon. Where they got their skates or what they used for material to make them if they fashioned them on the spot, he did not say. One can only wonder how they improvised skates in that land where they had neither proper materials nor equipment.

When work began the next day a number of Lapps again asked to be allowed to stay in bed because of their alleged sickness. Dr. Gambell gave them some foul-tasting medicine which they rejected with loud protests. What they asked for was a kind of patent medicine with a high alcoholic content that they had frequently drunk at home. They called this Hoffman's "draeber" which translates as "Naphtha." This couldn't have been gasoline, but what it actually was, Carl did not explain.[14]

The cold increased to the point that Kjellmann judged that finally it would be wrong to keep everyone in tents any longer, and allowed those men with wives and children to move into the cabins. The single men were told to stay in their tents until the headquarters building was finished. To everyone's dismay they next learned that they had run out of shingles to finish the roof, and could not get the building done until the shingling crew split some more.

At the end of the month of October, Wiig issued supplies for the next month, and the men were allowed to draw as much of their ration as they needed. The extra people he had had to hire, and the fact that almost everyone was still at Eaton forced Kjellmann to reduce the monthly allowance somewhat. Since Sacariasen was the cook, he had to listen to the men complain when he gave them their evening meal, and he did not like to be blamed for any skimpy portions of food on the plates. Once more he blamed Dr. Jackson for having allowed Kjellmann to violate the promises made at Port Townsend in June. Actually, the amounts of food they had demanded were far greater than one would ordinarily expect to eat. For instance, a man and wife would have eighty pounds of flour for the month, forty pounds of crackers (!), six pounds of oatmeal, forty pounds of potatoes, eight pounds of butter, a half-gallon of syrup for any pancakes they ate, thirty pounds of beef or reindeer meat, twenty pounds of pork, all the fish they could eat, plus two pounds of coffee, six pounds of tea, and six pounds of sugar to sweeten it. About the only thing they lacked was fresh vegetables, and they probably were not accustomed to eating them in Lapland in the wintertime, either. This was hardly a starvation diet, and Kjellmann knew it, but the men complained anyway. It is strange to realize that two people could exhaust their allowance of a pound of tea every five days, yet they thought that this was not enough! By a conservative estimate, their food ration averaged over ten thousand calories a day for two people.

Their problem was that they did not eat all that they were given, and the Superintendent had observed how much they threw away. The kinds of foods they would not use he reduced by as much as a half as the weeks went on. In one or two categories, he cut back to only one third as much as they had demanded and had been promised in the spring. They got all the dried or salted fish they wanted, and Carl did not tell which of the major items had been reduced. It certainly is not hard to visualize forty pounds of crackers being cut to twenty or less, or six pounds of tea being reduced to three. When one realized that it is possible to get well over a hundred cups of strong tea from each pound of dried leaves, this means that in addition to several cups of coffee a day, each person would have to have consumed ten or more cups of tea daily to use his or her ration for a month. A pound of meat a day does not seem too much in that cold climate, but is certainly plenty when supplemented by fish. The people were not starving by any measurement.

Just before the end of October, two gold hunters from New York City visited the Station. Both of them spent considerable time with the herders during the next few months, and became well acquainted. One was a Dr. Southward, and the other an engineer named Spring. Sacariasen never did give his full name, but always referred to him as "A." Spring. They had come to Alaska during the summer, and had built their cabin about thirty-five miles upstream from Eaton Station. Now that it was snowing every day, and the weather was so cold, they came down to Eaton for a visit, food, and to warm themselves in the wooden buildings that had good fires in them.

It was mid-November before the herders left their tents for better shelter. The shingles from the forest were at last nailed into place, and the door and window frames were shaped and installed. Some of the men had become wet from snow sticking to their clothes and melting later in the day, so those that were outside working frequently became chilled to the bone. A number of them caught cold as a result of the exposure.

Kjellmann finally learned why the Richardson reindeer mail had never begun. The Unalakleet entrepreneur named Englestad had received a contract to carry the mail between Nulato on the Yukon and where Fairbanks is presently located on the Tenana. This was to be done not by deer, but by dog team. The contractor used eight-dog teams, and had several of them. He employed an Englishman and an Eskimo to make the round trip from the coast, and planned several mail deliveries during the winter season.

Kjellmann also learned from several sources that the schooner *Louisa J. Kenney* had been wrecked on the coast of the Bering Strait. Some of the passengers and crew came to Eaton, which was not built to accommodate so many people, even though they were only temporarily housed there. Two of the passengers were themselves Norwegians from Port Clarence, and they had picked up considerable gossip on the way.

The news these people brought did nothing to discourage the herders from their plans to resign from the service and go prospecting. Rumors of Jafet Lindeberg's good fortune now proved to be true. He had organized a company which he called the Pioneer Mining Company for his claims on Cape Nome. These prospects gave excellent preliminary indications that they would prove to be very rich in gold. Since the herders could not speak English yet with any fluency, they had only a few Norwegians to translate information and it was exasperating to everyone not to know exactly what was going on. Once again, however, the men spent their evenings talking excitedly of the time when they could get away from Eaton and strike out for themselves.

What they did not yet know was that when Lindeberg resigned from the reindeer service on the previous July 31, he went independently to the Seward Peninsula where he knew there were tales of gold in the streambeds. His father had been both interested in mining, and occasionally involved in mining itself in Norway,[15] and Lindeberg had some knowledge of mining himself. He had taken some money with him, and when he reached Seattle he had invested it in a supply of canned groceries which eventually reached St. Michael. He sold that at a good profit, and was able to start his mining ventures at Cape Nome with a respectable amount of capital, which he proceeded to build into a fortune.

As early as 1866, Daniel B. Libby, an employee of the Collins Overland Telegraph Company, which was building a telegraph connection between San Francisco and Siberia by way of Alaska for the Western Union Telegraph Company, found traces of gold in the Niukluk River, not far from where Lindeberg's claims lay. In 1897, Libby returned to Alaska, arriving at

127

Golovnin Bay on September 17, almost exactly at the same time that the whalers had been frozen into the pack ice at Point Barrow.

In December of 1897 Libby, along with a man named H.L. Blake and two others whom Libby had added to his party, secured the services of Nels O. Huldtberg of Cheenik, who had been in Alaska with the Swedish mission since 1892. Huldtberg and an Eskimo guide known as Too-Rig Luck, went with Libby's prospecting crew to the creeks north of Cape Nome where Libby had sighted flakes of gold thirty years before. They reached their destination in January, 1898, where by chance they encountered Lieutenant Jarvis, Surgeon Call, and Charlie Antisarlook driving the reindeer herd north for the relief of the shipwrecked men at Point Barrow.

During the spring of 1898, Huldtberg led at least four different groups of gold hunters into low depressions drained by what were known as Anvil Creek and Snake River basins. Closely associated with Huldtberg was John L. Hagelin,[16] also living near the Swedish Mission at Golovnin Bay, who was representing a syndicate of Chicago Swedes who had organized the Good Hope Mining Company in expectations of making gold discoveries along the streams flowing into Norton Sound and the Bering Sea. Early in July, a few weeks before Lindeberg arrived, Huldtberg and Hagelin invited a third man, John J. Brynteson, to join them.[17] Brynteson was a twenty-seven year old coal miner from Ishpeming, Michigan, who had been working at Huldtberg's mission station. When the three reached Cape Nome they found Blake (representing Libby), and the other two men named Chris Kimber and Henry L. Porter already there. Both groups joined forces since no one had found gold.

The six men found "colors" in the Sinuk River, (from which Charlie Antisarlook's wife, "Sinuk" Mary received her nickname). Huldtberg also found good paying amounts of gold flakes in Anvil Creek. He did not tell Blake what he had found there, but persuaded him to prospect in other creeks nearby. After a few days the entire group returned to Golovnin Bay.

Immediately Huldtberg sent out three different men whom he felt he could trust to stake claims for him and for themselves on Anvil Creek. The leader of this trio was John Brynteson, the Michigan miner. The second was Eric O. Lindblom, a San Francisco tailor who had been "Shanghaied" in a San Francisco saloon after he had swallowed a drink loaded with "knockout drops." He had recovered consciousness aboard a ship headed for the Arctic, but had jumped ship at Golovnin Bay by climbing down the anchor chain and swimming to safety, which he found at the mission which gave him sanctuary.[18] The third member of the party was Jafet Lindeberg. They found him prospecting by himself on Anvil Creek, and after a moment of shock at finding him by chance working their best stream, talked with him and invited him to join them.[19]

Brynteson, Lindblom, and Lindeberg left Cheenik on September 11, and staked "Discovery" claim on September 20. All three men took this claim in partnership, and it was then that they formed the Pioneer Mining Company. During the following twenty years, they took out more than twenty-eight million dollars in gold from this claim and those immediately above and below it.

They staked additional claims above and below Discovery for their friends and for Huldtberg. For example, "No. 2 Below" was staked for William Kjellmann. "No. 4 Below" was claimed for John A. Dexter, the trader at Cheenik and a good friend and supporter of the workers at the Swedish mission. "No. 7 Above" was given to Dr. A. N. Kittilsen and "No. 10 Above" for Johan Sp. Tornensis. In all, more than seventy claims were marked with willow stakes for various Scandinavians at the mission and at Eaton Station. It may be noted that they staked no claims for Libby, Blake, or any of their acquaintances not of Norwegian or Swedish ancestry.

By October word of what Lindeberg, Huldtberg, and the others had done reached the ears of the outraged Blake. He had not found much gold in the streams that he had worked, but he came roaring over to Anvil Creek, spread the word of the discoveries made by the "lucky Swedes," and the stampede was on. Immediately the Scandanavians organized the Cape Nome Mining District.[20] After this they were attacked bitterly by Blake, and other Americans who repeatedly "jumped" their claims. There was violence, years of litigation, bribery of public officials, and even the imposition of martial law for a time.[21]

None of this was known at Eaton Station, other than that their former associate was going to become a rich man. Meanwhile, they worked as hard as possible in the short days left of the fall in order to get inside and keep warm to recover from their colds and aches.

Kjellmann and Regnor Dahl went inland for a few days to visit some herders who were in the mountains not far from Eaton Station. They told the workmen to insulate their tents against cold by piling earth and grass around the base of the shelters to protect them from the cold. Though this device was used frequently on the North American Great Plains, it was not pleasant, for it tended to become dirty and infested with rodents and insects. For a short time, however, it would provide insulation from the cold and protection from the winds of an Alaskan winter.

By November 11, the main building was declared ready except for finishing the interior rooms on the top floor. The sod tents were used only a few days, and the herders were allowed at long last to move into the building they had been waiting for. Some were thought to be getting scurvy from the lack of vegetables, but most of the sick men needed only to have a time of rest and warmth to recover from their various ailments. Kjellmann and Dahl returned in time to join in the celebration over the new arrangements. Dr. Gambell had his office and schoolroom on the main floor of the building, and Kjellmann occupied the rest of the main floor for his own office, files, and his private apartment. Upstairs were the rooms where the single men lived. One was a common kitchen-dining area, and another was used as a general living and meeting room. Several other rooms were used for sleeping areas, and Dr. Gambell had a single room to himself.

Now with the hard work done there was a lull in activities. The men held a dance in the second story living space, though Carl did not say what they used for music, and he did not indicate whether there were any feminine partners for the dancers. He did describe the affair as a "waltz," however, which may have meant that the men danced with each other. This was not particularly unusual, though, for there were plenty of examples where males danced with one another at fur posts and at the American fur Rendezvous earlier in the century. Kjellmann himself did not participate, probably because he thought this would affect the austere image he was trying to hold before the men, who now admired him as the skillful leader and "father figure" that he was. Instead, he celebrated the end of the construction by going for a swift ride across the snow seated on a Lapp pulka, drawn by a speeding reindeer.

With winter, the Eskimo at Unalakleet were able to venture out on the ice of the ocean, and at the mouth of the river to fish through holes they cut through to the water underneath. They caught a kind of white fish, about the size of a medium herring. Carl noted, as he wrote about them, that they tasted something like a cod. Obviously, he was no longer repelled by the Eskimo food, and was becoming more tolerant.

Several of the herders must have gone down to Unalakleet together, for Carl recorded the observations of a number of them as well as his own. They noted that the Eskimo men held cords about three feet long, "jigging" them up and down until some hungry fish would strike at the hook. The fishermen would then jerk on the line and pull the fish through the hole in the ice, knock it in the head, where it would quickly freeze, and then the process would go on for long periods of time, with both men and women participating. Since fishing was good, the local people saved some for their own food, and sold the rest to the herders or prospectors who would buy the fresh food gladly. Mothers would fish with babies held on their backs, and warmly wrapped in furs. The fishermen would eat a frozen fish for lunch without cleaning it, and were able to stay on the ice for long periods of time. They also used the frozen fish for dog food, and since they were plentiful it seemed that here, at least, the coming of the white man had not destroyed the native food supplies--at least not yet.

As a close observer of the Eskimo ways, Sacariasen noted the not unusual phenomenon among primitive peoples that women did most of the food gathering, and though the men fished through the ice in the winter, they did little to catch salmon when they were spawning during the late summer and fall months. The men would chop the holes in the ice, however, and sometimes in the early freeze would suspend nets under the ice of the river. The few salmon still swimming upstream could be caught by this device.

Barter had always been the way Eskimo obtained provisions from each other, but with the coming of the commercial operations of the whites cash was needed and the easiest way to get it was to sell fish to the Eaton herders. For this reason, the ice in front of the Station usually had a number of natives ice-fishing just beyond the warehouse. Their needs were few and simple. If they could supplement their former diets with flour, tea, sugar, tobacco, pork, and ammunition to hunt the larger sea animals they could do very well. They also bought cotton yardage for clothing for their wives, particularly calico and muslin. The commercial stores turned them from using furs for bedding to buying woolen blankets, and Eskimo had to pay money for these as well. If they did not have cash, they would gather furs, and even trade their own moccasins, fur boots, parkas, fur trousers, or their mittens for the goods they wanted. This was not wise, for they would trade things they needed to have to survive, for materials that were not as useful in that northern environment as what they had been accustomed to. After they developed a taste for alcohol, many deprived themselves or their families even of food in order to buy liquor. While the United States government declared this to be illegal because of its destructive effect on the natives, there were always heartless and greedy merchants indifferent to the suffering they caused if they could turn a profit by selling whiskey. A man like Sheldon Jackson complained bitterly to his superiors about what was happening, but Congress did not appropriate enough money to staff an adequate law enforcement, and the consequences of this policy were ruinous.   His opposition to the liquor smugglers was the main reason that Jackson was hated so much by the people whom he denounced.

Carl noted that when the Eskimo couldn't buy whiskey from the white traders, they made a home-brew of their own, compounded from syrup and a kind of brown sugar. Sometimes other substances might be added after fermentation. Occasionally these might include strychnine! This was the vile "hoochino" that even whites drank sometimes, and from which we get our colloquialism "hooch" to describe a powerful, alcoholic brew.

While the men lazied away the cold days waiting for a break in the weather, they were pleasantly surprised when some of the herders on duty brought in the carcasses of eight reindeer for their meals. These had been slaughtered because they had suffered accidents of some kind, and had to be destroyed.

Another pleasant surprise of a different kind came when three of the missionaries from Unalakleet came to visit. John Hagelin, of the Good Hope Mining Company, drove the deer and the sleds, but more to the liking of the celibate herders were Mrs. Karlson, the young wife of Axel Karlson, and the schoolteacher Malvina Johnson. They did not stay long, but promised to return later in the winter.

After about a week of virtual inaction, Kjellmann had the men trim the interior rooms with dressed boards. Others cut fuel for the roaring fires that burned day and night in the fireplaces that Paulsen had built. Neither of these tasks took very long with so many men to work at them, though they had none of the sense of urgency they had had when they were building their houses. The men took turns helping the cooks prepare the meals, but this did not take much time either, for the Lapp families did their own cooking in their separate quarters, and the few dozen people living in the main building did not require huge meals. Each man had to clean his bed, and wash his clothes each Saturday, which was not a very difficult thing to complete either, though how they dried their laundry other than in their crowded bunkrooms, the writers of the journals did not say. The move indoors had improved everyone's health and by a week after they had gone inside, most of the men with colds had recovered. Only Klemmet Nilsen and one other man did not get better, and Nilsen was obviously suffering from something far more serious than a common cold.

As they talked among themselves, they contrasted their situation with that of the prospectors living from one miserable day to the next in tents, just trying to survive until spring. Had they gone to Cape Nome when they first got the itch to go prospecting, they would have been in the same uncomfortable situation, but Kjellmann's good advice had spared them from doing this foolish thing. There was no way they could have earned money to get adequate housing, there would not have been adequate food for everyone, and prospecting in the wintertime was a discouraging thing at best.

On November 24, Kjellmann told the workers that this was a national holiday in the United States and no one had to work. While they had not been exerting themselves unduly in any event, to take a holiday on Thursday was a surprise to everybody. He explained to the bemused Scandinavians what Thanksgiving Day was all about and some of the traditions of the English Pilgrim fathers and mothers, and the herders agreed that it was a splendid idea, especially since it gave them a day free from work. They felt no identification with American customs, but were willing to go along in this case. As evening began to fall, to everyone's delight they heard the bells of a number of reindeer sleds, and going outside, watched a small cavalcade of sleds and passengers stopping in front of their quarters. The two Kjelsbergs,

Wilhelm Basi and Johan Tornensis, who had gone back again to Golovnin Bay on October 10, had returned once more bringing with them some of the government deer that had been held temporarily at the Swedish mission.[22]

Along with the four who had been gone from Eaton was the long missing Jafet Lindeberg. He was the most welcome visitor of all, for now they could hear firsthand of what had been going on in the gold claims to the north. Better, they could understand what they were being told, because he could tell them in their own language. Dr. A.N. Kittilsen was also with them. They had met him only briefly during the summer, but they had heard much about him because he held some of the better claims in the Nome district, and he was Dr. Gambell's superior in overseeing the health of the workmen.

They heard directly how Huldtberg had discovered the gold on Anvil Creek, and how, as he was panning a sample of the sand, Hagelin had watched him, and how they had agreed not to tell their American companions of what they had found.

While Lindeberg was not present at the time, he told how he and Olai Paulsen had gone upstream toward Council City to find a good prospect, and how they met Brynteson and Eric Lindblom, and how they joined forces. Now, with the information Huldtberg gave them, they purchased a flat-bottomed boat from the local inhabitants, attached a keel, hired an Eskimo woman to make sails, loaded a few provisions using Lindeberg's profits from his sale of canned food, and set sail, reaching Cape Nome in a short time. They tried other streams than Anvil Creek, such as Mountain Creek, Rock Creek, Snow Creek, and Glacier Creek, but found very little, though there were small amounts of gold present everywhere. At Anvil Creek, however, where Huldtberg had made his initial discovery, things were different. About three and three-quarter miles above where Nome was finally located, they staked "Discovery" and the rest was history. They also gave the name to the Snake River, returned to the Mission, made preparations as quietly as possible to work their claim, and borrowed a small schooner from the mission so they could get back to Nome in early October.

Seven men went this time--Lindeberg, Brynteson, Lindblom, Dr. Kittilsen, Tornensis, and Gabriel W. Price. They also took along with these six an Eskimo from the mission who had been given the name of Constantine. They anchored their schooner at the mouth of the Snake River, and hiked upstream to where they had discovered the gold. They then held the first public meeting of the Cape Nome Mining District, electing Dr. Kittilsen the recorder, then solemnly recording their claims before him. They used the customary American mining laws, with which Kittilsen was familiar; the size and recording of the claims was the same. They also adopted bylaws for the District which they intended to enforce on others who might come later. They required a $2.50 filing fee from each person who staked a claim. A prospector could file no more than one claim on each of the streams, and he could not file more than seven claims for others, even though he held "powers-of-attorney" from many more. The District was outlined as extending along the beach for twenty-five miles, and inland for the same distance. This considerable area would therefore comprise 625 square miles, which would presumably work out to allow 400,000 acres of tundra to be staked into claims for a large number of future prospectors, and by right of discovery they could claim the best ones. Each claim was about twenty acres in size, or 1,320 feet long by 660 feet wide.

During the month of October the seven men built a "rocker" to work larger amounts of gravel than the much less efficient gold pan. Anvil Creek and, to a lesser extent, Snow Creek, proved very rich in possibilities. At "Discovery" alone they took out $1,775 worth of gold in less than three weeks. By November they had filed on fifty claims for themselves and their friends on the various streams. They remained too long, however, and when the streams froze they had to abandon their boat in the ice, for they had been so occupied in trying to get rich that they had not sailed it back to the mission. They had to go overland to the mission, and found the place crowded with prospectors brought there by the tales spread by Blake of these "foreigners" who had found gold and were keeping it from American citizens.[23]

Of course when Lindeberg finished telling his story, the men wanted to leave immediately for Nome, but Kjellmann calmed them down once more with suggestions that they remember there was plenty of time until they could be able to search in the streams for places to locate their own claims. The big rush from the lower States, which was bound to come, could not start until the ships came up from Seattle in the spring. This, therefore, was a memorable Thanksgiving weekend for the herders, and since it was their first in North America, they always remembered that holiday. For the next weeks all anyone could talk about was "Gold," and "Nome."

Partly because of the weather, and mainly because of the gold fever, very little work was accomplished for the rest of the week. Carl noted that the men spent most of their time "hearing and talking about Cape Nome." And why not? It was "their" discovery, by virtue of some staking many claims, and by the fact that one of their own number had made the discovery. All that seemed to keep them from wealth was their contract with the United States government to herd deer until February first, and their agreement with Sheldon Jackson. In a sense their loyalty to Jackson was threatened by their dislike for him, but they still had a contract to complete.

On Monday, Superintendent Kjellmann and thirteen other men left for St. Michael to bring back supplies for the Station. The snow was now perfect for the reindeer sleds that they knew so well how to use. This was more of a vacation than hard work. The men enjoyed breaking their normal routine with the expedition south. Another reason Kjellmann did not have any trouble getting men to go was that St. Michael was a place where there was a judge who could grant the men their citizenship papers, although they had taken out first papers only five months before. As soon as they had their citizenship, they could locate gold claims on their own.

Parenthetically, it is interesting to note that in the original journal, there is evidence that Dr. Gambell's English language class was beginning to pay off. Although Carl continued to write his journal in the Norwegian language, more and more English words crept into it as the weeks went by. For instance, when he talked about "locating" claims, he spelled it phonetically as "lokete" but there is no such word in the Norwegian language when used with this meaning.

Lindeberg, Kittilsen, and Brynteson went along as passengers with Kjellmann and the others to St. Michael. The Superintendent was obviously not immune from gold fever himself, for he told them while traveling, that when he got back to Eaton he was going to take a short leave and go to Cape Nome himself to stake claims. Since he was already an American citizen this would mean that he could begin to work at once.

When he left, Kjellmann put Dr. Gambell in charge as Acting Superintendent, but Gambell's duties were not great. He did not give anyone extra duties of any kind. Probably not much would have been done anyway. His excuse was that it was so cold that the weather was not only unpleasant, but a strong Arctic gale was blowing, and it was not safe for anyone to go outside unless some pressing duty required it. Only a few men were needed at any one time to watch the deer, and the animals were able to live in extreme cold quite well. The buildings proved to be not only well built, but warm, so everyone stayed indoors by the fires and talked excitedly of their prospects for finding gold.

Since the men who had gone to St. Michael were as eager as those at Eaton to go to Nome, they did not tarry at the town but came back at once. Kjellmann, Lindeberg, and a few of the drivers reached the Station on December 3, after an absence of only six days. Spring, who was paying one of his periodic visits to the Station, asked to be allowed to join them when they went north.

They knew that they would have to be very careful along the Bering coast, and particularly so while crossing the ice of Golovnin Bay, for on their way to St. Michael two of the men had barely escaped having a dreadful accident. The entire party had moved out on the ocean ice to avoid the rough beach, and since two of the deer proved weaker than the others the men working this sled dropped farther and farther behind the rest. No one worried about that, for they were experienced men, but as they were camped in the open the ice broke away from the shore, and the wind drove them out to sea on a large floe. Fortunately the wind died down, and the ice stopped drifting westward, but it did not come back to the shore, and all they could do was wait to be rescued with neither fuel nor food for men or deer. They were isolated on the floating ice for more than twenty-four hours in the cold weather that kept the warmly dressed and well-fed men at Eaton indoors. The chill was what saved them in the end, for during the night new ice formed around their raft, and they were able to go cautiously to shore without anyone having to rescue them. They got to St. Michael just as the others were starting back to Eaton, and beginning to look for the missing drivers.

Regnor Dahl and Frederik Larsen stayed behind at St. Michael. Dahl now had the assignment of staking claims for the employees of the North American Transportation and Trading Company. Larsen stayed with him to keep him company, and to see that he came to no harm, for Dahl was not an experienced driver like the Lapps. The managers of the N.A.T. and T. gave Dahl their powers-of-attorney, and he declared that he would go to Nome immediately. Though Gambell had thought it was too cold to work out of doors, gold fever certainly seemed to raise the body temperature of those infected by it!

On Sunday, however, Larsen came in to Eaton with the two herders lost on the ice for his only companions. When Kjellmann asked him where Dahl was, the young man said he had left Dahl behind. It seemed that Dahl had reverted to the behavior pattern he had exhibited at Port Townsend. As Larsen explained it, his companion was already rich in his mind, and began ordering Frederik to do all kinds of unnecessary and unpleasant tasks. Larsen was much younger, but far more experienced, and he objected to being pushed around. His insubordination enraged Dahl, and he threatened to shoot Larsen dead on the spot unless he obeyed orders immediately. Larsen refused just as vigorously, and Dahl reached into his pocket for his gun, but found to his embarrassment that he had left it behind, when he put his hand into an empty pocket. Larsen realized then that Dahl actually meant it when he said he was going to kill him so he immediately took off toward Eaton, leaving Dahl to drive his deer any way he could.

Considerably after Larsen told his story, Dahl put in his appearance and tried to hire another man to take Larsen's place. Since everyone refused to work with him, he went to Kjellmann and demanded that the Superintendent assign someone to drive his deer. Kjellmann was totally in sympathy with Larsen, however, for he knew about Regnor's temper, and retorted that he had already given him Larsen, and if that had not been satisfactory there was no one else at the station good enough either.

Kjellmann's reply did not improve Dahl's disposition, but he swallowed his rage and went to several men again to try to get them to go to Nome with him. First he tried Otto Leinan, but Leinan refused until he had Kjellmann's permission to leave the service. Ordinarily this would have been no problem, for there was little to do now that winter was almost on them, and the Station was tremendously overstaffed as it was. Kjellmann advised Leinan to think well before he went with Dahl, but Leinan wanted to go to Nome as soon as he could, so he decided that it would be better to go with

Dahl than not to go at all. At least, since Dahl had forgotten to bring his gun, he wouldn't be murdered. Kjellmann agreed to let Leinan go if he really wanted to, but made Dahl pay the Reindeer Service $2.50 compensation for Leinan's lost services to the government. Dahl knew that Kjellmann was angry with him, and that this was his punishment, but he also knew that he was not popular with anyone after his foolish behavior toward Larsen, and reluctantly agreed.

To keep watch on him, the Superintendent appointed twenty men from the Station to go with Dahl and Leinan to Nome, and gave everyone permission to stake claims as soon as they got there. He decided to go along himself at the last minute.

They did not get away that evening, for just about dusk an inspection team consisting of an army corporal and two Eskimos from St. Michael came in to see whether they needed anything at Eaton. They also brought official mail for Kjellmann, which required answering immediately, so he had to work through most of the night to get the letters written and his reports filled out.

Early the next morning the mail carriers left with the dispatches and letters, and by ten o'clock the party left for Cape Nome with Lindeberg acting as their guide. Kjellmann had had but little sleep, but the excitement made him wakeful, and he was ready to join them.

In addition to Lindeberg, Kjellmann, Dahl, and Leinan, A. Spring went along, Alex Jornes, and "six Norwegians and the rest Lapps."[24] Dr. Gambell again became Acting Superintendent while Kjellmann was absent. Magnus Kjelsberg became work foreman if there was any work to do, and Wiig continued to be the storekeeper. Kjellmann excused his own absence because he planned to go to Port Clarence, where his father had died, after he left Nome.

In the confusion of leaving, some of the herders were not as particular about choosing docile reindeer as they should have been. Some of the young animals were barely trained, and when they started to pull the pulkas they became frightened with all the noise and the unexpected weight, and tried to run away. Since they could not do that without pulling their loads, they resorted to bucking, and to rushing around in panic. They did this until some collapsed from exhaustion. They were replaced with other animals, but it was not until early afternoon that the last of the sleds actually left with trained deer. The ones who had already gone were far beyond them, so the stragglers had to travel much of the night in order not to be left alone in case of accident.

NOTES

[1]56 Cong., 1 Sess., *Senate Doc. 245.* "9th Report on Reindeer in Alaska." pp. 19-20.

[2]*R. i. A.,* p. 100-101.

[3]*R. i. A.,* p. 107.

[4]*Basi Diary,* December 26, 1898.

[5]Kjellmann's journal and log of the station's activities duplicates Sacariasen's, but it is so much less colorful that Carl will continue to be the main source of information about Eaton.

[6]Basi, *Diary,* August 5, 1898. Basi gives the dimensions as 24' x 16'.

[7]56 Cong., 1 Sess., *Senate Doc. #245,* "Eaton Station Logbook."

[8]"Eaton Station Logbook," p. 79.

[9]*R. i. A.,* p. 120.

[10]Basi, *Diary,* October 12, 1898.

[11]*R. i. A.,* p. 125.

[12]Basi, *Dairy,* October 18, 1898.

[13]*Ibid,* October 25, 1898.

[14]*R. i. A.,* p. 130.

[15]Cameron, Mrs. Charlotte, *A Cheechako in Alaska and Yukon,* London: T.F. Unwin, 1920, p. 250.

[16]Basi, *Diary,* September 15, 1898.

[17]Carlson, L.H., "The Discovery of Gold at Nome Alaska," *Pacific Historical Review,* XV:3, September 1946, pp. 259-278.

[18]Davis, Mary Lee, *Sourdough Gold, The Log of a Yukon Adventure,* Boston: W.A. Wilde Co., 1933, p. 327.

[19]Basi, *Diary,* September 15, 1898.

[20]Basi, *Diary,* October 25, 1898.

[21]Carlson, "The Discovery of Gold at Nome Alaska," *Op. Cit.:* Lomen, Carl J., *Fifty Years in Alaska*, New York: David McKay Company, Inc., 1954, p. 15; Clausen, Clarence A., ed., "Life in the Klondike and Alaska Golds Fields," *Norwegian-American Studies and Records*, v. XVI, Norwegian-American Historical Association, Northfield, Minnesota, 1950, pp. 121, 253-54; 56 Cong., 1. Sess., *Senate Doc. #236*, "Preliminary Report on the Cape Nome Gold Region, Alaska," p. 31.

[22]*R. i. A.*, p. 139-143; Basi, *Diary*, November 28, 1898. Basi gave the date of their return as Monday, the 28th, instead of Thanksgiving afternoon.

[23]*R. i. A.*, p. 139-143.

[24]*R. i. A.*, p. 147.

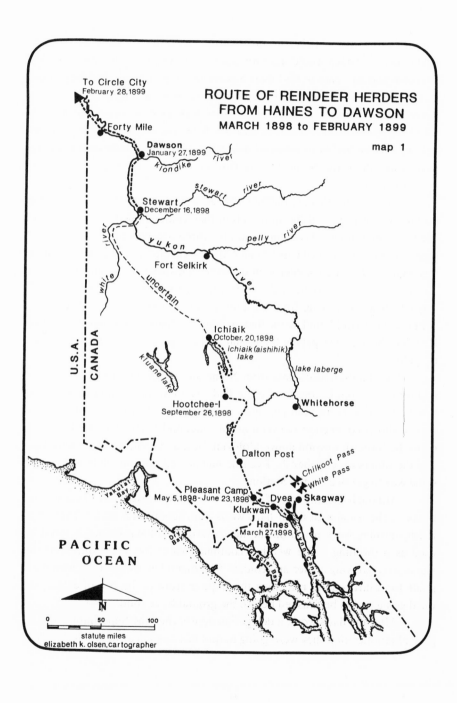

ROUTE OF REINDEER HERDERS
FROM HAINES TO DAWSON
MARCH 1898 to FEBRUARY 1899

map 1

To Circle City
February 28, 1899

Forty Mile

Dawson
January 27, 1899

klondike river

stewart river

Stewart
December 16, 1898

yukon river

pelly river

Fort Selkirk

white river

uncertain

Ichiaik
October, 20, 1898

ichiaik (aishihik) lake

kluane lake

lake laberge

Hootchee-I
September 26, 1898

Whitehorse

U.S.A.

CANADA

Dalton Post

Chilkoot Pass

White Pass

Pleasant Camp
May 5, 1898 - June 23, 1898

Dyea   Skagway

Klukwan

Yakutat Bay

Haines
March 27, 1898

Dry Bay

Glacier Bay

Lynn Canal

PACIFIC
OCEAN

N

0   50   100

statute miles
elizabeth k. olsen, cartographer

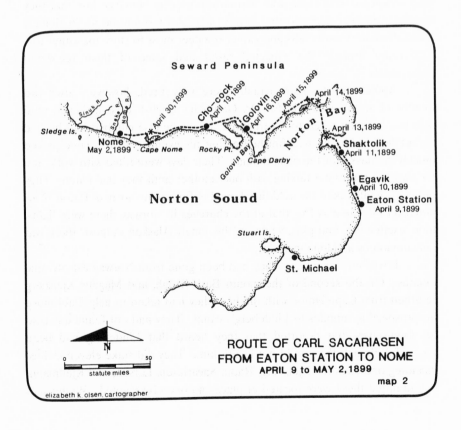

Seward Peninsula

Sinuk R.
Snake R.
NOME R.

Sledge Is.

April 30,1899

Cho-cock
April 19,1899

Golovin
April 16,1899

April 15,1899

April 14,1899

Norton Bay

April 13,1899

Shaktolik
April 11,1899

Nome
May 2,1899   Cape Nome   Rocky Pt.

Golovin Bay

Cape Darby

Norton   Sound

Egavik
April 10,1899

Eaton Station
April 9,1899

Stuart Is.

St. Michael

N

0   50
statute miles

ROUTE OF CARL SACARIASEN
FROM EATON STATION TO NOME
APRIL 9 to MAY 2,1899

map 2

elizabeth k. olsen, cartographer

Reverend Sheldon Jackson landing the first reindeer at Port Clarence, July 4, 1892

William A. Kjellman and reindeer, Teller Reindeer Station, Alaska

Reverend Sheldon Jackson

Laplander and wife on skis in Alaska

Reindeer, Eaton Station, Alaska, 1898

Michael Nakkila and a group of reindeer, Alaska, 1898

A herd of reindeer in Alaska, 1890s

Laplander housing in an Alaskan village, 1898

Reindeer being used as pack animals

The beach at Dyea, Alaska, 1898

E.A. Hegg photograph of Front Street, Nome, July 1, 1900.

Snake River, Nome, June 29, 1900

Beach scene, Nome, June 28, 1900

Laplanders milking reindeer at Port Clarence, Alaska, 1900

Church at Unalaska, Alaska

Eskimos drying fish, Nome, ca. 1900

Eskimo in kayak

Chapter Five

WINTER AT EATON STATION

At this point, Carl lost track of Lindeberg and Kjellmann's party as far as his journal is concerned. For several weeks there was no way of knowing what was happening to them. All he reported as the December days went by was that everyone "rested awhile," doing nothing. The snow started falling again and the weather became slightly warmer, but still there was almost nothing to do except for a few of them to watch the deer, and the rest to keep the fires going. The two men who had been ill did not get any better, and Gambell finally diagnosed their trouble as scurvy. There is no record as to what they had actually been eating, and why in 1898 it was possible to get this disease with enough food to eat, though little was known about balanced diets and vitamins. It is possible that the men who suffered from scurvy refused to eat anything except what they liked, and neglected the kinds of food that would have prevented the trouble.

Dr. Southward, Spring's partner, came in to Eaton during the week, along with the dog-sled mail that now was to be delivered each month. Everyone who got a letter was delighted as only those isolated in distant places can be when they hear from home. When they left, Dr. Gambell suddenly realized he had forgotten to give the mailman his own letters, for he was not feeling too well himself that day. When he remembered that he had prepared them to send out, he had Alfred Hermandsen catch and harness a deer to catch the mail. The deer could run much faster than dogs. He was so pleased to get something to do that he got the animal harnessed and the sled in place in only a few minutes, setting "off over the ice in a cloud of flying snow."[1]

Because Gambell felt indisposed most of the week, Missionary Karlson came up from Unalakleet to see whether there was anything he could do to help. Gambell was not that sick, however, so Karlson contented himself by telling of news from Nome. According to his information, many prospectors living near Council City waiting for the spring had abandoned their camps, and headed for the gold bearing creeks near the Snake River in the coldest, darkest part of the winter. These were neither properly dressed nor equipped for such rigorous climate, and many froze hands, feet, or parts of their faces on the way and had to turn back badly disabled. Some actually never did recover. They showed once more that the Seward Peninsula was nothing to trifle with in winter.

On December 13, the men moved the entire reindeer herd to a small forested valley about three miles from the Station on the north bank of the river. Here the animals would be protected from the wind, and they could find plenty of moss to eat. This was the kind of terrain reindeer were familiar with, both in Siberia and in Norway, and they knew how to survive and even prosper with only minimal human assistance under conditions like these.

The next day Gambell felt well enough to begin to plan for a Christmas celebration for the people at the Station. He sent five men to St. Michael to buy provisions, and told them to come back by way of Unalakleet to bring some of the missionaries who promised to put on a program for the herders and their families. Sacariasen was used to weeks of preparing for the holiday in Norway, and he noted in his journal that the Americans didn't seem to be looking forward to much of a celebration at Christmas. He saw no obvious bustle of Christmas housekeeping, or of any plans to make special treats for the day.

Dr. Southward now declared that Gambell was almost entirely recovered from whatever his illness had been, so he left for his own cabin up the river. He did not know much about driving deer, so he loaded a pulka with supplies and planned to pull it himself to his camp. As he left he told everyone he would be back the next day. He was back, but so exhausted from hiking fifty miles in two days, and pulling the heavy load, that he collapsed into a bunk without undressing or eating anything. Carl broiled a little reindeer meat and bouillon to give him some energy, and had to awaken him to get him to eat even that much. It was hot and steaming, and Southward was hungry enough to rouse himself, but he did not wait long to get back to sleep when he had finished eating.

143

For the next days it seemed to have been Carl's job to keep a record of the weather. It gave him considerable satisfaction to be chosen for some kind of responsible work, for just cooking was not enough to keep him busy. Gambell claimed that he himself was not yet well enough to make the weather observations for the Station. Carl faithfully recorded temperatures and weather conditions long after Gambell was completely well, and kept them in his own journal as well. Until Christmas Eve the cold ranged from 25^0 Fahrenheit to -30^0 F. Mostly the weather was calm and clear. The men did almost nothing but cut firewood, which was plentiful. "With nothing else for Christmas, we could at least be warm," wrote Sacariasen. On the 21st, he couldn't read the temperature for the mercury was frozen in the thermometer.[2] The night before it had been -30^0 F. again. It might well have been ten or more degrees colder on this beautiful, clear, starlit night. He noted in the official journal that on the 22nd there were exactly two hours and fifty-four minutes of daylight on this, the shortest day of 1898.

When the men who had gone to St. Michael returned they were in a rage. Gambell had written a note to the storekeeper there telling him not to sell the herders any whiskey. Carl wrote: "The Lapps were now cursing the new administrator at the station, for Kjellmann had never forbidden them a drink for their thirst as long as they paid for it out of their own money."[3] He himself agreed with Gambell's actions for he did not drink, disapproved of it, and had noted that the Lapps' behavior became very erratic when they were drunk.

Christmas Eve was a quiet time at the Station. The disgruntled Lapps had writted in ungrammatical English, "Not Whiskey," [sic] in the frosted window of the living quarters, but by now they were laughing about it. Olai Paulsen and Thoralf Kjelsberg came back to Eaton in the afternoon after taking the United States Collector of Customs, a Mr. Hatch, and his wife to the Swedish Mission at Unalakleet. During the evening the army corporal inspector came through with the return mail, and stopped for the night on his way back to the Fort.

Around six o'clock someone came into the bunkhouse with the unpleasant news that Anders Klemmet Nilsen had died.[4] His wife lived in Karasjok and had not accompanied him to America, so he was alone when he died except for Dr. Gambell. Since there was no Christmas celebration this night anyway the Norwegians experienced a somber mood of deep gloom, to think of this happening the night before Christmas.

Christmas Day was on a Sunday, but no one had done much work for quite a while so no one had any sense of taking a holiday from work. Besides, the missionaries did not come, but sent word they would be there in a few days. The single men were given a piece of reindeer meat to boil or fry any way they wanted to eat for their Christmas dinner. That was the total celebration. Gambell held to his rule of abstinence, and there was neither whiskey nor revelry. Only the Eskimo celebrated. They did not know much of the religious significance of Christmas but they knew it was a white man's holiday, and that if they made themselves very conspicuous they would receive gifts. Accordingly they made pests of themselves at the station for much of the day. Finally, Gambell told Carl to prepare extra rations, and to give every Eskimo all he or she wanted to eat by way of a Christmas feast. There were no gifts for them, but enough food for all. The Lapp families in the small cabins dressed in their best clothes and visited back and forth between houses as was their custom, but they did not give gifts either.

On the 27th the belated Christmas celebration actually took place. Late or not, it was welcome. Miss Malvina Johnson, the missionary teacher, sent word that if someone would come to get her, she and Alice, the Eskimo teacher, would be glad to come up to Eaton, decorate a tree, and put on a program for anyone who wanted to attend. The herders were only too glad to cooperate.[5] Early in the afternoon of December 27, the two women arrived and went to Dr. Gambell's office where they were to spend the night. Someone had cut an evergreen tree, and after the girls had rested and changed their clothes to party dresses, they came out and began trimming the Christmas tree with paper bags of candy they had brought with them. When they were done each man "harvested" one of the bags of homemade candy, which the women must have spent some time preparing. Afterward, the teachers showed "lantern slides" and sang for the people crowded into the large living room. The Eskimo girl, whose name turned out to be Alice Omegetchake, could speak good English, so most of the songs were in the English language, since while Alice knew both English and Eskimo, Malvina knew very little Eskimo. The celebration finally ended, and the two women slept in their makeshift bedroom in the doctor's office.

The next day the two were joined by Axel Karlson from the Mission, and the Hatches returned to visit a little more. Miss Johnson and Alice cooked a special dinner for them in the absent Kjellmann's apartment, where all the rooms were heated, and which Gambell had designated as the guest quarters for the evening.

Gambell asked the herders to put on a program for their guests when evening came. Since none was much of an actor or singer they made a parade of themselves in their colorful clothes, and also went across the river and drove the entire herd of deer past the headquarters in a kind of review. None of the visitors had ever seen this large a herd before, and it was as entertaining for them as the lantern slides and songs had been for the men the night before. Before people went to bed this night they took the deer back to their sheltered forest valley.

Now with the Christmas season ending Karlson, Brynteson, and Hagelin, who had stayed in the dormitory with the men, prepared to return to Unalakleet. They ate a final meal with the herders, and when Dr. Gambell came upstairs to wake them he found everyone already eating and enjoying one another's company. During the short daylight of this day, all of the visitors except the Hatches returned home. The driving snow and the below zero temperature was a little too austere for these two so they decided to stay a little longer until things warmed up a bit, or until the snow stopped falling.

It was not until the temperature rose to a balmy -5° that they finally left on December 30. Alfred Hermandsen took them back to the Mission. The other men took turns digging a grave for the deceased Klemmet Nilsen's body and spent most of the daylight hours cutting into the frozen earth. Kjellmann had selected a spot for a cemetery on the hillside back of the station when he laid the plans for the various sites, but though Carl referred to the spot as a churchyard there was no church nearby. This certainly differed from the custom in Norway.

The last day of the eventful year of 1898 was no more exciting than Christmas Eve had been. Sacariasen noted that they had eaten about seventy deer since they arrived seven months before, but since their Eaton herds were nongelded deer from Siberia, they reproduced in large numbers, and the fawns that would be born the next spring would far more than replace the ones eaten.[6] Interestingly, the Eskimo were not allowed to kill reindeer for food, but the Lapps could. Carl also noted that each man reminded one another solemnly that their adventurous year was behind them, and now nothing lay before them in the coming twelve months but riches and good fortune. Apparently they were not accustomed to making loud noises at the stroke of midnight, for nothing happened at all when 1899 came in.

By now Sacariasen was tired of trying to find something exciting to write about in his journal at the end of every day. During the long winter nights in 1898-99, he tried to summarize Alaskan history from the Russians to the goldrush as he had learned it from his own observations and other somewhat inaccurate American sources.

For example, after describing Vitus Bering's voyage from Kamchatka in 1728, he jumped to Russian settlement of Alaska, which he said had occurred "soon after this," although in fact almost two generations elapsed before any European settlement began. In addition, although Bering discovered St. Lawrence Island and explored much of coastal Siberia, he did not do extensive exploration along the Alaskan coast. Two ships built at Petropavlovsk sailing under the name of the *St. Peter* and *St. Paul* made the voyage. The *St. Paul*, commanded by Alexei Chirikov later got as far south as Mount St. Elias. The *St. Peter*, which was Bering's ship was wrecked on the return trip, and Bering as well as almost half of his crew died on the lonely rock still known as Bering Island just east of Kamchatka. Chirikov had little to show for his efforts, but he did return to Petropavlovsk and was able to report his geographical discoveries as well as bringing several hundred furs obtained by trading with the local Indians.

A German naturalist named Georg Wilhelm Steller accompanied this expedition, and his discoveries were of vital importance to the future of the Bering Sea and Alaska, though they did not seem so at the time. He spent the winter of 1741 and part of 1742 observing animal life on and near the island where the Bering party was stranded. He described the fur seal and the sea otter, which were to be the cause for the coming of hundreds of Russians who traded and settled along the coasts of North America hoping to gain wealth by trading for these furs. Incidentally, Stellar also observed a bird known as the Stellar Jay, a lively and beautiful creature, still very common on the Pacific Coast. He also noted the sea cow, a good food source for the Eskimo, but now extinct because of their slaughter by whalers and others who wanted fresh meat in the Arctic.

In his account, Sacariasen next noted the voyage of Captain James Cook and later of Captain Charles Clarke, who assumed command of the expedition after Cook's death. These English expeditions were followed by the Spanish who came in the middle 1770's and 1790's as a reaction to the activities of both British and Russians. By now the Russians were in firm control of the Aleutian Islands and what is today called Southeastern Alaska. Russian presence caused the Spanish to back off, though their expeditions were half-hearted at best. The French Revolution also slowed Spanish exploration, and the Nootka Sound dispute with Great Britain over trading rights off the Pacific Coast created a political vacuum for a few years into which the Russians moved vigorously.[7]

By 1784 Shelikof had built a trading post and settlement on Kodiak Island and made Alexander Baranov the manager of the post. Shelikof's son-in-law, Count Rezanov, obtained a charter from Czar Paul I in 1799, allowing him to establish a trading monopoly for the Alaskan fur trade as far south as the 55th parallel. For the next sixty-eight years the Russian-American Company, as it was called, was the government and exclusive commercial operation in Alaska. Priests of the Russian Church established missions and settlements in the Aleutians and along the Bering Sea coast, of which St. Michael was one. Baranov dominated the operations of the Russian monopoly as the General Manager of the Company, and also as governor of Russian America until 1818.

In 1799, the Russians under Baranov moved their headquarters from Kodiak to Sitka, which he made the capital city of all Alaska, and where he built his home. A wooden cathedral was also built here, which stood at its original location until it was burned in the middle twentieth century. Most of the Russian trade and ship traffic gathered in the port of Sitka, where many a gruesome tale of mistreatment of the natives by the Russians has become legend.

One of these, credited to Chirikov, tells of a Captain Soloviev who tied a group of Aleuts together, and for his amusement made bets with other Russians as to how many of them he could kill with a single bullet fired at point-blank range. "He was unable to pierce more than to the ninth man," reported the amiable Chirikov. Especially poignant are the stories about the dreadful deeds of two characters named Sholikov and Trangolikov who were reputed to have so abused the Alaskan Eskimo that the bitterness between Alaskan and Siberian natives around Bering Strait became fixed. Sacariasen said he had heard tales told by the Eskimo of a war between the two Eskimo groups in the Diomede Islands that lasted for many years. Some historians, he claimed, estimated that ninety percent of the coastal Eskimo died during this shameful period.[8]

In 1825, the Russian and British governments signed a treaty fixing the boundary between the Russian-American Company and its British counterpart, the Hudson's Bay Company, at 54° 40' north latitude. The Hudson's Bay Company evaded the spirit if not the letter of the agreement when it sent a small ship with a party of traders to open fur posts on the Stikine River east of Alaska. The Russians retaliated by building a tiny fort at the mouth of the Stikine that they called Redoubt St. Dionysius, but became known later as Fort Wrangell in honor of an official of the Russian-American Company. When a brig under the command of Peter Skene Ogden sailed into the north of the Stikine on the brig *Dryad* in 1834 he was stopped, and the British withdrew only after loud protests. It required a meeting of diplomatic importance between Governor Pelly of the British and Baron Wrangell of the Russian Company to settle the dispute.[9] The two men and their staffs met in Hamburg, Germany, and it was an impressive occasion indeed.

Things quieted down for a time but the English invaded the Yukon valley and began trading with the interior, Athabascan-speaking Indians at Fort Yukon and operated here for quite a time before the Russians discovered what was going on. Another conference resulted, and the Alaska border was moved several miles west of where it had been established in 1825 to accommodate the ambitions of the Hudson's Bay Company, which enlarged the Yukon Territory somewhat in consequence.

In 1853-55, the Crimean War brought a bad case of jitters to both Russians and Englishmen along the Pacific Coast. Both Sitka and Victoria expected attacks at any time, and their officials made appropriate arrangements for defense. No attacks materialized. On Kamchatka Peninsula, however, there was actual bloodshed. On August 20-24, 1854, a combined squadron of British and French naval vessels bombarded the fortifications at Petropavlovsk, and silenced its guns quickly. A landing force of marines and sailors went ashore, and were ambushed by the Russians who had fled to the forest. One hundred seventy of the attackers were killed or wounded before the crestfallen allied commanders ordered them to withdraw. Shortly after their victory, however, the Russians withdrew from that part of Siberia, and abandoned the Fort until after the war. When a new British force attacked the place the following year they found everything deserted and the landing party burned the buildings of the town as well as demolishing the fort. This was the Crimean War on the Pacific.[10]

Carl noted in his journal that "relief and peace came when the territory passed into the hands of the United States." This allegedly happy event took place in the early spring of 1867. The correspondence between Sheldon Jackson and the Department of the Interior after he went to Alaska would seem to contradict Carl's generalization, for his letters and reports are full of tales of injustice to the natives, unethical behavior on the part of some of the American traders and trading companies, and the destruction of the natural resources of The Great Land. His vigorous protests to Washington were noted at the highest level, and he made frequent trips to Washington to back his charges. This bellicose little man did not mind being in the midst of a perpetual storm, but "relief and peace" was not exactly the state of affairs in the North before the gold rush. Nevertheless, the history of the Russian mistreatment of Aleuts, Eskimo, and Indians is not a happy tale, and perhaps the Indians and others were better off after the purchase in spite of American governmental neglect and the shoddy practices of many Americans. Certainly the autocratic Romanoff corporation was no model of enlightenment.

Carl noted by indirection that the American jurisdiction was not entirely without flaws. He said that the natives were able to enjoy more peace and "greater fairness" in trade with Americans than Russians. He claimed that American missionaries were a force for good, and their schools in Sitka, Yakutat Bay, and Haines were helping the local people. The European missions on the Bering Sea also worked to bring religion and education to the Eskimo, such as those at Unalakleet, Golovnin Bay, and Kuskokwim Bay.

The Americans came north to Port Clarence, and they also had a mission station and school at Cape Prince of Wales. At the latter spot Harrison Thornton, an American, was murdered one night in front of his wife and children by Eskimo whom Sacariasen described as "wild." He gave the reason for this sad event as a feud that had begun in 1877 between a group of whites and townspeople when the Eskimo boarded and plundered a trading schooner. When another ship came to the same place in 1879 the local people decided once more to raid the ship. The women were secreted back of the town and the men boarded the steamer. The Captain ordered them to leave at once, but they refused to obey. He then ordered his crew to drive the Eskimo away and a brawl resulted in which fifteen Eskimo lost their lives. Others were wounded and thrown overboard. Uninjured survivors jumped over the side in retreat. The only casualty among the ship's company was one man wounded. After this no ships were robbed, but the natives took out their spite on the white missionaries who exercised a kind of "muscular Christianity" by taking axes and destroying native "stills" or seizing contraband liquor brought in by the traders. Whether Americans should have been involved in such activities, or even informing law officers, is a matter of opinion. Carl thought they should have, but said the touchy situation cost Thornton his life. Another opinion holds that there was strife between two bands of Eskimo living in the same area of Cape Prince of Wales, and that Thornton had broken an Eskimo custom by treating both factions equally, which meant that he did not favor either. On the theory that "he who is not for me is against me," some of the young men of the feuding groups killed the missionary.[11]

Had the United States government taken any responsibility for Alaska and sent in civilian governors, this tragedy might have been avoided, but it did not. Only the missionaries and the trading companies did much except at the few forts and naval bases along the coasts, and government regulations stopped the commanders of military forces from acting on anything other than routine matters.

The Alaska Commercial Company hired Eskimo to slaughter the seal, and at that time gave no thought to conservation. All they paid the American government for their profits was a small annual license fee to the federal treasury, and a subsidy of food to their hunters. When the missionaries came in 1877 the company opposed educating either the hunters or their children lest the new learning upset the arrangement between the company and its suppliers. When the missionaries objected to selling liquor, the company resisted their interference. Carl agreed that Sheldon Jackson was the best source of information for those wanting to know more about Alaska, and that he tried to promote the general welfare of the native population, without concern for profits of California-based exploiters of the land's natural resources. In spite of his approval of Jackson's actions, however, Carl continued to dislike Jackson himself.

After this long preface to 1899, the journalist finally got down to summarizing the first week of the new year at Eaton Station. It was a somber New Year's Day, since the body of Klemmet Nilsen was buried that day. The Reverend Axel Karlson from the Unalakleet came up to conduct the services. William Basi translated his remarks from Swedish into Finnish so that the Lapps might understand what was going on. After the dead man was decently interred there was little else for anyone to do.

Early in the week, however, fourteen men went to St. Michael to bring back supplies to the station, but others did only the usual chores of chopping firewood, sawing boards, and keeping warm. All Carl reported this week was that the wife of John Tornensis bore him a tiny daughter.[12] Basi put the child's birthday on January 8.[13]

Peder Berg had intended to go to St. Michael along with the others but his special deer, whom he had named "Moses," was a stubborn beast and this time showed that it had a mind of its own. His objections were violent and to the subject. On the evening of the second day after he left Eaton, Berg returned complaining that Moses had kicked him and tried to gore him so many times that he lost count. His overcoat was badly torn and his sore foot was trampled, making it very painful for him.

By the beginning of the second week of January, Doctors Gambell and Southward were so bored that they took a measuring tape to determine the distance between Eaton and Unalakleet. When they returned they announced that the two places were seven and three-quarters miles apart. In addition, Gambell picked up some mail, and in it found a letter from the absent Superintendent William Kjellmann. Kjellmann was sick in an Eskimo hut about fifteen miles north of Golovnin Bay, and he wrote that he needed a doctor badly. The Reverend Anderson, one of the Swedish missionaries, had given Kjellmann some simple medication but it had not helped. As acting superintendent, Gambell picked two men and had them drive three reindeer to go to Kjellmann, sending Dr. Southward and Ole Bahr with them in case the Superintendent needed to be brought out to the Station. When this small party left, the routine settled down once more in non-activity, though the "mild weather" continued, for temperatures got as high as 4^0 to 10^0 F. for nearly a week. Southward did not agree that it was "mild" however, for he put on a complete set of winter gear of the kind worn by Lapps. As he knew he would have to sleep in the open for several nights before he got to where the sick man was, he wore the fur coat, the bulging trousers and the peaked cap of the Lapps, complete with knife and bright sash at the waist. Since he was a tall man compared with the shorter Lapps, he appeared to be even bigger than he was. His clothes were so bulky and so new that he could not run beside the sled in his stiff garments, and was totally unable to drive the deer himself. He had to lie down instead, and Bahr drove the lead deer, with Southward's sled and the supply sled tied behind him in a kind of reindeer train. The people at Eaton roared with laughter as the party left.

On Thursday, the 12th, Gambell consulted with Kittilsen at Unalakleet about Kjellmann's illness. Since Sittilsen was going to the Seward Peninsula himself, he agreed to visit the sick man and if necessary consult with Southward about what was to be done. Before he left Eaton, however, he had another patient; Isaac Nikkila came into the Doctor's office badly injured. He had gone on a bird hunting junket for food and pleasure, but instead of returning with some edible bird, he had fallen, his gun had discharged, and he caught the entire charge of shot in his elbow and left thigh. He had fainted from the shock and loss of blood, but eventually recovered consciousness enough to get back, and Gambell and Kittilsen spent much of the night picking shot out of the wretched and suffering Nikkila. Within a week the wounded man's leg became badly infected, and at first the doctors feared it was gangrene. Fortunately it was not, and Nikkila must have been in excellent physical condition for although it took some time, he eventually recovered fully.

When Gambell finally got away, he spent a few days at the Mission, but when he returned he tried to find some kind of work to fill the

153

unoccupied time of the men at the Station. He sent two men to St. Michael to get additional supplies to send on to Cape Nome by reindeer freight. Another party was sent to find how Kjellmann was doing, and to discuss with him the request of a man named Anvig for a loan of government reindeer to be used at the mission where he worked. By now the deer at Eaton were running a regular supply route between Unalakleet and Nome, and Gambell did not feel that he should loan any of them, but proposed to dump the request in Kjellmann's lap.

Reporting what he had heard about Nome while he was gone, Gambell told the men that there were rumors of widespread claim jumping in the gold fields. Since most of the claims up to this time were staked by their friends and associates, they were particularly concerned that some of the herders had claims of their own staked by a power-of-attorney. Some of the miners at Anvil Creek sent a letter to Captain Walker, commander of the post at St. Michael, asking him to send soldiers to the gold fields since there were no civilian policemen of any kind in this part of Alaska. Gambell was as concerned as the herders for the main reason they might have trouble was that none of them had actually received their naturalization papers, and until they had actual proof of their citizenship they were vulnerable. The American miners challenged the right of "foreigners" to stake claims, and especially those whose claims were taken in the name of their friends. Any claims staked by or for Eskimo were usually "jumped," for whites had cheated Indians and Eskimo for so long that they automatically excluded the native people from any benefits they might get from their lands. The Americans who came in found that the Norwegians used only two stakes to mark their claims, and they leaped on this technicality to insist that it took six stakes for a valid claim so all original claims were invalid. Sometime in the future there would probably be a court decision on these matters but at present, with no one able to maintain law and order except the miners themselves, the potential for violence was very great, with the newcomers preparing to fight for gold and the first claimants equally prepared to fight back.

Walker realized the danger and acted swiftly. Although the number of men under his command was small and most regular soldiers were still involved in the Philippines, he sent a small squad of soldiers to the new town of Anvil City, or Nome as it was coming to be called. This was the first time any kind of authority appeared in this part of the country.

For the next few days no one brought any more news to Eaton, and no one at Eaton knew what was happening on the peninsula to the north. There was much activity as soldiers passed back and forth between St. Michael and the Nome area, however. Language barriers still kept the herders from learning much from those coming down from the gold camps.

Scurvy still bothered them. Two of the Lapps had been complaining about feeling ill, and finally Gambell decided that they were suffering from this needless ailment. This could be very serious during the dark days of winter unless the invalids changed their diet at once. One of these men was Anders Balto, the brother of Samuel Balto, the polar explorer. On February 12, Samuel came into Eaton from his work elsewhere to nurse his brother back to health.

Before January was over, however, a Mr. Kvidsted, a clerk for the N.A.T. & T. Company in St. Michael, came to the Station on his way to Nome to look after his own interests there. He had heard that his claim had been jumped by one of the Americans who was raiding the claims of those not actively working them. It turned out that only three claims had actually been jumped, and the rumors greatly exaggerated the situation. One of the claims was that of the Kjelsberg brothers and two belonged to Olai Paulsen.

Now passing prospectors coming back from the frozen wasteland to the north brought a different kind of news. Along the Snake River, Kjellmann and Spring had staked out the entire shoreline on both sides of the tiny stream, and it was here that the new city of Nome was growing up. The two men permitted newcomers to stake building sites one hundred feet wide by three hundred feet deep along the west side of the river bank. They could either dig for gold or construct a building on their lot. The privilege did not cost much, and the lots were selling, though not yet at boomtown rates. Kjellmann had assumed that the business section of the future city would be built on the east bank of the river, so they neither sold lots nor permitted construction of cabins here until spring, which they assumed would bring in a big influx of miners and businessmen. Spring surveyed the plotted streets while Kjellmann was recovering from his illness, so that he and

Kjellmann could make their profits in land speculation in addition to anything they might make from their gold claims.

January was a dreadful time to arrive in this rugged country. When several of the herders returned from visiting Kjellmann they told of a nameless young man who had frozen both feet while looking for gold. There was no fuel to build a fire and his partner placed the injured man in a sleeping bag while he went into Nome for help. On his way to Nome the second man had fallen through some thin ice and thoroughly soaked himself. Nevertheless, he went on in grave danger of perishing, and finally came to the cabin where Kjellmann was living. The men there dried and warmed him. Kjellmann, although still not able to go himself, immediately sent Ole Olsen, one of the herders working near him, with a deer and sled to the rescue of the frozen prospector. As soon as he reached the young man Olsen built a fire and, after warming him, put him on the sled and drove swiftly back to where Dr. Southward could look at him. Southward examined him and said that he was so badly frosted that there was no chance of saving his feet. Before he amputated he wanted some surgical instruments, which he borrowed from Gambell at Eaton. Kjellmann was impressed by the skill with which Southward saved the patient's life, and asked him to serve with the Reindeer Service at a salary of ten dollars a day, which was an excellent salary in 1899, even in the Yukon.

At Eaton they had intermittent requests for deer to transport men or supplies between St. Michael and Nome. Captain Walker relieved some of his law-enforcing soldiers of their assignments at the gold fields, and he did not want his men to have to march between their posts when the deer sleds made moving them so much faster and easier.

Similarly, men who were not connected with the Service would come to Eaton for tools to work on the buildings going up at Nome. Two men whom Kjellmann hired to saw driftwood into planks to build houses and business structures came down to borrow equipment. They reported that many foolish people were coming even this early in the spring without thought about how they were to be fed or housed. Nome was not a city, and the few people who were there had not built hotels or restaurants, or even stores where supplies could be purchased. The Swedish mission, and Karlson, at Golovnin Bay, had its work totally disrupted when it turned into a continuous rescue mission for destitute prospectors who insisted on coming across land from Dawson and elsewhere in spite of the weather. Ships were not yet able to come from Seattle that early in the year, and supplies were very scarce. It was only fortunate that the number of people who came through were still numbered in the dozens and not yet in the hundreds or thousands as they would be in a few short weeks. The one storekeeper at Golovnin Bay, a merchant named John A. Dexter, had a good reputation because he generously aided those in need. He gave food to those in genuine poverty, and "grubstaked" others who could not pay cash, but who had claims and might have perished without his aid. Precipitation that covered the ground with four feet of snow in some places did not help the situation any.

New cases of scurvy still appeared from time to time among the herders who simply refused to eat what the Acting Superintendent told them to eat. Not enough men were stricken to be a threat to the efficiency of the Station, but it was unpleasant to know that so many could be ill from a wholly needless ailment. Gambell prescribed medicine which would stop the condition, but the childish herders would not take it, demanding that he give them whiskey instead. He refused to give them what they wanted, for alcohol would do nothing for what was wrong with them. Sacariasen was disgusted with his companions, who even refused to admit it was their eating habits that brought them to where they were.

Since their contracts with Jackson had been signed in Norway in early February, 1898, their year of service was almost at an end. Accordingly, the men began gathering supplies to make an "outfit" for themselves as soon as they could leave for Nome. They knew enough about the Arctic, however, to understand that there was no point in leaving on the very moment their contract was over, for temperatures were very cold, and it was a long hike to the gold fields. One bitter evening the thermometer registered forty degrees below zero, with a tremendous chill factor, for a strong wind was howling from the interior of Alaska. Even the Eskimo people, Carl noted grimly, came into his kitchen to warm their noses to prevent them from freezing. He noted one afternoon with amazement as he watched the Eskimo women fishing through the ice of the river how one of them, sitting in the snow, loosened her clothing and exposed her breast to the biting wind so that she

157

could nurse her infant. The child was warmly dressed, but how the mother kept from injuring herself, he did not know.

Two of the Norwegians found something to do during the long winter darkness. The Lapp girls who came over with their parents were a year older than they had been when they arrived and now, although still very young, some of them were marriageable. The young, single herders had courted them, and at the end of February, two of the couples had agreed upon a wedding date. The first such celebration any had held since leaving Finnmark, it was to be a gala occasion. The night before the wedding seven soldiers from St. Michael came through Eaton along with twelve non-military prospectors who wanted to travel with the military company. Seven soldiers was not exactly a major police force to control hot tempers or criminal activity in Nome, but it was all that Walker could spare at that time. These nineteen people decided to join in the marriage celebration along with the herders.

Sacariasen had almost stopped grumbling by this time, but he did feel abused to have to cook for nineteen hungry men who arrived just before he thought he was done working for the day. He said it took him most of the night to get the fires built up again, to prepare and cook the meal, and to get the guests satisfied before he could finally get some rest. Sometime after midnight everything quieted down, and he got to sleep, but had to cook an early breakfast for those who had eaten at a normal time. Early in the morning the civil judge from St. Michael came to Eaton on his way to Nome, and he decided to stay for the wedding feast as well.

At nine o'clock in the morning the two couples to be married climbed into sleds to go to Unalakleet to be married by Karlson. Their attendants and other guests each drove a reindeer and sled, and they all made quite a procession as they left Eaton with sleigh bells jingling in the traditional way. The weather was a bitter thirty below zero, but everyone was in a holiday spirit and was dressed for it. Carl did not go, for he had to stay at the headquarters building to cook for everyone who would be coming back happy and hungry and expecting a feast.

There is no record of the ceremony itself. It was nearly five in the evening when the deer were heard coming back along the snow-covered trail with their jingling bells. While they had been gone, the people who had stayed behind had set several large tables in the main living room, so more could be seated as they ate, for even the families living in the cabins wanted to be there for the party.

Finally everything was ready, and the brides and grooms were seated in the honored places. As many of the others as could do so sat at tables, and the rest crowded along the walls all the way around the dining area, sitting on benches that had been placed there for the occasion. The first course Carl served was hot chocolate for everyone. He noted later in writing of the event that one bridal couple was dressed in Norwegian peasant clothes, described as "ordinary." The other couple, however, including the Norwegian groom, had dressed in full Lapp costume. The bride was decorated with silken ornaments. On her head she "wore a lady's cap on which was fastened a crown of silver stars from the back of which hung a silk bow and long streamers. On her feet were neatly sewn Lapp boots of reindeer skin." The presumably happy groom appeared desperately uncomfortable in his strange clothes, and looked like "a strained, stiff officer in his broad, silver-studded belt with a heavy white scarf around his neck, crossing over the chest and caught under the belt so that the long fringes hung below his jacket. He had a Lapp hat on his head and snow white dress boots on his feet."[14]

At the proper time, however, the two grooms got up, and as was the Norwegian custom at such celebrations, served all of the guests a small glass of whiskey. There was plenty, and it was not long until everyone glowed with the pleasure of the happy occasion. Sacariasen noted with distaste that some of the women drank too much, and commented editorially that "when a Lapp woman gets a little drunk she becomes very affectionate, and throws herself at any man, regardless of who he is." He then concluded primly, "This now began to be the order of things."[15]

Soon the people began to sing, and as the whiskey continued to flow their singing became more and more boisterous, until it degenerated largely into mere shouting. Carl hustled in the food to quiet things somewhat. The staple diet of fresh reindeer meat was the main course. After the tables were cleared, the guests quickly resumed the more serious activity of getting drunk as thoroughly and quickly as possible. They toasted the two couples until about eleven o'clock. Not until then were wedding presents of money given and received. Finally, after one more drink, everyone started home. Two of the Lapp couples began to quarrel as they left the banquet hall, and their screams of rage could be heard as they yelled at each other. Both wives were struck by their enraged husbands, and pushed over a bank by their mates, who later could not remember what the quarrel was all about. Unfortunately one of the women was injured severely enough that Dr. Gambell had to give her emergency treatment. The other woman was drunk enough to be relaxed when she fell, but continued to lie there, either unconscious from drink or knocked senseless. She soon came to, however, after her friends returned for her and put her to bed to recover from the fall and to sober up. Thus ended the celebration, which was almost at the end of Carl's service as the cook for the employees of the Service at Eaton Station.

Sacariasen did not leave until the end of the month of March, but Basi left a month earlier.[16] Carl said that Kjelsberg and Basi left on the last day of February. They had learned by now to use sled dogs, and they piled three hundred pounds of supplies on a sled leaving for Nome. After shouting that they would be waiting for the others when they were ready to come, they cracked their whips and headed north.

The soldiers left the next day. Their equipment required twenty-six deer to pull the pulkas, and three herders went along to drive the animals. Civilian freight was usually carried for a charge of thirty to forty cents a pound between Eaton and Nome, but since the War Department had put up the money to bring the herders to Alaska in the first place, the army paid nothing. Olai Paulsen, Ole Stensfjeld, and Isaak Tornensis were the three drivers who went with them.

Two new scurvy cases developed toward the end of February, and several of the small children at Eaton became ill with the mumps. Carl made no comments about the mumps, and did not speculate where they got the disease, but he did give a frank and unfavorable opinion of the childishness of the men who refused to eat canned vegetables because they liked to eat a straight diet of dehydrated potatoes.[17]

The rest of the month was quiet and cold. One day it warmed to sixteen degrees below zero, but the rest of the week the temperature hovered around the minus forty level. On Thursday, however, at the last day of the month, sixteen herders gave notice to Gambell that they were quitting, and would leave as soon as the weather permitted.

160

Gambell was a busy man. He was not only acting as the executive for the Station, but was occupied with his medical duties as well. The woman pushed over the bank by her drunken husband on the night of the wedding party was still in bed, and it soon became evident that her trouble was complicated by a pregnancy, and that she was in danger of having a miscarriage. Some of the men ill with scurvy did not feel better, and turned away from Gambell to take advantage of the "herb doctor" who lived there. John Petter Johannsen from Kvalsund, Norway, claimed to have learned some folk medicine in the Old Country, and he brewed a large pot of herbs, which he gave to the men. Probably they did help, for these cooked plants would likely contain some vitamins. He also practiced a little primitive blood-letting, still used at that time in some parts of Europe. The sick men claimed that Johannsen's methods were better than those of Gambell, and that they felt much better. They probably did, for a combination of new goods, the "placebo effect," and confidence in their own doctor would certainly have operated here. By this time, because of his own overwork and the fact that most of the herders did as little work as possible, Dr. Gambell probably had become short-tempered, and the patients he treated could have sensed it and resented it. Johannsen, however, visited his patients two or three times a day, and his bedside manner must have been excellent. When everyone had recovered from his sickness, Johannsen collected a small fee from each one, and anyone else who thought he or she needed attention. In this way he collected almost one hundred dollars of extra income, which was about four months pay at a regular job. When he left for Nome, he was reasonably well supplied with personal funds.

On Tuesday, March 14, Frederik Larsen came back to Eaton, having driven a dog team all the way from Port Clarence. He was living with his wife's Eskimo family, and had come down to buy supplies at the store in St. Michael. He had visited briefly with Kjellmann while on his way south, and he told the herders at Eaton that the Superintendent would be along the following day. Since it had been weeks since anyone at Eaton had talked with Kjellmann, they awaited his coming and the information he would bring with eager anticipation.

It was on Wednesday evening that Kjellmann and Spring arrived. Their faces looked terrible. They were grimy, and the skin was peeling from their noses and cheeks where they had been frostbitten. The new skin under their frostbitten faves was showing as blotches of light against the dark and weather-beaten faces of the men, which gave them a sort of piebald effect. Kjellmann was gaunt from his recent sickness, and not totally well even yet. In fact, Dr. Southward had told him he would have to have an operation if he wanted to feel like himself again. They were pleased, however, over the way their speculative ventures were progressing at Nome. Both men planned to leave the government service as quickly as they could and spend full time looking after their business interests. They also reported that Berg, Greiner, and Amund Hansen who had gone to Nome to stay with Kjellmann were still there, and had sent notice that they were resigning and would not be back.

The men waiting impatiently for the warmer weather had little to do except complain. They did this with enthusiasm, grumbling about scanty rations and the dried beans they had to eat, and declaring that they had been foolish by leaving "impoverished Norway" (as they sarcastically described it), to come to Alaska which was supposed to be so rich, in order to starve to death. No one was starving at Eaton Station and with a flash of humor Carl predicted that when they were able to travel to Nome, their health would be restored almost miraculously. It is clear that Sacariasen had become adjusted to Alaskan life, and that from spending much of his time complaining about his own misery he had changed to criticizing those who talked almost exactly as he had done a year before. While there is nothing in his journal to say that he planned to stay in North American, there is also nothing about going back to Norway, either.

Otto Leinan returned from Nome with word from Basi. He and his companions had reached Nome safely. He also told everyone that Regnor Dahl had staked eighteen claims on the Nome River by virtue of the powers-of-attorney the herders had given him. Ole Krogh had the most of them, and Dahl quite a number of the others. Krogh and Dahl had also staked a claim for Nils Balto, the Lapp boy who had gone with them, who was too young to be able to hold a claim in his own name. Leinan said that the judge who had gone through Eaton on the night of the wedding would hold court in Nome in the very near future to try to settle disputes over ownership of claims. The Scandinavians did not know whether to be relieved or apprehensive, for what American courts might do to their claims was a total mystery to them.

As usual, when Kjellmann was in charge of things, the morale of the men improved immediately. He found work for them to do, sending some up the river to cut lumber, and others with Spring to help him bring back furnishings and supplies from his cabin. He told the others that if they had a project of any kind they wanted to do on or off the Station, he would give them leave to do it. He certainly did not believe that sitting around doing nothing was going to make anyone feel better. Unfortunately, he forgot on one day when he sent men out into the forest that it was Good Friday. They forgot it themselves until noon. They were not a particularly religious lot, but they were accustomed to taking this holy day off from work, and felt highly abused that Kjellmann had ordered them to do something. The ones in the forest were particularly enraged when they learned at the end of the day that Kjellmann had remembered after they left, and had stopped only those at the Station from working for the rest of the day, while the woodsmen worked the entire day.

After Easter, however, the men began drifting away more and more rapidly. Otto Leinan took his family down to Unalakleet to get ready for their trip north at the first break in the weather. The usual route they had learned to use did not go directly north from Eaton, which would have forced them to cross a range of hills, but go to Unalakleet and along the beach as far as they could, then cross the frozen water of Golovnin Bay to reach Cape Nome. At the end of March the ever-falling moisture came in the form of rain instead of snow. While it was still not warm, this seemed an encouraging sign, and everyone felt it would not be long until they could get away.

In spite of gold fever, life and birth went along in its normal way. The wife of Anders Balto gave birth to a little girl on March 25, as did the wife of the Eskimo herder-apprentice, Tenaja Donnak, who had come to Eaton so that Dr. Gambell could deliver the child.

At the time of the Easter holiday Carl commented that this occasion showed a considerable change in circumstances and comfort from the Easter spent at Klukwan village the year before. There is no question that their physical condition was vastly improved, and to Carl it seemed that their financial state was about to improve dramatically. In a sense he was experiencing the American Dream before he had even heard about it. The most obvious improvement apparent to one reading the journal is the change in Carl's own spirits and attitude.

Several of the more impatient young herders began to build Lapp sleds. Kjellmann had no objection to this, but he refused to sell them anything from the supplies of the Station, for he feared that if he did they would immediately start for Nome and they might easily lose their lives because of storms, cold, or hunger.

As March came to an end, more good news came from the gold fields. The judge who had gone to Nome had completed his court session, and had declared the claims of most of the men legal. Hagelin, Huldtberg, and the Reverend P. H. Anderson got their claims restored to them. Two of the Americans, one who had seized Johan Sp. Tornensis's claim, and a man who had jumped that of Mikkel Nakkila, refused to abide by the judge's decision, and he had had the soldiers arrest them for their defiance. Tornensis and Nakkila had to appear as witnesses against them, and when they got back to Eaton they declared that American justice was fair and impartial in dealing with law-breakers.

Finally, on the last day of the month, Kjellmann announced that weather was favorable and he would sell supplies to those who had money enough to pay for them. Now those who had neither dogs nor deer could make the trip by dragging a loaded Lapp sled behind them, pulling it themselves. Those who had been preparing casually to make the trip immediately began packing goods into their sleds, and eighteen men applied for their back pay and their release. Five of the men who had drawn on their money in advance and spent it at the store for nonessentials were denied credit, and these had to go to St. Michael to work for enough to buy supplies. In only a few weeks, however, they could make enough to buy their provisions, and book passage to Nome. The ships would be arriving again very soon. On that happy note, the month of March came to an end.

NOTES

[1]*R. i. A.*, p. 148.

2 Basi, *Diary*, December 21, 1898.

[3]*R. i. A.*, p. 151.

[4]Basi, *Diary*, December 24, 1898.

[5]Basi, *Diary*, December 26, 1898; *R. i. A.*, p. 152-154.

[6]*R. i. A.*, p. 154.

[7]For a much more detailed and a considerably more accurate account of this period of Alaskan history than Carl put into his journal, see Cook, Warren L., *Flood Tide of Empire: Spain and the Pacific Northwest, 1543-1819,* New Haven: Yale University Press, 1973; also, Ray, Dorothy Jean, *The Eskimos of Bering Strait, 1650-1898*, Seattle: University of Washington Press, 1975, pp. 17 ff.

[8]*R. i. A.*, p. 156.

[9]For a full account see Galbraith, John S., *The Hudson's Bay Company as an Imperial Factor, 1821-1869*, Berkeley: The University of California Press, 1957. Part II. "Relations with Russian America," pp. 113-174.

[10]Jackson, Sheldon, "The Introduction of Domestic Reindeer Into Alaska," *Annual Report, 1899.* p. 29.

[11]Montgomery, Maurice, "The Murder of Missionary Thornton," *Pacific Northwest Quarterly*, 54:4 October 1963. Ray disagrees with Montgomery's account. Ray, *Eskimos of Bering Strait*, pp. 218-220.

[12]*R. i. A.*, p. 158.

[13]Basi, *Diary*, January 8, 1899.

[14]*R. i. A.*, p. 166-167.

[15]*R. i. A.*, p. 167.

[16]Basi, *Diary*, February 26, 1899.

[17]*R. i. A.*, p. 168.

Chapter Six

THE NOME GOLD CAMP

Sacariasen left the Reindeer Service officially on April 8, 1899. Along with eleven others, he left early that morning for the jumpoff at Unalakleet. Helping Carl to pull the sled were Alfred Nilima and Johan Petter Johannsen, the herb doctor who had once carried mail between Alten and North Cape before he agreed to go to Alaska. He had been perhaps the most northerly mail carrier in the world. After 1900, he delivered mail between St. Michael and Kotzebue at least three times a year, which was a 1,240 mile round trip each time. According to Carl Lomen, a reindeer entrepreneur who lived in Alaska for many years, Johannsen eventually lost his life in an Alaskan blizzard.[1]

On the second sled were Otto Leinen, Ole Krogh, and Johannes Ravna. The third sled was pulled by its crew of Ole Rapp, Lauritz Stefansen, and Johan Losvar. There was a fourth sled as well, and Lauritz Larsen, Hilmar Hansen, and Rolf Wiig, the former storekeeper pulled that one.

Carl and his partners planned to leave as quickly as they could get their things together, but the other three crews had their departure scheduled for a later time. These four pulkas were heavily loaded, holding almost eight hundred pounds of supplies on each.

The three men on the first sled were able to push and pull their load the seven miles to Unalakleet the first day. They rested at Karlson's mission for the night, and spent a few minutes talking to some of the herders who had gone from Eaton to carry freight from St. Michael to Nome. Donnak, the Eskimo, was there too, for he had finished his apprenticeship and was ready to pick up some deer to form the basis of his own herd. Only a few snow flurries had bothered them and, by Bering Sea standards, the weather was mild.

Now away from the supervision of anyone or from Dr. Jackson who believed that Sunday was a day for no work, the impatient Norsemen loaded their sled on Sunday forenoon in preparation for their departure as early Monday as they could get away. To their consternation, however, they had added enough weight to their sled after they reached Unalakleet that it was far too heavy. Carl admitted that he had piled his load so high he couldn't see over the top. Since they had no way to get their supplies to Nome except by pulling the sleds themselves, they knew that a load of nearly a thousand pounds was too much for three men to pull over the rough ice and snow covering over two hundred miles. No one wanted to leave anything behind, however, so overloaded though it was, the three men started out, pulling on lines attached to the sled. As Sacariasen put it, "We shuffled along, hoping to keep abreast of the drivers, since we were able to pass them at Unalakleet where they were resting."[2] By "drivers," he was referring to the reindeer freight operating between St. Michael and Nome.

They traveled about fifteen miles their first day out, and that evening camped at Egavik, a small Eskimo village north of the Mission. They had to stop in the early evening for they were utterly exhausted from their exertion. While they were resting they heard the reindeer sleighs rushing by them to gain extra distance before dark.

One hospitable Eskimo of the village showed them to a small wooden shack on the shore of the beach. Another Eskimo helped carry their sleeping bags, some of their food, and a coffee pot, while the trio of whites walked empty-handed to their quarters. In return for the shelter, the three travelers invited an ancient Eskimo who was living in the shack to share their meal with them. After eating the usual bland fare of pork, pancakes, and hot coffee, they crawled into their sleeping bags and went to sleep at once in the warm hut.

On Tuesday morning their Eskimo host got up before they did, laid a fire in the fireplace, and had the room warmed by the time they crawled out of their sleeping bags. They all cooked breakfast over the fire he had built, shared some of their food with him, and left in the cold of the early dawn to try to overtake the reindeer drivers who had camped a few miles north of them. By the time they had reached the reindeer camp, however, the drivers were ready to leave, and did not want to wait for the men trudging along slowly pulling their overloaded sled, so the three were left alone to travel the best way they could.

All day long they pulled and lifted, and heaved over obstacles, and over the smooth snow on the beach. They knew that a few miles farther was the next Eskimo village, called Shaktoolik, and they wanted to get there by evening. The daylight hours were still short, for it was only April, and by the time darkness fell, they were still unable to see anything resembling human habitation. They were talking about having to sleep in the open on the beach when in the distance they heard the welcome sound of a barking dog. This meant that they were near humans somewhere ahead. Summoning their last reserves of energy, they seized the sled ropes again and struggled on. With the sun gone the cold settled around them, and the frost forming on the iron runners of the sled made the going unusually difficult. They were so tired that they found this more than a vexation. The drag of the overloaded sled simply proved to be too much for them, and finally they collapsed in the snow, telling one another that they simply couldn't go another step, even though it might mean that they would freeze to death.

Once again the friendly Eskimo came to their rescue. They were near enough to the village that when they quit walking the natives heard the noise of their approach stop suddenly, and a crowd of the local people came rushing out to see what was the matter. Since they could barely talk to each other, the Eskimo told the sledders by way of signs that they would help pull the load into the village. In their exhausted condition Carl and his companions could not have objected even if they wanted to, and they staggered behind the cheerful Eskimo as best they could. The happy crowd of natives made a party of it, and their load was drawn almost magically into the center of Shaktoolik. One of the older men showed them where they could sleep. This was in an underground hut that appeared to Carl from the outside to resemble a midwestern root cellar.

They crawled through a small opening and down a few steps to a passageway which led them to another hole about four feet deep, with a second passageway leading into the living quarters. Here they found a group of local people seated around the wall with a fire burning in the center of the room. The walls of the dwelling were lined with turf. The room was very warm, so warm indeed that many of the people had taken off their outer garments and were sitting partially nude, which startled Sacariasen, since some of their hosts were adult women.

It is interesting to note once more that Carl, who objected so much at the beginning of his travels to black or Japanese cooks, was quite willing by this time to eat the food that the Eskimo had cooked for their evening meal. His sense of cleanliness was offended, however, by the grime of the unwashed kettle in which the Eskimo women cooked their evening meal. The visitors were offered food, and they ate it with a good appetite. Sacariasen evaluated the meal with his professional judgment as a cook, and pronounced it quite pleasant to the taste. One of the older women made coffee for them in their pot, and everyone shared it. Then the weary travelers leaned back against the dirt wall content and ready to sleep. They did not eat any "dessert" which was frozen wild cranberries, dipped in seal oil.

As other travelers have noted, the Eskimo women used human urine to tan seal skins, and stored it in various vessels inside the house.[3] With their hunger satisfied the men became aware of the powerful and unpleasant odor, and when Carl saw one of the women bathing her baby in the urine he said he almost vomited, for immediately he wondered how the kettle in which the seal had been cooked had been washed! Nevertheless, the men crawled into their sleeping bags spread out on the floor among a roomful of natives. Only the banked cooking fire furnished any light. In the faint glow the men soon lost track of their companions, the odors, and the "filth" that surrounded them.

The culture shock of the night before could not have been severe, for when the travelers woke in the morning after a refreshing sleep, they ate a hearty breakfast and went outside to see what the weather was like. To their dismay they found that it was snowing, and they knew that it would be poor sledding for them. In the distance they could see through the slowly falling flakes that the reindeer drivers were camped only about a half mile away. They, of course, had reached the Eskimo town before the three men pulling the sled, but had made camp and waited for the weather to clear and make traveling easier. Sacariasen put on his skis and quickly covered the distance between the village and the camp. He asked the drivers whether they were going to try to travel that day, and they said they were. They planned to reach the shores of Norton Bay that night so that they could cross the twenty-one mile stretch of open pack ice the following day without having to make camp on the dangerous crossing.

Carl hurried back to his two companions, and told them to be ready to go along; in case of accident each party could help the other. They loaded their gear hastily on the sled, seized the ropes, and pushed off after the reindeer drivers. It was not long, of course, until they gave up for, as usual, the deer traveled much faster than they could, and after only a few miles they were once again exhausted. During the afternoon they saw an Eskimo hut, and the hospitable family invited them in to rest until the snow stopped falling. Gratefully they accepted the invitation. Carl observed that "the following day conditions were much better, enabling us to reach the shore of Norton Bay by early afternoon."

The drivers had crossed the Bay by this time, so the three were alone when they reached the bleak shore, without fuel to build a fire and in the wake of an Arctic storm. They pitched their tent, however, and crawled inside expecting to have to spend the night cold and with uncooked food. To their delight, however, by dark six of their friends from Eaton Station came to their camp site. These were not the same men who were following Carl, but John Brynteson and Hagelin, (two of the "lucky Swedes,") Johan Tornensis, Isak Hatta, and Ole Klemmetsen, all on their way to the gold fields. Inga Baldo was the sixth person, and she was going to Nome to serve as cook for Dr. Kittilsen. This party was more affluent than Sacariasen and his friends, for they had dogs to pull their loads.

In the morning when everyone was ready for the difficult crossing on the ice, Tornensis took off about two hundred pounds of the load on Carl's sled and put it on his own. He told the men that when he reached the other side he would leave the supplies on the beach where Carl and his companions could pick them up when they finally arrived. The reduced load made it much easier to pull, and during the morning a stiff south breeze came up behind them. Accordingly, they were able to rig a temporary sail from their tent which helped them more, and they could walk at a normal pace without so much exertion. After a time, however, the ice became much rougher, and they had to push and tug at their load using the total strength of the three men. Had the wind not been at their backs, and if they had had to pull the whole load, it is difficult to say when they might have reached the other side, for it was a full twenty-one miles and in spots was extremely rough. It was well after dark when they arrived at the north beach. Hungry

170

and tired as they were, they set up camp without any delay. They had eaten nothing since breakfast, for they were far more concerned about crossing the ice than eating.

This night they camped beside an Eskimo sod hut whose owner had just returned from a successful seal hunt, so they were able to buy a chunk of meat from him, which they cooked and ate on the spot. They crawled into their bags in the tent, but were so sleepy that they let their fire go out during the night. About midnight they woke so chilled that they had to get up, relight the fire, and walk around swinging their arms to get their circulation going again. After a bit they went back to bed, but all the activity had aroused them too thoroughly, so they cooked some coffee, drank it, and now wide awake decided to resume their travels in the dark. Their weariness, and the hard work of pulling their sled had depressed them, but they agreed that if they could only reach Cape Nome, all their efforts would have been worthwhile.

Hours later, about noon, they came to another Eskimo village, and the people there pointed to a kayak pulled up on the beach into which Tornensis had piled the packs he had brought across the ice. At no time did Carl ever complain that the Eskimo, poor as they were, ever stole anything from them, or even tried to take advantage of their guests. He makes no particular comment about this, but again and again he found only hospitality and honesty among these people, even though they had been badly abused by Russians and Americans alike during the time of imperial governments.

Carl knew a few words of the Eskimo language from spending the winter at Eaton near an Eskimo village, and in halting speech he asked them how far ahead Tornensis was camped. The natives pointed to another camp about four miles distant, and said that the "Lav-Lakker," as they referred to the Lapps, were there. The three companions hastily threw the sacks packed in the kayak onto their sleds and pulled away from the village, almost running in their haste to join their fellow travelers.

While they were "loping" through the snow they noticed movement almost out of visual range, but paralleling their own route. After a short time they realized they were seeing reindeer and loaded sleds coming up behind them. The speeding animals soon caught up with them, and they recognized the lead driver as the same man with whom they had talked at Shaktoolik.

171

The drivers had not crossed the ice when they said they were going to after all, but had rested their animals during the snowstorm, and Carl's group had passed them in the falling snow and darkness without sighting them. They spent the night together, except for Brynteson and Hagelin who had not yet arrived when Tornensis pitched his camp. Somehow they had become separated from the other five, and everyone assumed the deer of the missing men had become tired and refused to move farther forcing them to camp at the spot.

Carl estimated the temperature to be about twenty-five degrees below zero when they woke the next morning, but he had no thermometer to check his guess. With his partners, he decided not to spend another night in their tent, which barely protected them from the cold. The deer drivers stayed in their own camp, however, because there was plenty of moss near at hand for their animals, and they needed a good meal of fresh food. The two men and Carl hoisted their "sail" as soon as they could get away, and the three pushed their sled westward toward Nome. Their objective this day was a tiny Eskimo village known as "Moses."

They reached this place just a little before noon, and decided not to go any farther that day. They were tired again, and beyond the place there was no natural shelter for anyone.

Once again a friendly Eskimo offered them hospitality, which they accepted. They were heating coffee when the drivers and deer came along, so everyone took a break and visited with each other for a little time. The deer freighters went about five or six miles farther where there was again enough moss for their animals. Carl and his companions stayed with the Eskimo.

The next day was Sunday, but no one even considered resting that day. They paid an Eskimo thirteen dollars to bring his four dogs and help pull their load to Golovnin Bay. He might have been the same man who took them into his house. By evening the dogs and men had gone far enough to pass the camp of the drivers. Then both parties camped about a mile apart at the foot of a hill that led them to the Bay. Monday morning the dogs pulled them up a slope which the journalist declared to be "pretty steep for about a mile and a half."[4]

It took several hours before they reached the top, but to their delight they could see down a gradual slope all the way to the sea. They paid the Eskimo, who took his dogs home again, and then they jumped on top of their load and like small children, slid down the several-mile-long hill to the beach. Carl did not say how they steered the sled while sitting on top of a five foot pile of supplies, but they reached the shore without mishap. They stopped, lit a fire, brewed the inevitable coffee, and plodded on toward the next village. As they entered the tiny hamlet they were met by Jafet Lindeberg, who had come out to see whether everyone was all right. He was staying with the Andersons at the Swedish Mission, but he had already arranged for an Eskimo woman and her son and daughter to take care of anyone coming up from the Unalakleet River settlements. Sacariasen noted with approval that the interior of this Eskimo house was clean and the furnishings were in good repair. The people were neatly dressed and clean as well. He gave no opinion as to whether this was a result of the missionaries' influence or whether it was the woman's own inclination to be clean.

Inside the house they found another of their friends, Karl Suhr, who had left Eaton a month before they did, but had only just arrived. How he had been able to get there at all was a miracle. He had left the Station alone, pulling his heavy sled, and in a bright sunlight he became snowblind. Since he had no companion, his predicament was very serious indeed. He felt his way along the beach trail as best he could, camping when he had to, and he had survived. Of course, having lived in northern Norway he knew fairly well how to cope with a disaster of this kind. There is nothing in the official records to show how he was saved, but in the light of what the experience of Sacariasen, Nilima, and Johannsen had been it is not unlikely that he was rescued and cared for by friendly Eskimo.

Thanks to the speed of their descent down the mountain slope, they reached the Eskimo hut before the reindeer drivers did. Brynteson and Hagelin did not get there for three more days.

The town at Golovnin Bay where they stopped was sometimes known as "Dexter's." Like other Eskimo villages it contained about ten native houses and huts. Beside these was the house and store of the merchant, Dexter, and the schoolhouse and main building of the Mission. Compared with the utter desolation of the frozen ice of Norton Bay, the activity and travelers coming and going made it seem like a bustling metropolis. This village was located on a low headland extending into the still-frozen ocean from the east side of the Bay.

By now it was almost the end of April. The days were getting noticeably longer. It was possible for the first time to travel after their evening meal, and it was also warmer than it had been. From time to time both the drivers and the trudging sledmen went on through the semi-darkness over the crusted snow. This not only made their work easier, but was a pleasant way to travel.

Tuesday evening the drivers, with Jafet Lindeberg going with them, left for Anvil City. They still did not go very fast, for on Wednesday evening the Sacariasen sled caught up with them at a place called Chocock. This night the three partners found an unoccupied Eskimo hut, and were told by the local people that they might use it, which they did. The reindeer drivers left at midnight, but the sledders slept on until they heard a fire crackling in the fireplace where they were staying. They woke to find it was morning and an unknown Eskimo was melting snow for coffee water. They crawled out of the sleeping bags, Carl made some coffee, they shared their breakfast with their guest, and set out once more.

Suhr went with them. He did not want to chance having his eyes go bad again. Although they were not far from Nome, he did not want to take the risk of another experience like the one he had been through. He complained that his leg hurt, and admitted that his eyes still bothered him, but said he could see a few things. This meant that they had to slow down to let Suhr keep up with them, but from time to time they would find good sledding, and come whooping down a short slope without effort. Since the deer were hitched to their sleds at all times on the trail, the drivers could not easily slide down hill, and even though the men pulling the hand sled were normally much slower, from time to time they passed several of the reindeer sleds on downhill slopes before they were passed again on a level place, where the deer had the advantage.

Once more they spent the night with an Eskimo family. Carl noted with some wry amusement that this Eskimo not only had two wives, but he clearly favored the young and attractive one over the one who was "old and ugly." When bedtime came the man got into bed first, then his young wife came and lay beside him, and finally the older one crawled over against the wall of the hut. By this time the Norwegians must have been pretty well acculturated, for neither any uncleanliness in the house, nor food the native people ate, nor the nudity of the sleeping Eskimo family seemed even worth mentioning.

In the morning no one wanted to stay any longer than necessary, however, for they were approaching Nome, and they wanted to get there as soon as they could. As soon as everyone had breakfast, the three herders started out once more. They were still very tired from traveling so far the day before, so this time they stopped after only a few hours of pulling their load. Carl Suhr seemed to be worse again, hardly able to see. They used this as their excuse to stop. They pitched their small "drill" tent in the snow between some stacks of wood that the Eskimo had gathered from beachwood, and camped there for the rest of the day and the following night. The weather was still milder now, so they were able to stay warm in their tent. Johannsen had caught a nasty cold while in the stuffy Eskimo house, and he coughed so hard that Carl became alarmed lest he be nurse to two disabled men on the open trail. Johannsen even coughed blood in one of his paroxysms of coughing. They had only the simplest of medicines in their supplies, so that all the sick men could swallow were a few drops of "Hoffman's Draeber," (which Carl identified as "naphtha") but this was at best only a poor cough syrup. They all took turns rubbing the suffering man's chest with a few drops of camphor but this would be of little help if his cold turned into pneumonia. While the two sick men rested, Sacariasen went outside to see whether he could risk trying to make Nome where they could get some better medicine and care. He found that a storm was developing, and if it grew worse there would be no chance at all to do anything for his friends. He walked back three miles to the Eskimo village where they had stayed the day before to see whether he could buy some cranberries to feed the sick men. When he reached the tiny village he found the first hut unoccupied by natives, but outside were two reindeer sleds of the kind that the people had built at Eaton Station early in the winter.

He climbed to the roof and peered down the smoke hole, and saw with pleasure that Mikkel Nakkila and his wife, Bereth Anna, were inside. He then joined them and asked how they got there. They told him that they had resigned from the Service on Wednesday, the 26th, and by using a trained sled deer they had already come as far as Carl and his companions had in almost three weeks pulling their own sleds. They were obviously much faster than the reindeer freight as well.

Nakkila harnessed his reindeer while Bereth Anna brewed some coffee. After the three of them drank it they rode back to the tent where the sick men were, with Nilima looking after them. Since the Nakkilas had no medicine either they pushed on, for Nome was only twenty-five miles beyond Sacariasen's tent. The other four remained in camp.

The following morning, which was their third day of staying in their camp, both Suhr and Johannsen seemed to be better. Carl judged them well enough to travel and they agreed. On the last day of April they started west once more. That night they reached a cabin used by the recorder for the Bonanza Mining District. He was pleased to see them and, since he was Norwegian, they could talk to him. He told them they were only fifteen miles from their destination.

It was May 1 when they reached the summit of the small hill that was the ridge of Cape Nome. This ridge formed the boundary between the Nome and Bonanza districts. It was only a short haul to the town and the Nome River, where they knew Regnor Dahl had gone, and they thought they might be able to live with him. They had not been fond of Dahl either in Port Townsend or at Eaton, but here in this northern land among people whose speech they could barely understand, the former reindeer herders thought that they could tolerate him much better!

Dahl was not at his house when they reached it, but two of their friends, Otto Greiner and Amund Hansen, were. Dahl had hired these two men to saw lumber for a building to be rented by the North American Trade and Transport Company in Anvil City, and for Dahl's own buildings that he was constructing on his mining claims up the river. Suhr took refuge in the sod hut the two sawyers were using, while the three original men in the party went on to Anvil City.

Carl said the town, now known as Nome,[5] had three hundred inhabitants when he arrived, but in general the agreement is that there were only a little over two hundred by the first of May. The town was located on a "weird and majestic spot,"[6] between the Nome and Snake Rivers, which were about six miles apart.[7] Between the two rivers were a series of small creeks, Grove Creek, Lindblom Creek, Sunset Creek higher in the mountains behind Nome, and near the beach, Anvil Creek whose name came from a kind of highland known as Anvil Peak because of a curious rock formation on the top. This was the best placer creek in the area at the time. These creeks and rivers emerged from the mountains behind Nome, about fifteen miles from the sea. Some were from three to five thousand feet high with sharp crests and glaciated slopes.[8]

When the three herders came into the town of Nome they found Lindeberg, the two Kjelsberg brothers, William Basi, and Ole Berg, all in good health and all claiming to be doing well in their mining ventures. Lindeberg certainly was, though it is doubtful whether the others were making any fortunes. Across the river from the Kjelsbergs were the tents of those who had bought town lots from Kjellmann and Spring. Those who were already there planned to erect store buildings when the ships and passengers arrived in the next few weeks, but until they could get supplies and good lumber everyone lived in tents. In order to hold a lot, the regulation governing the town said that the owner had to live on his land within a framework of at least twelve logs laid out in the form of a house. Most of these "logs" were driftwood timbers dragged up from the beach, but at least they had the pattern of walls, and formed a tiny stockade around each man's tent which was pitched inside.

On May second, eager to get rich as quickly as possible, Carl and his two companions went around visiting "old timers" in the tents asking them for suggestions as to where they should stake their claims. Since they spoke English very badly, probably they did not learn much. They did learn that everything along the Snake River, "that sluggish, unnavigable stream,"[9] had been prospected and staked, but that there might be some gold claims along the Nome River to the east. Some spots had probably been overlooked in the tiny creeks flowing into that river, or some might have been looked at, but not examined carefully. The three men proposed to set out the following morning to begin their search.

They traveled without much gear, for they did not want to be slowed down carrying huge packs, as they had been when they came from Eaton. They took only a little food, their mining tools, and their sleeping bags.

When they reached the Nome River they found Carl Suhr feeling very perky, and he was out of the cabin with Amund Hansen ready to take off on his own for the gold. Hansen went with the others, leaving his log sawing job for the day.

The five of them climbed the ridge beyond the river, and swung up Osborn Creek. To their disappointment, they found the stream completely staked, and at noon they gave up and made camp. They boiled water in the heavily used coffee pot over a fire of tiny twigs, since they could find nothing else to use for fuel. They rested miserably that night on the hillside in their sleeping bags with no tent for shelter, and in the following morning hiked to the end of the claimed area. Clumsily they began to pan for gold, but found nothing, and staked no claims.

All the next day they ranged over the hills and in the tiny ravines on their slopes, still finding nothing. They spent another chilly night in the open, then turned back toward Nome, reaching Dahl's tent before dark. Dahl was still gone, but Greiner invited them in for the night, and the six of them crowded inside to get warm and to eat a decent meal.

The Nome that Carl had reached in that May of 1899 was not the city that it would be by fall, but its general appearance was already evident. By fall, when Sacariasen had finished his journal, the tent city of the spring had become a chaotic boom town. Some of the paths between the tents had originally been platted with names of local citizens, but these had been changed. For instance, Steadman Avenue was known during that summer as "Hogan's Alley."[10] Most of the "streets" were ankle deep in mud. Emigrants noted the "confusion, waste and filth"[11] in the town, which had been built without any plan "upon damp and muddy soil hitherto covered by the deep and marshy moss."[12] Kjellmann had plotted the lots and streets, but few paid much attention to things like sewers, fire protection, or a police force. Nome was a mining camp much like hundreds of others that had sprung up in the American west since 1848. There were two or three frame buildings, but for the most part people lived any way they could in any kind of shelter they could get along the river or the beach. The beach was described as a "low sandy beach, without a tree for fifty miles," sidewalks, such as they were, and the streets varied in height and width,[13] depending on the whim of the one who had built a portion. By the end of the summer, one observer noted that "tents were pitched everywhere on the sand. Men were milling among them, stepping around piles of refuse and broken-down equipment. Most of the men had rocker outfits, set up for mining. Some had strung barbed wire around their claims. Washing hung from clothes lines."[14] It was impossible to keep dirt out of the tents or even the frame structures along the beach and Main Street. By mid-summer the business establishments were saloons, gambling places, dance halls, restaurants, steamship agencies, stores, and lawyer's offices. There was no church until the end of August, and then the pastor spent most of his time operating a makeshift hospital.[15] Even the mud of the streets, however, had some "color" in it, and it was a grim thought that amid the squalor and discomfort of the place this one town in all the world came closest to approximating the popular 19th Century concept of heaven with its "streets of gold!"[16]

By the fall of 1899, some semblance of law and order had emerged and there was even a town election. However, the chaos of shacks, dogs, men and women, reindeer, claim stakes, claim jumpers, sluice boxes, and heaps of unsorted freight piled on the beach almost overwhelmed those who tried to support organization in the mining areas. This was, indeed, a time when strong men and a few women made their own laws, where might made right, and where the unity of cultural ties, kinship, friendship, and language gave the reindeer herders an advantage over the thieves and those, who came to be known as "spoilers," who tried to dispossess them.

Carl Suhr and Amund Hansen prospected near the town, but Johannsen and Sacariasen went back into the hills to try again to find a likely looking prospect. They found only a little "color," but did find enough to encourage them to stake their first claim on an unnamed creek which Carl called Darling Creek. They worked around it for another day or two.

One morning after a few days of gold panning, they heard the familiar sound of approaching reindeer. Again it was someone from Eaton with outfits which took them to the gold. Per Larsen and Alex Jornes were in charge this time. Jornes also had a big dog named Gypsy, which was pulling another load. Jornes, now known only as Jones from this time on, was not with Nilima, who was usually prospecting with him, so Carl and Johannesen joined forces with him and Larsen to be able to stay out longer. Jones could speak English and he examined their signs put up to claim their holdings to make sure that they had been written correctly. Later in the week the four men went down Clark Creek and found a likely looking spot only a few yards above its mouth. They called this claim "Cuba" after the victorious war that was concluding in the Caribbean. Their other claims were merely numbered.

On their way home they visited Osborn Creek again, and once more found nothing. That night they stopped at Regnor Dahl's tent, and found that while at last he had returned from his own prospecting trip, he was temporarily absent on a trip down the river, so once more they missed seeing him.

On May 9, they returned with food enough to last them four days on their prospect on Osborn Creek, but a storm caught them in the open. The heavy fog was so dense that they could see no landmarks in the barren wasteland, and they became totally confused. Fortunately they found their own tracks from the previous day, and went back to their campsite waiting for better weather. The storm continued, however, and by morning snow was falling heavily. Since by this time their food was almost all gone, they knew they either had to get back to Nome or go hungry. In spite of the storm and snow, they had caught such a severe case of "gold fever" that Johannsen and Sacariasen both staked two more claims there. Carl admitted that they did this only for a lark to pass the time until the storm let up.

On the morning of the eleventh their food was finally gone, and they packed their gear and began to hike downstream. Although the fog was still heavy, they could not become lost again as long as they stayed along the banks of the creek and river. When they reached a spot they believed they recognized they cut over the ridge to Anvil Creek. It was late evening when they reached Kjellmann's house on "Number Two Below" as his claim was named. In the house were some of their former herding associates who quickly invited the four hapless prospectors inside to dry out and eat something. Since they had eaten only a breakfast, they were hungry and gladly accepted the invitation.

They reached their own tent in Nome on the morning of the twelfth, and found that their pile of possessions had remained untouched all the time they had been gone. The storm that had chased them from the mountains continued without letup for nearly a week, and no one did anything but stay under cover. Only in Lindeberg's camp was there any activity. Here a group of men worked through the storm at hauling lumber they had sawed from the drift logs on the beach. Lindeberg was now operating a kind of lumber yard until better logs and sawed boards could be brought from outside.

During the bad weather only those with reindeer were able to go back and forth to their claims with supplies. Again, this favored the Norwegians over the American prospectors, who resented their disadvantage and grumbled about "foreigners."

The record of names and identification of the claims on Anvil Creek shows that Jafet Lindeberg, of course, had staked the "Discovery" claims, as well as "Number Two Below." "Number One Above" was Brynteson's, and "Number Two Above" belonged to Missionary Anderson. "Number Three Above" was in the name of Hagelin. "Number Four Above" was being worked by Axel Karlson, the missionary they had known at Unalakleet. "Number Five Above" was Huldtberg's. Lindblom had "Six Above" and Dr. Kittilsen was working "Number Seven Above." Claim "Number Eight Above" was staked by G.W. Price. "Claim Number Nine Above" had originally been taken for the Eskimo boy, Constantin, but the rules of the mining district were changed to discriminate against all natives in places where whites were prospecting. In order to prevent this injustice, Price's brother became the absentee owner of the Number Nine claim so that Constantin could have it.

J.S. Tornensis had "Number Ten Above," eleven was in the name of Mikkel Nakkila. J. Kvidsted worked half of "Number Twelve Above Discovery" and the other half belonged to Stefan Ivanoff of Unalakleet. Ole Olsen Bahr had no superstitious dread of staking "Number Thirteen Above."

Beyond Anvil Creek, at the upper end of Eleven, was a tiny creek called Nakkila Gulch. This had two claims on it--one staked by Isak Nakkila, and the second by an elderly American named Derring.

On the upper side of Lindblom's Number Six off Anvil Creek was Specimen Gulch. Again it was the same story. With only a few exceptions, all of the better claims had been taken in the name of the herders or their friends. Specimen Number One was claimed by Sacariasen's cousin, Wilhelm Basi. Number Two was that of Olai Paulsen. Quartz Creek was opposite Specimen Gulch, and there Thoralf Kjelsberg and Magnus Kjelsberg had claims. William Kjellmann and Doctor Gregory from Saint Michael had claims nearby. So it went down as far as the mouth of Anvil

Creek. Altogether the herders had forty-four claims on this best of all gold producers at that time. It is no wonder that, with normal human greed being what it was and is, the Americans from outside resented these "prospectors" being there first and gathering the gold that they thought should have been theirs. They thought of Lapps and Norwegians as being little better than the Eskimo boy Constantin, and were determined to gain control of the rich gold claims by any means they had to use.

Carl was not particularly involved, for his own claims seemed almost worthless. He and Johannsen grew so discouraged when finally they left their own "diggings" that finally they asked Lindeberg whether they could work for him. He agreed to hire them. In fact, anyone from Eaton who needed work could get it, for labor was in extremely short supply. He gave each man a share of whatever they could recover from the streambed, and his workers were satisfied with this arrangement. Carl and Johan Petter were assigned to chopping ice from Anvil Creek at "Discovery" so that the prospectors could get to the gold-bearing muck at the bottom of the stream. Other crews were doing the same thing in places like Snow Gulch, Mountain Creek, Rock Creek, and Dexter Creek.

At the beginning of the last week in May the storm was almost over, and four of Lindeberg's employees went over to Snow Gulch to try to get claim "Number One Above" operating. This belonged to John Brynteson, and seemed to show promise of yielding good profits quickly. By now they knew pretty well what had to be done. J.D. Morgan, a non-herder, was appointed foreman for the crew, but he didn't have to give many directions. Two chopped ice out of the creek, and the other two practically quarried chunks of frozen muck from the stream bed as soon as it was exposed. During the brief spell of good weather after the gold discovery, almost two thousand dollars worth of gold was recovered from this claim, and now with summer coming, thousands of dollars more seemed highly possible. There was a contest among the prospectors to be the first to take $10,000 from a claim. The prize, offered by the N.A.T. & T., was a free trip to Seattle as a guest of the "Company." Lindeberg wanted to win, but the weather was not good enough to work "Discovery." Many of his workers had refused to work at all during the storm, but stayed in their tents.

A few days before the first of June, the larger chunks of muck had thawed enough so that the men could begin to wash gold out of the dirt. Price, who was Lindeberg's chief rival for the prize, took almost $5,000 from his claim on "Number Eight Above." Brynteseon cautiously informed his friends that he had taken about $4,500 from his claim at "Number One Above." The Norwegians working for Lindeberg built sluices at their assigned spots, and when they would total their recoverings for a day it was not at all unusual to announce that $400 worth of gold could come from one claim during a single working day. These days were very long, however.

It was only a short time until the news of their success got to the other people in Nome. Consequently trouble came very close to erupting into violence, when a rush of outsiders brought scores of men to Anvil Creek determined to get rid of the foreigners who were sitting on the best locations. Lindeberg, Price, and their employees were numerous enough to drive the claim-jumpers away with threats alone, but soon the ships from Seattle would bring more and more people in, and they would no longer be able to hold them away. When the commander at St. Michael learned of what was brewing, he sent a message for everyone to remain calm, and as soon as he could he would send a squad of soldiers to maintain order. He also promised to get a judge there to hold court again, and to decide who owned what. When Lindeberg complained that unless a judge arrived soon, thieves and claim-jumpers might easily steal thousands of dollars in gold from his claim, the Captain tartly responded that the Pioneer Mining Company, which was what Lindeberg called his operation, probably had broken the law anyway! Because he could not watch all the claims on Anvil Creek, Lindeberg leased some of his claims, but the covetous claim-jumpers defied the new leasees to do any work if they honored a lease from Lindeberg. Therefore, little work was done on these claims lest Lindeberg's men find too much gold, and the human vultures, now watching from the nearby hillsides, should move down and take what they had cleaned from the mud.

Now that the topsoil was thawing, the miners could dig holes up to four feet deep in the muck before striking frozen mud again. The watchful observers wandered up and down the slopes of the low mountains with pick and shovel and gold pan, trying to find other spots where they could stake a claim themselves. Even Lindeberg and his employees searched for other spots lest when court finally be held, they might be forced to relinquish what they had discovered originally.

By the first of June several ships arrived from the south and anchored offshore beyond the ice which still extended for a considerable distance out to sea. The inhabitants of Nome eyed these vessels longingly, for they knew they carried needed supplies that would be put up for sale as soon as they could be brought ashore. They needed fresh vegetables and fruits as well as merchandise for stores or tools to work their claims. Scurvy had developed among the people because they had not had a proper diet all winter. The more seriously ill men had to be taken to St. Michael to the crude, ill-equipped hospital the army kept there. Carl noted that most of the scurvy cases were among Frenchmen.[17] What this signified is hard to guess, but it does raise the question as to who the "Frenchmen" were, where they came from, and why they had scurvy more than others.

On Sunday, June 4, the ice finally broke up and was blown out to sea. The first sailing schooner immediately came as close to shore as it could and landed its supplies and passengers. There was no harbor and no docking facilities at Nome, but the ship could get close enough to allow small boats to go back and forth from the open beach to unload her. Supplies and the new load of passengers made Nome bustle with activity and its night life even more turbulent.

Sacariasen observed events grimly and felt that there was a kind of poetic justice at work, for when the new arrivals sized up the local situation they soon learned that there was no kind of law enforcement in Nome. Almost instantly those who had jumped the Norwegian claims were themselves pushed aside and some claims were jumped as many as five or six times before the first week was over. To counter this move some of the original "crooks," as Sacariasen labeled them), went over to Sinuk--or Sin-Rock, as the miners called it--and organized a new mining district whose boundaries included the Cape Nome District where all the gold was. They then sent word back to Nome that all previous claims had been voided and, unless they were newly staked and recorded at Sinuk, anyone would be free to move in on anyone's previous claim. Of course they planned to charge a fee for making this service available!

184

The audacious scheme came to nothing, however, when the indignant citizens of Nome, themselves little more honest than the others, held a hastily called miners meeting, and sent word to the Sinuk "recorder" giving him ten hours to vacate his post or be called on by a delegation from Nome carrying a rope. He got the message, complied hastily, and the whole dishonest scheme collapsed.

Price, whose successful gold operations were best known in town, was able to defend his property by having enough armed employees nearby that jumpers were discouraged from trying anything threatening his interests. By June 10, he had his $10,000 in gold cleaned from the mud, and left for St. Michael to claim his prize. Lindeberg grumbled in Carl's hearing that someone else might have won except that Price had borrowed enough dust from all of his other claims to win. Price's use of a private army made it clear that with no police available and with abundant riches available for the taking, only brute force could protect a man's property.

The same week that Price left for St. Michael, diligent prospectors found gold on the beach at Sinuk, about twenty-five miles west of Nome. Immediately a curious prospector decided to try his luck washing the sands on the beach in front of Nome. He seems to have been one of the unnamed Frenchmen living in Nome whom Sacariasen claimed were more subject to scurvy than others. He found considerable gold in the beach sand, and immediately other prospectors tried the sands also and, although it seemed impossible that any gold could be in the ocean, this actually became "unquestionably the greatest poor-man's diggings ever found."[18] The beach was about one hundred fifty feet wide, and perhaps six miles long. During the year that Carl spent there, five hundred men took out half a million dollars worth of placer gold--an average of a thousand dollars worth of the precious dust apiece. Their holdings were small--they were limited by custom to a circular amount of land not much larger than a man could reach with his shovel from the point where he first began to dig.[19] On these tiny areas men pitched tents, ate, slept, and worked their claims. Strangely, Carl never did stake a claim or work the beach itself, but continued to search the rivers and creeks coming from the mountains beyond Nome.

There was very little formal staking of claims on the beach, however. By August, one observer noted that there were a hundred beachcombers for every claim owner. The Nome Mining and Development Company tried to charge the "combers" and squatters a fee of fifty cents a day to work the beach in front of the town, but the miners laughed at them. By August the "diggings" stretched for eight miles at the water's edge. These "ruby sands," a combination of normal sand mixed with iron ore and gold, provided enough to keep most miners minimally solvent,[20] but not everyone was successful, of course. One of the disgruntled failures penned the mournful lines

> Break, Broke, Bust,
> On the ruby sands of Nome.
> Break, Broke, Bust,
> Three thousand miles from home![21]

To all of this feverish excitement, a new fervor heightened tensions and raised the noise level when several sailing vessels unloaded a cargo a liquor for the miners. New tent houses for saloons and barbershops appeared overnight. Both the N.A.T. & T. and the Alaska Commercial Company bought lots from Kjellmann and set up stores in tents until they could get their permanent structures built. Although supplies were now plentiful, prices were high. By modern standards they were not exhorbitant, but by the price indices of the day, they were frightful.

For example, a twenty-five pound sack of flour cost $20. Roast beef was 50 cents a pound in cans, and fresh beef was unavailable. A drink in a saloon was 50 cents, while a similar drink in the lower states was only a fraction of that. A cigar cost 50 cents, and a haircut, $1.00. Wages in Nome were from five to seven dollars a day for twelve hours work. (Basi made $10 a day as a carpenter.) A bed to sleep on went from a dollar to ten dollars depending on the quality of the surroundings. A man might pay as much as two dollars a night to rent a blanket. Eggs were $1.35 a dozen. Potatoes cost ten cents a pound. These were unheard of prices at the turn of the century.

Meanwhile, back at the fort in St. Michael, Major P.H. Ray and Captain Walker were still being bombarded with letters demanding that they send soldiers to control the growing horde of prospectors and set up some kind of police force. It is somewhat surpising that there seems never to have been any demand for a vigilance committee of the sort sometimes used in California or Montana mining camps. Since Walker had dispatched a squad of troops under Lieutenant Oliver L. Spaulding to Nome in March, the first discoverers assumed that this would be the way things would be handled from then on. While Huldtberg, Lindblom, Brynteson, and Lindeberg, who had organized the original mining district fumed, the American squatters presented a totally different point of view. They argued that the "Lapps" had received only their first citizenship papers, some as far away as Port Townsend, and others at St. Michael. These persons had then acted as though they were already citizens, transferring their mining rights by "power of attorney" to those at Nome. They had come to Alaska at government expense from their Norwegian homeland, which had given them a tremendous advantage over persons who had to finance themselves, only to find that government-subsidized aliens had taken all the good claims.

On July 10, Willoughby Clarke, one of the newcomers, called a meeting of all the non-Norwegian miners. He had been elected chairman of a miners' court which met on July 3, and this gave him as much authority as anyone held in town. Lt. Spaulding was still there, but he kept out of sight, and did not try to stop the meeting. Ostensibly, the July 3 meeting was called to reduce the size of the claims originally established when the District was organized. This could potentially double the number of people who could hold claims. Who Clarke was, there is no information, but he operated from the good democratic premise that what was good for the greatest number was good for all. He must have been the most eloquent spokesman, and probably told the gathered miners that since the Nome District required a notice of five days before a general meeting could be held legally, they would have to adjourn until July 10. They did recess after electing Clarke their presiding officer.

On July 4th, there had been a town celebration in Nome. There was no unusual disorder, which encouraged Lieutenant Spaulding to believe that everything would soon be calm. On July 5th, however, Anderson who was working "Number Nine Above" found that an Irishman named Ryan had moved onto the claim with a crew of cronies and was taking gold from the creek as fast as he could. Ryan threatened bodily harm to Anderson when he protested what was going on. Anderson then went to Spaulding who took a couple of soldiers with him to Anderson's property, and confronted Ryan, who was ordered to leave at once. According to Sacariasen, Ryan's crew was just preparing to eat its evening meal when the soliders came, and had to leave it uneaten. Since the soldiers were armed and the claim jumpers were not, all they could do was to grumble loudly.[22]

Five days later Ryan was back with nine additional men. Spaulding had heard of his new plans, and was there to meet him. This time the military not only chased him away, but broke up his equipment as punishment. He had not been willing to wait until a judge arrived to decide who owned the property.

Everyone in town heard about the fracas at Number Nine Above, and when Clarke called the meeting to order in the Northern Saloon on July 10, three hundred and fifty men were present. According to Spaulding, before the meeting ended, over five hundred tried to get into the place. The saloon was not meant to hold such a crowd, so everyone had to adjourn to the street outside. Most of the people there were only observers.

A man named Milroy began by reading a statement drafted during the week's interval between the first informal meeting and this one. The preamble noted that the Powers-of-Attorney were illegal because "foreigners" with the connivance and assistance of "certain officials were depriving citizens of mining on the public domain."[23]

The two most important resolutions he asked the group to vote on were one which would have voided the authority of the local Mining District operators, meaning the Norwegians, and the second which called for voiding all claims previously staked, and allowing everyone there to scramble out and restake the claims and record them afresh. When Milroy had finished, and before a vote was taken, Spaulding announced that he had been sent from St. Michael to support local government and prevent disorder. If these resolutions were adopted there would certainly be disorder, and he could not allow this to happen. Hence, he adjourned the meeting. His warning was "greeted with a howl of rage and derision," according to the deposition of the Deputy Collector of Customs who happened to be present at the time.[24]

Spaulding was annoyed by this defiance and reminded everyone that his orders were to permit no meetings without proper notice, and that any notice could be issued only by a Board of Official Representatives. He then demanded that the street be cleared within the next two minutes. No one moved. Spaulding next called in a loud voice for "all law abiding citizens to leave." Still no one budged an inch. Spaulding then turned to his tiny army of ten men and gave the order to "Fix Bayonets." Next he ordered them to advance on the crowd. The soldiers did not point their bayonets at anyone but placed the rifles across the chests of the first men they met and began to push. Although there were some curses and threats from men farther back, those in front more or less amicably began to move backward. What might have been an ugly confrontation ended when the crowd "just melted away," as the Army report put it.[25]

Since Spaulding was very young and held the rank only of a third lieutenant, he was concerned about whether he had done the right thing, and whether there might be a more serious rumpus the next day. To his relief, Clarke called no meeting, though a so-called "citizens committee" drew up a letter which they sent to the Major at St. Michael demanding to know by what right Spaulding had interfered in a meeting of civilians on civilian business.

On the 12th, Spaulding's worries were increased when he heard a rumor that all along the beach, men were piling wood into heaps to light as signal bonfires when it became dark if Clarke gave the word to start seizing the claims by force. The fires were not lighted that night and, though matters were still tense, no riots took place.

By July 12, however, Willoughby Clarke had had enough. He was apparently not a man to enjoy flouting authority. He relinquished his chairmanship of the miners' meeting to a man named Rawlins, who had been very busy at the meeting which the soldiers had dispersed, and was now fiercely determined to have one of the good gold claims. That night as the darkness fell, Spaulding was tremendously relieved when Captain Walker and Lieutenant W.C. Cragie arrived in Nome with thirty additional enlisted men of the 7th Infantry. The presence of this considerable additional force quieted things momentarily, and there was an uneasy truce until morning. The following day Walker issued a proclamation that in the future no one could attend any miners' meeting unless he were an actual claim holder with a registered claim in the Nome Mining District. This would pretty well eliminate the claim jumpers from any consideration. He did not even reply at first when the letter asking him about Spaulding's authority was handed to him. When he was pressed for a response he replied that, since the Congress had never created a territorial government for Alaska, the military was in charge, and that was that. He announced that he would stay in Nome until Judge Charles S. Johnson could get there and his court would decide the claims disputes. He also announced that if either Rawlins or Milroy were to make any trouble they would be arrested instantly.

Whether Walker was on sound Constitutional ground or not, there was no one to whom the miners could appeal his decisions, and the camp returned to normal immediately.

At Snow Gulch, in the meantime, Brynteson seemed to be having trouble with his employees. The men he employed frequently quit because he was such a hard taskmaster, and tried to get as much out of the men with as little pay as he could. Carl expressed disappointment that Brynteson had become greedy with his prospects of fortune, and had changed into a different person from what he was when they first met. This might have been said of many people in Nome, however, especially those who actually made money. He was also displeased to note that during that month about thirty women had come to Nome from Dawson hoping to stake gold claims themselves. After they had hiked inland in their long dresses they found that all the good claims were being worked, and were forced to go back to the "profession," as Carl referred to it, that they had been following in Dawson. They had plenty of clients, but Sacariasen could note that while Brynteson was money crazy, he "was not a man to visit saloons or houses of sin." While this man was neither a miner nor a missionary, he must have been something of a Puritan with his strict behavior, his hard work, and his desire to make money.

Lindeberg was much better with his employees. He paid good wages-- eight dollars with food, plus a percent of what the worker panned, or ten dollars a day plus percentage if the worker paid for his own food. Usually the worker allowed Lindeberg to feed him.

The steamships *Roanoke* and *Garrone* arrived in Nome in mid-summer to add to the already large population in the town. By now full-scale mining was going on all over the district, and the sluice boxes needed only water to wash out the gravel. Lindeberg's competitor, a man named Lane, tried to furnish the water for his own claims by pumping water up the creeks and gulches to his sluice boxes.[26] One writer said he also built a railroad the four miles from Nome to his camp on Anvil Creek,[27] before the excitement died down.

Every rapid increase in population meant that the newcomers started jumping claims almost as soon as they came ashore. It is not difficult to see why these claim jumpers acted as they did. They had come a tremendous distance at considerable expense, only to find that not only the best claims were already being worked, but even the beach claims were a solid mass of tents and holes in the sand for miles. Profits were tremendous, and as rumors spread the value of the claims grew by leaps and bounds in the imagination of those who described them. The actual profits were good enough. When Lindeberg's crew cleaned the sluice box for the first time at Number One Below, they took out $600 worth of dust. The second cleaning showed over $10,000 worth of gold in dust and nuggets! Two weeks later "Discovery" Claim produced a thousand dollars of gold in two days. Numbers One, Two and Three in Snow Gulch showed $37,000 during one single week. Another week Number One Below, the big producer for the Pioneer Mining Company, brought in $14,000. The only thing that made the work difficult was that after digging only a few feet the ground was still frozen, and even in the third week of July the hillsides back of Nome were subjected to severe storms. One storm during this month was so severe that five vessels anchored in the roadstead just beyond the beach were driven ashore. No one was drowned, but the ships themselves were a total loss. Other ships, also anchored in the open Bay, made their escape by moving into the shelter of Sledge Island about twenty-five miles away.

Work was so difficult that Carl scarcely found time to write at all. He did note several changes in personnel at the mines. Some foremen quit to work for other companies, some men were fired, and some of these went to work on the very next claim.

On the 23rd, the storm finally ended and, when the next passengers disembarked, among them was the stubby figure of Dr. Sheldon Jackson. With him was Jeremias Abrahamsen who had spent several months on St. Lawrence Island. As was his custom, Jackson was trying to do three or four jobs at the same time. He continued his work as United States General Agent of Education for Alaska, he was the person officially in charge of the Reindeer Service, and he took some time from his other duties to make a trip to Siberia to buy more deer.[28] He continued to serve as the informal adviser to many officials in Washington, D.C. on Alaskan affairs. He also took time to go on one of the periodic trips of the *Bear* to St. Lawrence Island to bring out W.F. Doty, the missionary, and Abrahamsen back to Nome. An Eskimo, who was imprisoned aboard the ship, was accused of trying to murder Doty, and Jackson wanted to get that matter settled.[29] As befitted his interest in the Reindeer Service, Jackson found a few minutes to consult with Kjellmann about affairs at Unlakleet and Eaton Station before he returned to Juneau to meet with his friend and associate, Governor John Brady.

When Abrahamsen reached Nome he was in a state of semi-shock. He had not heard a word about the gold frenzy of the place. He was particularly annoyed that, when Jackson stopped to pick him up, he had said nothing about the gold rush and the part his Norwegian and Lapp associates had had in it. As soon as he could, he resigned from the Service and immediately Lindeberg hired him.

The former herders enjoyed the excitement of Nome, even though their own claims were not very rewarding. They made enough money for others to enable them to pay expenses and save a little for a trip to the lower States, since they shared to some extent in what they obtained for Lindeberg.

When the last storm of July was behind them, the brief summer season came with a vengeance. The warm spell was mercifully brief, but it was astonishingly hot. Carl claimed at the end of July that one day the thermometer registered 118° F, though this is doubtful. Yet he remembered that only a few weeks before they had had to wait to work and dig the creek sand because it was frozen solid.

The hot weather was particularly hard on elderly people who had left Seattle without the remotest idea of what they would face in the Yukon or at Nome. Now they found themselves alone, penniless, and suffering in a hostile environment in their old age. Carl's own words describe their plight vividly:

> I watched the people come ashore from the steamer *Sadie* from St. Michael. Among them were a number of women, some of them so old that their hair was white and they walked with a cane. So bent and stooped that they could barely

walk, they had money on their mind and one foot
in the grave.

Alaska is anything but a place for the
aged. It is hard enough for the younger people
who through the past few years have streamed
into the north with gold fever. Healthy and
happy, they have left their good homes to search
for riches, only to discover that the riches are
gambled away and that it is very difficult to build
up a fortune. Many who have had to get along
on only what money they brought with them have
cursed themselves and Alaska that they were so
foolish as to enter into this misery which for
many has meant an early grave.[30]

During the final week in July, the tremendous value of the ocean
beach claims were fully understood. "Gold is where you find it," and now as
summer was coming to an end, sums amounting to ten or as much as thirty
dollars a day were taken from these same sands along the shoreline, which
allowed the destitute latecomers to make enough to survive. Hundreds of
men working for wages on the older claims inland quit their jobs and headed
for the beach, though only a few weeks of panning were left until the winter
snows and freezing weather stopped everything. Innumerable quarrels
erupted as greed and even need destroyed prudence, and men fought for the
right to wash sand from tiny sections of the beach. Up on Lindeberg's claims
the Norwegians who kept working for him had their own sense of cultural
identity and personal acquaintanceship to keep them from the troubles that
other more lonely persons got themselves into. In almost a detached way,
Carl wrote how profiteers brought building supplies to Nome and charged
outrageous prices for things the local people did not need, and seemed to
have little trouble getting people to buy their wares. Those without money or
prospects of making any were beginning to talk of returning to Seattle or
California for the winter, and many of these would never come back.

Early in August, "Number One Below" produced a gold nugget worth
$312. At the price of gold in 1899, this meant that the gold weighed almost a
pound and a quarter. By the prices of the 1980's, this would have brought
between four and six thousand of today's dollars.

The near neighbor of Lindeberg's operation was the San Francisco
investor, Charles D. Lane, who had "grubstaked" Price, one of Lindeberg's

associates in 1898, and who received half of whatever Price should find. The Price claims on Anvil Creek and in Snow Gulch were proving so valuable that Lane put together a gold mining corporation that eventually became the Wild Goose Mining Company, and made him, like Lindeberg, into a millionaire.

As summer faded into autumn, the newest prospectors swarmed over the hills once more, hoping that their predecessors had missed some tiny pocket of gold along the creeks. Generally these showed as poor a return in September as they had in May. Nevertheless, since it was possible to dig much deeper than earlier, enough gold could be taken out to get a good case of gold fever going again. Regnor Dahl's claims were nowhere as productive as either Lindeberg's or Lane's, but Carl reported that they produced more richly when the topsoil was removed. Carl himself went out to one of the claims he had abandoned the winter before, and panned twelve large nuggets in one pan of top sand. Since he had no food along with him, he said he had to leave his search for more temporarily.

Ironically, for the next seven weeks he went out to his claim to try to duplicate his fortune on that one day but, while he panned many shovels full of dirt, he found virtually nothing. He would hike out to his claim after he put in his day's work at Lindeberg's and try his luck. Finally, in October, when he was ready to go south for the winter, he sold his claim in disgust for only $750. The purchaser dug three feet deeper and took out more than a million dollars in gold.[31] That, unfortunately, is the usual story in this kind of frenzy. Lindeberg was the exception rather than the rule.

The disgruntled prospectors, scouring the hills for new discoveries or vainly working abandoned claims, continued to view the Pioneer Mining Company successes with envy and covetousness. Once again, the sharpers among them challenged the powers-of-attorney that the judge ruled legal in July. They also raised the interesting point that Lapps were simply European Indians and, since Indians and Eskimo were barred from working gold claims in Alaska, even on their own tribal lands, a Lapp should not be allowed to hold any claims either. In this case, the Americans lumped Norwegians and Finns with the Lapps to allow them to confiscate everything that the former herders had staked. They demanded that a judge be sent to Nome to make an adjudication of this point.

In response, Governor John Brady, a friend of Sheldon Jackson and a supporter of the Reindeer project, along with a judge arrived in Nome shortly afterward, and the complainers were summoned to present their views before the Court. The judge did not talk to the Norwegians, but Governor Brady and Captain Walker of St. Michael spent the night on Discovery Claim talking to Lindeberg. Sacariasen noted that the subsequent court session produced "good results" for the Lindeberg supporters. Once again the judge ruled that the powers-of-attorney were legal, and that Lapps or anyone else could keep the claims they had staked the previous year. They were not to be treated as the Indians and Eskimo were. The judge conceded that first papers obtained in St. Michael or even Port Townsend did not automatically make the immigrants citizens but, since they did have their first papers, the holders were correct in assuming that they were valid. Since they had also had their claims legally registered they had acted in good faith and the claims were still theirs. Only one claim jumper was permitted to keep working his claim, and the reason for that was that the original owner had never recorded his claim with the district record keeper.

In the early fall the days began growing noticeably shorter. In the early darkness, thieves turned to extra-legal ways of getting gold. In the absence of genuine law officers, and with only a handful of soldiers stationed in town, it was comparatively simply for unscrupulous men to attack the claims of people who worked many miles from the coast. As always, in frontier situations like this, the miners themselves were expected to guard their own property and to take what steps were needed to insure that they kept what belonged to them, even if it resulted in violence.

In Nome itself reports of crime began to increase. One young man was held up in his tent where he was living alone just outside of town. When he told the bandits that he had not been able to find any gold, they began to pistol-whip him. As he finally collapsed, they ransacked his belongings and found that he had been telling the truth. There was nothing worth stealing. He was badly injured by the beating, but he did finally recover.

Other thieves raided the sluice boxes out at the camps. They could do this at night, or even when the men were eating their meals. At "Number Eleven" on Anvil Creek, thieves took over $400 from a sluice while the workers were in the mess tent eating supper. Axel Karlson, the missionary,

195

lost $800 the same way to robbers who struck his camp while he was temporarily absent. At Snow Gulch a watchman, possibly from the Wild Goose operation, saw the official guard taking nuggets from the box he was supposed to be guarding. He reported this to Brynteson who rushed up to the scene, attacked the guard, and forced him to disgorge over $1,500 worth of nuggets. Probably the culprit was fortunate only to have lost his job as a guard. Men had been killed for less than that in other places and at other times. Strangely, for all of the reported crime, generally Nome itself was an amazingly law-abiding gold camp during these free-wheeling months.

For example, a miners meeting was called by aggrieved claim holders, where they discussed what they could do to stop the raids. One proposal was that any known thief be driven from the district. However, when another disgruntled mine owner proposed that even suspects be expelled, the idea was rejected after some debate on the grounds "that many innocent people might be accused and expelled."[32] Thus, even in this remote outpost, a majority of decent people knew enough about civil rights that this particular violation was not adopted. It is curious that they felt no reluctance to violate the civil rights of the Eskimo, however.

Eventually, Discovery itself was struck by robbers. This time the cook seemed to have been involved. About 2 a.m. the night watchman, an honest but unidentified employee, saw a man leaving the tent used as the office. The watchman called out, "Is that you, Lindblom?" The man responded, "Ja," and walked toward the tent where Lindblom slept. Since Dr. King and Rolf Wiig also shared the tent, it seemed logical that the unknown man was actually who he said he was. The stranger lifted the flap, called "Goodnight" in Norwegian, and entered the tent.

Suddenly the watchman heard a commotion from the tent, and Wiig began to yell that the camp had been robbed. The gold chest strongbox had been taken! The watchman was armed, and he rushed up the hill where he caught the cook and two strangers at the edge of the ditch where the sluice box was placed. He held them at gunpoint until Dr. King came up. As King started to question them, they made a sudden break and pulled a revolver and fired two shots at the watchman who returned the fire, but missed in the darkness. One of the culprits must have fallen over something in the way, for they heard him utter a cry, and curse in pain, but all of them kept on running and the three disappeared.

Everyone sleeping in the camp was awake by now, and those with guns were told to search for the strongbox, but to be careful for the thieves were armed, and were obviously willing to shoot. It is a marvel that no one was injured, for those who had guns were so jittery that they fired at bushes, and probably at each other as they moved gingerly up the hill. By now Dr. King had found a rifle, and Carl noted that he, too, "bombarded away with his rifle." Finally Lindblom came up with a lantern, and they did not go more than thirty feet when they found the strongbox which the robbers had dropped in their haste to escape. A pick lay alongside, but they had not had time to use it to break open the chest, so the entire fortune was recovered intact.

As they reconstructed the attempted robbery, they decided that the man whom the watchman thought to have been Lindblom entered the tent, cut a hole in the wall and passed the chest through the slit to his waiting accomplices. In a scene smacking of an old-time comedy, however, after the successful move was over, he stumbled over a guy rope on the corner of the tent. He fell to the ground and, in his attempt to catch his balance, he struck the wall beside where Wiig was sleeping. Wiig immediately reached out his hand to the chest, found it gone, and gave the alarm. Not more than three minutes elapsed until the watchman gave chase. Carl estimated that the loaded chest weighed more than two hundred pounds, which was far too heavy for even the most muscular thief to carry at a dead run up a hill. Two men would have had even more trouble keeping step with one another while carrying a heavy box, so they were forced to drop it. He made no estimate of the value of the gold inside, but if there were even fifty pounds of precious metal it would have amounted to a haul of $150,000 modern dollars, which would have been, indeed, a tidy sum.

Eventually everyone got back to sleep.

Sacariasen noted that just before the first snow fell a man whom he named "A. Hansen" (possibly Amund Hansen) prospected a small stream that he named Seattle Creek since he had been in that city. He was of Norwegian origin, and had attached himself to the Norwegians from Finnmark. Ole Rapp and Lauritz Stefansen of the original herders went with him on his prospecting expedition. They did not find much, for their average was only about ten cents worth of gold to the pan, but the three of them could make about five dollars a day with hard work, and they figured that as soon as they reached bedrock or hardpan it would begin to pay handsomely. Hansen himself staked two claims and Rapp and Stefansen hastily staked eleven more, which took up the entire tiny gulch which they had found.

They did not get a chance to dig deeper, however, for on Thursday, September 14, the first snow of the season fell to remind everyone that winter was close. Summer had been short. Only six weeks before the temperature had been over 100°F. Now it was freezing. Frost could be seen everywhere when the men came out of their tents, and there was a scum of ice on the ponds in all of the gold claims.

A week later operators decided winter was there, and the mines and sluices in Snow Gulch and Dexter Creek were shut down. Carl describes the prospectors he saw who "came stumbling down the hill, carrying their bedrolls on their shoulders, driven toward town in flocks like birds of passage going south at the approach of winter."[33]

Only the crews at Discovery and the even richer "Number One Below" on Anvil Creek kept working. Lindeberg, Wilhelm Basi, and Olai Paulsen had to stop, however, for the three of them contracted typhoid fever. Nowhere in the gold camps was there any provision made for adequate sanitation, and both in town and out on the hills and gullies, typhoid was rampant. The crowded conditions in the Nome business section, and the lack of any sewage system or clean water to drink or use for cooking spread the epidemic. Perhaps the miners thought that copious quantities of whiskey would disinfect their digestive tracts, but if they did they were disappointed.

Some of the people began to talk about leaving while they were still healthy. About forty Lapps wanted to go back to Norway. Some of the Norwegians would have settled for Seattle but, since most of the mines had shut down, they didn't want to stay idle in the middle of an epidemic. Those who were actually serious, and this included Sacariasen, announced that they would sell their claims to the highest bidder. Charles Lane was consolidating his holdings, and he sent agents to those willing to sell. Sacariasen wrote with scorn of two Lapps who sold to Lane for $70,000. In view of the fact that he sold his own best claim for only $750, it would appear that the Lapps were shrewd businessmen, but the difference was that his claim was unproven while theirs was producing richly. Lane also acquired the claims of Regnor Dahl and Ole Krogh on the Nome River in the same way. No purchase price was named. Kjellmann sold his "Number Two Below" claim on Anne Creek to Lane for $75,000, and made plans to leave Alaska for the needed operation he had been postponing for months. Altogether, Lane acquired nine claims of various value from the Norwegians, in addition to other claims he bought from people the herders did not know.

At the end of September Lindeberg, Basi, and Paulsen were still sick, though their lives were no longer in danger. If they wanted to make a complete recovery, however, they knew they would need better medical attention than was available in Nome where the harrassed doctors could give little more than first aid, and the only hospital was not a genuine hospital at all, but a row of beds in a large building constructed for the soldiers, but now used by the typhoid patients.

Hundreds of miners driven from their claims on the Yukon River by the winter began to arrive in Nome in early October, but there was no chance for them to make any major strike in the freezing weather of the Seward Peninsula. Their coming made the problems created by the epidemic more difficult to solve. More than two thousand newcomers, many without funds, arrived in late September and early October. These people soon became desperate when they saw that Nome was no place for poor people to be, and some turned to crime. The journalist reported that a woman was murdered in her tent while her husband was in a downtown saloon getting drunk. Tents were too cold to live in, but with the tremendous influx of transients, wooden buildings were not being built fast enough to care for everyone. Even those board structures were not very warm, for their insulation was almost nonexistent. The thin walls let heat out almost as fast as the fires inside the stoves radiated heat into the crowded rooms. Some of the windows inside the restaurants frosted so badly from the moisture given off by the cooking kettles plus the body heat of the men and women crowded around the tables eating, that after a day or two the frost built up into solid cakes of ice several inches thick on the inside of the glass windows. From time to time someone would go outside with warm water and scrub down the glass, which freed the blocks of ice, and these fell with a loud "thunk" onto the floor of the room.

With darkness, cold, discouragement, and sickness, many gave up. Three steamers, the *Roanoke,* the *Laureda* and the *Cleveland,* sent agents who sold tickets for passage to Seattle. The *Portland* and the *Bertha* sold tickets for passage to San Francisco. Nearly all the tickets were snapped up as soon as the agents appeared. By October first none of these ships was at Nome, and the purchasers killed time as best they could until they could actually board the steamers. About all there was to do was to gamble or drink in the saloons. Carl did not say whether he lost any money himself, but he did watch a young man lose $300 in a gambling game in less than five minutes, which apparently was all the man possessed. This would mean that he would have to stay in Nome all winter without resources, which made his survival doubtful and, if he did survive, his misery would be intense. Eating at the miserable restaurants was dreadfully expensive, and even those who had money could not wait many days, or they would begin to run short of cash. The Coast Guard ship, *Bear,* sent word that it would carry out one hundred fifty "indigents" who could not pay for their passage, but these accommodations were far from first-class. In spite of this, almost two hundred fifty persons, like the young man who lost his money gambling, applied for passage. This was a hundred more than the *Bear* could take, and they had to reject the overflow.

Sacariasen was healthy enough or lucky enough to keep from catching typhoid, but he estimated that a third of the population of Nome was sick with it. The death rate was not high, but people were dying. He said that every day one or two deaths were reported and there may have been others. On October 8, five people died.

The following day the first issue of *The Anvil News* appeared. This was the first newspaper to be published in Nome, and the copies went fast. Naturally, there was no current international news, but there were advertisements, and much local gossip and predictions about the state of the future economy. The editors had to work to find enough to fill their pages, but they gave accounts of high-life in the saloons and dance halls, of life in general, and of typhoid. Carl was skeptical about the amount of gold reported by the newspaper to have been taken from the hills and beach during the short summer season, but even his estimates were spectacular. The *News* claimed that Anvil Creek had yielded a million dollars, and the beach one and a half million. The Snake and Nome River valleys and tributaries were said to have produced three-quarters of a million in gold in only three months. This totaled three and a quarter million for the whole district, and Carl said this was too high by at least $750,000. Nevertheless, he believed that Lindeberg and the Company he controlled had taken six hundred thousand dollars from the claims he had helped to work. Lane and the Wild Goose had made enough to pay $200,000 for claims on the Snake and Nome, and he had enough left over to charter his own private ship to take him to San Francisco. He would be back. In contrast, one of the otherwise unidentified Cleveland brothers who had organized a third, smaller company, committed suicide. No one knew why he had shot himself, but the assumption was that he was facing business failure.

Only a little over two weeks later a second newspaper appeared. This was known as the *Nome Gold Digger*, and Volume 1, Number 1 was published October 25, 1899. It reported much the same kind of news as the first paper. It talked of rich production at "Number One Below" where nuggets were common only four or five feet under the surface that were valued at three to four hundred dollars apiece. It praised the ruby sands on the beach under the headline "Rich Beach Mines." It reported the illness of the leading citizens, including the sickness of Axel Karlson. It also stated that the two Tornensis brothers had sold to Lane for $90,000. A week later, the editor's chief story was that thieves had stolen the safe from one of the stores on the main street.[34]

It was not published by the newspapers but, to the consternation of those who had bought tickets for Seattle, the rumor began to circulate through Nome that the steamship *Laureda* coming to Nome to carry them south had been caught in a storm on the Bering Sea, and had sunk. The rumor proved to be true and, while no one had been drowned since the Captain had beached her on a convenient island, those who had bought tickets to Seattle feared that they would have no way to get out of the Nome area before winter. Since the steamer also carried a cargo of food to supply those who planned to stay, this would mean short rations for all unless some could leave. The *Portland* came in, carrying many of *Laureda*'s passengers from the barren island, but this ship could not take both its own and the other steamer's passengers. Unfortunately for some, they were so ill that they could not go with the *Portland* in any event. Among these was Olai Paulsen.

Lindeberg was too weak to walk unaided, so he was carried to the *Roanoke* and put to bed in his cabin. He had enough funds after his successful summer to hire a full-time private physician, a Doctor Miller, to go to Seattle, and take care of him. He now left Dr. Southward as the only doctor for the entire district, and he was in charge of the military hospital which was jammed. Southward had been urging the inhabitants of Nome to boil their drinking water for weeks, and now that he was going to be alone he insisted upon it. When finally the people there took his advice, the number of new typhoid cases dropped immediately.

Wilhelm Basi, who also had typhoid, was much improved and was well enough to board the *Portland* when it left for San Francisco. Sacariasen went with him to take care of him in case he were to become worse. In his journal Carl noted with regret that others, such as Thoralf Kjelsberg, Emil Kjellberg, Lauritz Stephansen, and Mikkel Nikkila were too ill with the infection to travel, so they had to be left behind along with Paulsen.

Basi and his cousin climbed into a barge, and were taken out to their ship by a crew using poles to propel the conveyance. There were almost four hundred people who had to be put aboard this way. Twenty-five of them were ill with typhoid, but protested that they were well enough to make the trip. Both the *Bertha* and *Roanoke* had other patients than Lindeberg, also.

On Sunday night, three days after they left Nome, the two ships reached Dutch Harbor. They waited here for twenty-four hours, taking time to put provisions and water aboard, and to conduct burial services for two of the sick passengers who had died in spite of claiming recovery.

The *Portland*, that legendary ship that brought the first cargo of gold to Seattle touching off the whole Alaska-Yukon gold rush, was the one on which Basi and Sacariasen had chosen to travel, and it had auxiliary sails to add to its speed. With a good southwest breeze blowing, the ship hoisted six sails to increase its speed to eleven or twelve knots. The breeze stayed fair all the way to San Francisco, and they anchored in the Bay on the morning of November 2. This was excellent time, but it took almost two weeks to come from Dutch Harbor.

The local health authorities were aghast at the amount of illness aboard, and quarantined the vessel in the Bay, refusing to give anyone permission to go ashore. After a two day delay, however, they changed their minds and those people well enough to walk were allowed to disembark. The sick ones stayed under observation.

The *Roanoke*, with Lindeberg aboard, got to Seattle some time before the *Portland* reached California. Lindeberg came by train to San Francisco, and when Basi and Sacariasen came off the ship, they were surprised to be met by their friend. Carl reported him quite recovered. Dr. Kittilsen and William Kjellmann had also come down on the same train with Lindeberg. Not long afterward, while they were all still staying in California, Thoralf Kjelsberg arrived. He had recovered enough to get passage on another ship, and while not feeling strong, wanted to leave Nome so badly that he took the first ship he could get, which was going to Victoria. From there he had gone to Seattle, then joined the others after a train trip south, where his brother, Magnus, was already living. After a few weeks of recuperation, the Kjelsberg brothers and Lindeberg left for Norway to visit their families. Johan Sp. Tornensis came through San Francisco, also, but did not plan to return to Norway. Instead, he left for a visit with an uncle in Iowa, who was pastor of a Norwegian church there. The others who had left Nome stayed in California for a few weeks longer.

Since the weather in California even at that time of year was mild, and since Basi felt much better, the two cousins decided to indulge in some social life. They were registered in the Humboldt Hotel in San Francisco and wanted to get in touch with others of their countrymen living in that part of California. The best place they knew to begin their search was in a Norwegian church, and three days after they arrived they dropped in on a worship service conducted in the familiar language of their homeland. There, to his delight, Basi met a woman he had known as a boy in his home town. She was married to a man named Jacobsen, a California miner, but since they had been good friends as young people they had a good visit, and Basi enjoyed meeting her husband as well.

Two weeks after this, the cousins left for Portland. Why they chose that city, neither Carl nor Basi said. They reached Oregon after two days on the train, and when they got off the train at the Portland station they had made up their minds to buy some land and settle near other Norwegian and Finnish families living near the mouth of the Columbia River at Astoria and Illwaco.

They did not find anything at first on either the Oregon or Washington shore, and on the last day of the year they went to a Finnish church in Astoria. There the pastor, the Reverend John Lumijarvi from Hammerfest, told them of a small town just east of Astoria where he knew of good land for sale. The next day, New Years 1900, they followed his suggestion, and found a farm offered for sale by a Joseph Mustola. They bought it in a matter of hours. The town was Quincy, Oregon, between Astoria and Clatskanie. The two partners spent the next weeks getting the farm ready for spring planting, repaired the house, and then changed their plans once more.

By the time the trees started to get green, they turned north to return to Nome. They arrived on the steamer *Nome City* on June 18, just about two years after they had left Haines to return from the ill-starred reindeer expedition to Dawson.

NOTES

[1]Lomen, Carl J. *Fifty Years in Alaska*, New York: David McKay Company, Inc., 1954, p. 51.

[2]*R. i. A.*, p. 175.

[3]Freuchen, Peter, *Arctic Adventure: My Life in the Frozen North*, New York: Farrar & Rinehart, Incorporated, 1935. pp. 106; 108-9.

[4]*R. i. A.*, p. 180.

[5]*R. i. A.*, p. 183; Carlson, Leland H., "The First Mining Season at Nome, Alaska--1899," *Pacific Historical Review*, XVI:2, May 1947, pp. 163-175; Carlson, Leland H., "Nome, From Mining Camp to Civilized Community," *Pacific Northwest Quarterly,* July 1947, v. 38; 3, pp. 233-242. The name was changed officially by the postal authorities in 1899.

[6]Lanier, McKee, *The Land of Nome*, New York: Grafton Press, 1902. p. 7.

[7]Harrison, E.S., *Nome and Seward Peninsula*, Seattle, Metropolitan Press, 1905. p. 19.

[8]Critchfield, Howard J., "Seward Peninsula," *Economic Geography*, 25:4. Oct. 1949. p. 275.

[9]Lanier, *Op. Cit.*, p. 30.

[10]French, L. H. (M.D.), *Nome Nuggets, Some of the Experiences of a Party of Gold Seekers in Northwestern Alaska in 1900*, New York: Montross, Clarke, & Emmons, 1901. p. 44.

[11]Lanier, *Op. Cit*, p. 30.

[12]Lanier, *Ibid.; R. i. A.*, p. 185.

[13]McLain, John Scudder, *Alaska and the Klondike*, New York: McClure, Phillips & Co., 1905. p. 150.

[14]Hines, John Chesterfield, *Minstrel of the Yukon*, New York: Greenberg, 1948. p. 2.

[15]Carlson, Leland H., "Nome: From Mining Camp to Civilized Community," *Pacific Northwest Quarterly*, 38:3, July 1947, pp. 233-242.

[16]Lanier, *The Land of Nome*, p. 47.

[17]*R. i. A.*, p. 191.

[18]Harrison, E.S., *Nome and Seward Peninsula*, p. 15.

[19]Underwood, John J., *Alaska: An Empire in the Making*, New York: Dodd, Mead & Company, 1928, p. 137-138.

[20]Nome, *Gold Digger*, 1:1, October 25, 1899.

[21]Lanier, *The Land of Nome*, p. 96.

[22]*R. i. A.*, p. 196; Spaulding Report to Adjutant General, July 14, 1899, IDTP:AK Roll 6.

[23]Spaulding Report. *Loc. Cit.*

[24]Deposition of E.T. Hatch, Deputy Collector of Customs at St. Michael to Interior Department, July 14, 1899. IDTP:AK, Series 48, Roll 6.

[25]Spaulding Report, *Op. Cit., Loc. Cit.*

[26]McLain, John Scudder, *Alaska and the Klondike*, New York: McClure, Phillips & Co., 1905. p. 159.

[27]French, L.H., M.D., *Nome Nuggets, Some of the Experiences of a Party of Gold Seekers in Northwestern Alaska in 1900*, New York: Montrose, Clarke, & Emmons, 1901., p. 77.

[28]56 Cong., 1 Sess., Senate Doc. #245. *Ninth Report on Reindeer in Alaska*, Jackson Report.

[29]*R. i. A.*, p. 197.

[30]*R. i. A.*, p. 198.

[31]Interview: Carl Sacariasen with Author, October 25, 1958.

[32]*R. i. A.*, p. 202.

[33]*R. i. A.*, p. 204.

[34]*Nome Gold Digger*, 1:1, October 25, 1899; 1:2, November 1, 1899. University of Washington Library; *Lopp Papers*, University of Oregon Library.

Chapter Seven

EPILOGUE

Carl Sacariasen never again kept a detailed record of his activities, although Wilhelm Basi did for few more years. Anyone who wants to find what happened after the first flurry of activity in Nome has to consult other sources for information. For a few more years after 1900, officials of the Reindeer Service continued to make trips to Siberia to buy deer from the Eskimo there without much success, and some of the herders worked for the Service for several decades into the Twentieth Century.[1] Governor John Brady again tried to get the federal government to organize some kind of civilian Territorial status for Alaska but again he had no success. Part of his problem was that he and Sheldon Jackson were close friends, and their enemies were determined not only to move the center of power from Sitka to Juneau, but to discredit the two men at the same time.[2] The Army made some efforts to ease the plight of the native people who continued to be abused by both commercial companies and miners.[3] Although the Secretary of War did authorize fourteen tons of military rations to be distributed among the destitute natives for their use after the miners burned their fuel supplies and destroyed their stored food, some tight-fisted Congressmen objected to this reckless waste of public funds, and the local Commanding Officer, safe in his headquarters, denied that there was any starvation among the natives, and that these were only rumors spread by a "hysterical missionary spending his first winter" in Alaska.[4]

The summer that Basi and Carl returned to Nome with a neighbor woman, Hilma Mustole, was the infamous summer when the late-comers made their last attempts to drive the Norwegians from their gold claims. A Judge, Arthur Noyes of Minneapolis, combined with an enterprising local man and president of the Alaska Gold Mining Company named Alexander H. McKenzie to try to get rid of the Europeans. Judge Noyes overruled the decisions of the courts of 1899, and placed all claims in receivership, making

McKenzie the "receiver" of Lindeberg's claims on Anvil Creek. McKenzie then sequestered the gold already obtained from these claims in 1900 still in the office safe. At once Lindeberg and the other first-comers, including Lane, retained the firm of Johnson and Knight as attorneys to recover their gold and their mines. Since the Nome District had produced more than a million and a half dollars worth of gold in 1900, the amount involved was very large. The affair had a happy ending for the aggrieved original claimants who all got their property returned to them. The story has been written into a highly colorful fictional account by Rex Beach in his novel, *The Spoilers*.[5] It also made Judge James Wickersham of Tacoma into a national figure of importance, when he was sent to Alaska to resolve the problems, and did so.[6] Governor Brady was deeply involved in seeing that justice was done for the Lindeberg-Lane group.

When Jackson was indicted by a Juneau Grand Jury in June 1899 for his failure to spend appropriated money on white children of Southeastern Alaska, the one genuine charge his enemies brought was that he was so busy doing many things at once that he had little time for his educational functions.[7] This was hardly a criminal offense, however, and Brady said so. For this he was again attacked by the Juneau group. The rumors of malfeasance continued for years, and long after Jackson was dead, one writer referred to the "grave scandal" when reindeer were brought from Siberia "at great expense . . . for the benefit of the needy natives and miners," and "were appropriated by missionaries without authority."[8]

Basi and Sacariasen returned to Portland in September, 1900, having decided that conditions were too turbulent in Nome to be able to do anything on either their own claims or on Lindeberg's. Meanwhile, at the same time, twenty-five Lapps returned to Norway. They included eleven men, seven women and seven children who had had enough both of Alaska and the gold rush. They crossed Canada to Montreal, boarded the steamer *Tunisian* for England, then they crossed to Norway where they reached Hammerfest, October 3. The chief of police of that town reported all Lapps in this group safely at home by mid-October. For this group, at least, the adventure was over.

While neither fame nor fortune came to Basi or Sacariasen, it did come to Lindeberg. The Pioneer Mining Company paid out handsomely.

His career in the Twentieth Century continued to be a stormy one, but to him personally, it was a highly profitable one. He died on November 5, 1962. Perhaps his obituary tells something of what happened to him as much as anything can:

> Jafet Lindeberg, shipwrecked Scandinavian seaman who parlayed a $200 grubstake into a multi-million dollar mining empire in turn-of-the-century Alaska, died here yesterday at Children's Hospital. He was 88.
>
> Mr. Lindeberg, key figure in several titantic legal battles over mining and banking operations in Alaska, Washington, and California during the 1920's, was active in running a group of tungsten mines in Nevada until shortly before his death.
>
> The colorful miner's early career was marked with a frantic series of suits and countersuits with his operation of the Blue Goose Mining Company of Alaska, and the failure of the Scandinavian-American Bank of Tacoma, Washington, of which he was president.
>
> Several times Mr. Lindeberg's San Francisco attorney fought off extradition to Washington by waving authorities away with a shotgun.
>
> The energetic miner traveled to St. Petersberg in 1910, sued the Governor of Siberia for $77,000 lost in a gold concession, and won.
>
> Mr. Lindeberg made his home in San Francisco since the early 1900's. He is survived by his wife, Josephine. . .[9]

The trouble with this obituary is that much of it is sheer fiction. Lindeberg had never been shipwrecked and had not been a "seaman" either. He was not president of the Scandinavian-American Bank of Tacoma--Ole Larson was. His company was not called the Blue Goose Mining Company, but rather the Pioneer Mining and Ditch Company--or at least it was when the bank failed. The shotgun story may have been correct, for Lindeberg had been indicted by a Grand Jury for financial irregularities. He had apparently borrowed $60,000 secured by a note, which was approved by the bank's president, while engaged in a struggle for control of the mining company's assets against Eric Lindblom with whom he had developed a feud of some kind. The jury tried to get him to come to Tacoma voluntarily, but he refused, and his attorney supported him.[10]

In the years after he left Nome to live in San Francisco, his company had expanded to furnish light and power to Nome. In the 1930's he invested in the Lomen Company which was attempting to make reindeer meat competitive with beef in Pacific Coast meat markets and restaurants, thus furnishing a financial base not only for the Eskimo herders, but also for their private corporation. When leasing deer to Caucasians ended, the marketing idea ended as well.[11]

Nome itself continued to be a roaring mining town for a decade after most of the herders had left Alaska. In October 1900 the question of having a city government was posed to the miners for a vote by the army commanders who thought they had had enough of trying to be a police force, operators of the hospital, and running a fire department and sewer system on the side. The residents liked things the way they were, however, and voted to have nothing to do with something that would cost them taxes. Randall, the officer in charge, was so annoyed that he testily informed the town that he was returning to St. Michael, and would leave only enough men "to guard public buildings and property."[12] For the rest, the Nome citizens could look after themselves any way they wanted to. Gold deposits were found to extend under the ocean itself, and hard-rock mining began to supplant the placer mining along the inland creeks and the beach. Eventually the placer deposits played out, and the tunnels under the sea had a continuous problem with flooding which finally made further mining impossible. After World War I, the town dwindled to a few hundred Eskimo and white inhabitants. Although there was a short revival of mining when dredges came into the peninsula after World War II, it was not the kind of operation that would bring thousands of people to the fields. Few of the present inhabitants are involved in gold recovery.

Sheldon Jackson was an old man by 1901, and although he lived for seven more years, his office of Commissioner of Education for Alaska was given to another official. He made no more trips to buy deer in Siberia, for the Alaskan herds were large enough to show the success of his idea to introduce the animals to the native peoples. Lieutenant Bertholf, who had been with the Revenue Service almost from the time Jackson brought the first deer from Asia, made probably the last successful trip to Siberia in 1901. He had made arrangements in St. Petersberg in early February of that year, and left Moscow for Irkutsk on February 27. There he bought a covered sled and with horses, reindeer, and dogs, traveled to Okhotsk in a two-week period. He bought more than 500 deer, though he had the usual trouble getting the United States Treasury Department to advance him enough cash to pay the people who sold him the deer and wanted immediate compensation. After a tricky manuever, in which the deer herders were christened "Industrial Teachers" he was able to get the Interior Department to transfer three thousand dollars from the school fund to the Reindeer Service, and was then able to pay the $15,000 it took to finance the trip. By July 21, 1901, he was back in Alaska with fifty bulls and four hundred fifty female deer. He had learned his duties well from Sheldon Jackson.[13]

The problem was that everything had to be done with skimpy appropriations from the federal government. Though American citizens were taking millions of dollars from that rich land, no one wanted to put anything back. For instance, on August 30, 1901, the Treasury Department reported that after Bertholf had paid for the deer, there was only $349.58 in the Alaskan education fund,[14] and Congress stoutly refused to appropriate any further money for this purpose. Again and again concerned people involved in either education or the reindeer work had to pay for supplies out of their own meager salaries, and Washington was so far away that it might take years for them to be repaid.[15]

Bureaucracy also annoyed the Alaskans with its petty regulations. In 1902, D.H. Jarvis, now a collector of Customs in Sitka, wrote Jackson telling him that he had received a Department of Agriculture regulation issued in February 1900 that required all animals imported into the United States on the Pacific Coast to be taken to San Diego, California, for quarantine and inspection. Since a high proportion of commerce in those years came through San Francisco, such a regulation might have made sense, or at least have been of minor inconvenience, but for Siberian deer landed on Cape Prince of Wales, such an order was preposterous. When Jackson protested the stupidity of the regulation, Jarvis was told to send him the curt memorandum, "You are informed that the ports of your district are not excepted from such requirement because of their geographical location."[16] The former Commissioner had enough influential connections in the national capital, however, that after a year of argument, he was permitted the grudging concession that if he would let the Secretary of Agriculture know a month in advance when another expedition to Siberia would take place, they would send an inspector with the purchasing agent, but the Interior Department had to pay his expenses from the appropriations made to buy deer. The question became moot, however, when in April 1903 the Russian government announced that it would permit no more purchases of Siberian deer by Americans.[17]

The subsequent history of the reindeer herds was also a stormy one. Before 1910 the system introduced by Dr. Sheldon Jackson and William T. Lopp was a complete success. It was based on the principle of pride of ownership that possession of a herd gave the Eskimo, and the prestige that wealth and material possessions brought along with it in that society. After a hesitant start, a considerable number of native people wanted to become involved in the program. When Antisarlook died in 1901, his widow inherited a herd of three hundred seventy animals, and was considered the richest Eskimo in Alaska.[18] In addition, a few of the Lapps who did not return home stayed to own and manage their own herds. The very increased numbers of reindeer that resulted from the continuous care and protection of the animals proved the undoing of this phase of the work. The Eskimo had traditionally lived close to the sea, and unlike the Lapps or Siberian Chukchi, they did not like to follow the herds inland. About the only herders willing to use inland grazing sites for summer feeding were the employees of the meat companies, or other non-Eskimo who believed that the inland tundra might make an Arctic reindeer range equivalent to the cattle range on the Great Plains of the Mississippi basin during the 1870's and 1880's. As the number of Eskimo deer increased, the tundra along the seashore became increasingly scarce, and when vandals deliberately burned the moss along the seacoasts to get rid of animals and Eskimo alike, this contributed to the native reluctance to follow their herds inland.[19] Overgrazing began very early, but by the First World War, the destruction of this food source seriously jeopardized the herds. Nevertheless, the system of apprentice training and assigning deer to native herders was a success. This lasted only while the Eskimo were willing to live in what was essentially a subsistence lifestyle.

After 1910, the government tried to solve the problem of overcrowding and overgrazing in the tundra near the coasts by consolidating the herds into single units for each village. In this way, the larger herds could be moved to richer feeding grounds. Instead of private, family ownership with special markings for each owner, the deer were not divided and branded, but ownership by each native was now indicated by a stock certificate. The advantages of the new system were obvious to the government bureaucrats, but less clear to the Eskimo. The work of government supervisors was expected to become easier because they would have fewer Eskimo owners to deal with. Presumably this change should have resulted in an economy of manpower, as fewer herders could care for all the deer belonging to a village, leaving the other men to hunt or fish for supplemental food. Federal officials predicted that this would make greater efficiency possible through better equipment purchased by a corporation rather than having each owner buy his own materials. Grazing lands in the interior could then be assigned arbitrarily, and this would in turn permit better land management. Finally, it was argued, setting up a village corporation would teach the primitive Alaskan the rudiments of capitalism.

Unfortunately, this reasoning was thoroughly unacceptable to the natives themselves. When the Nome mines and placer claims shut down, there was a marked decrease in demand for fresh reindeer meat. Eskimo herders assigned to care for the deer objected to working for the village corporation far from home, while others in their own village hunted, fished, or loafed. Possession of stock certificates carried neither the prestige nor the satisfaction among the natives that owning live, marked deer did. The influenza epidemic of 1918-19 killed many of the older herders, putting much of the work in inexperienced hands.[20] In 1928, a disastrous fire in the office of the Reindeer Service destroyed some of the records, and disputes arose as to who owned the animals. Many young Eskimo lost interest in the whole affair, and killed their deer for meat, or neglected the herds entirely. Wolves and other predators harrassed the unguarded beasts. A hoof disease kept many of the wretched animals from digging through the snow for winter food.

213

When the Eskimo began to work for wages and to buy "white man's food," however, the reindeer industry almost disappeared because the animals that had been turned loose without herders began to wander. At its peak number in the late 1920's, the herds were estimated to number 600,000 animals. The decrease after that year was swift. By 1940, there were only 200,000 deer left.[21] For various reasons, the government blamed the independent, non-Eskimo corporation, and particularly the Lomens, for the woes of the reindeer industry. In addition, some individuals, still fighting missionaries in general and Dr. Jackson in particular, long after his death continued to attack the whole concept of reindeer for the Eskimo as a kind of plot to replace Eskimo with Europeans in northern Alaska.[22] It was true that the village herds, neglected and roaming at will, tended to merge with the company herds, and no one bothered any longer to sort them out. "Bitter conflicts" over ownership took place, and with the records destroyed they could not be resolved. The Interior Department then proposed that the Caucasian-owned commercial companies be forced to sell all of their herds to the native corporations. This proposal solved nothing, since native herding had virtually ceased. The simple fact was that times had changed, and the Eskimo were no longer content to live at the subsistence level they had existed under from time immemorial, or when their food supplies might become uncertain, as they did after 1890 when they faced possible starvation.

In a letter to the President of the Indian Rights Association, dated January 1, 1937, William T. Lopp, who had been associated with the reindeer service almost from its beginning, pointed out that the system of routine care of deer which had been taught by the Norwegian and Lapp instructors was now almost a thing of the past, and there was at least a fifteen percent greater loss of newborn fawns than had been the case thirty years before. He also noted that there were too many bulls for the size of the herds, and this led to fights and consequent injuries among the deer.[23]

The phase-out of corporation herds seemed to work for awhile. In September 1937, the last private corporation went out of business, and for the next six years a modest increase in reindeer was reported each year.

World War II brought many employment opportunities for Eskimo. Defense requirements included an airfield at Point Barrow, and many natives were employed there. The winter of 1943-44 was a severe one which killed the weaker animals and made predators more bold. It also drove the wild caribou from their accustomed ranges, making it easier for the deer to mingle with the wild herds. Subsequent to World War II, radar stations were built along the Arctic Ocean, and these were also built with native labor. The Eskimo were paid more handsome returns in cash wages than they could ever get from deer herding.

The 1960's brought extensive exploration for oil, which also created jobs for the Eskimo. The mechanical tractors, known as "weasels," used by the oil technicians stampeded the herds, and both military personnel and oil company employees made frequent "mistakes" while hunting, shooting many reindeer for meat or sport. The herds shrank almost to the vanishing point.

From time to time a few native herders made half-hearted attempts to find what had become of their deer, but to no avail. By 1951, the great Point Barrow herd descended from those not slaughtered during the relief expedition for the whalers in 1897-98, was reduced to only fifty animals under the care of a single herder. By this time, refrigerated ships were bringing frozen beef from Seattle, and even the Eskimo stopped eating venison when they could use their wages to buy the same kind of food served to the navy, radar operators, or in the oil construction camps.

Thus, Dr. Jackson's reindeer herding idea of the 1890's was all but overwhelmed by changing times and changed conditions.

All that remains is to tell what happened to some of the herders who came to Seattle and Alaska with Kjellmann and Jackson.

A few of those whom Kjellmann hired stayed in Alaska, but others came to Washington or Oregon. For example, Andrew Bahr herded for a time, but in 1929 drove a herd of deer from Kotzebue to the McKenzie River by way of Point Barrow and received considerable publicity for this feat. Johan Petter Johannsen, sometimes called Stalogargo, who had carried mail in Norway, and was the "herb doctor" who accompanied Sacariasen from Eaton to Nome, stayed in Alaska, and carried mail there making three round trips a year from St. Michael to Kotzebue. As has been recorded, he died in a blizzard on one of his mail carrying expeditions.[24] A number of herders and their families came to Poulsbo, Washington. Per Alaksen Rist, who came to Alaska in 1894 as a mature man of fifty, died in Poulsbo early in the century. Peter Hatta, who lived at Candle, Alaska, for ten years after the

215

Nome gold rush, also came later to Poulsbo, and died there. Johan Sp. Tornensis, one of the original group of herders, died in Poulsbo in 1933 at the age of 76. Alfred Nilima, who sold his herd to the Lomens, came to Poulsbo with the others, but finally left the United States and returned to Norway sometime between the two World Wars. He and his wife ran a hotel in Kautokeino. Nilima himself died before the Nazi invasion of Norway, but his wife stayed on, and when the Germans destroyed most of the towns and villages in Finnmark, they did not spare the Nilima's hotel. Marit Pentha Nilima was forced to hide in the hills behind the town and she watched her enemies burn her property to the ground. She returned after the Germans left. As far as is known, she may still be living in Kautokeino.[25]

Hedley Redmyre died in Seattle. His daughter, Mary, stayed in Alaska as the wife of Anders Bahr. He died in Unalakleet. Mike Nakkila lived in Poulsbo for a time, became a logger at Kingston, Washington, and was killed in a logging accident.

The two journal keepers who have been the chief sources for this account of the reindeer project and the gold discoveries, Wilhelm Basi and Carl Sacariasen, have both left a brief record of their later years.

Basi returned to Quincy after he came back from Nome in 1900. He sold part of his land to Thomas Basse and his family, and still had enough money to work the rest of his farm. In 1901 after he returned from Nome, he learned that William Jacobsen, the husband of Wilhelmina whom he had known in Norway, had been killed in a mining accident. Very soon afterward, Basi got in touch with Jacobsen's widow, and on June 9, 1901, he married her. She must not have liked Quincy, however, for the following year they bought a farm in the state of Washington on the plateau just north of the Columbia River, eight miles southwest of Goldendale. The Basi's lived here until 1922, when they sold their farm and moved to Portland. They were restless, however, and next they returned to Quincy and Clatskanie. For some reason that Basi failed to explain in his diary, he decided after he was almost sixty years old that he wanted to become a Lutheran pastor. He did not say where or when he took his theological training, but soon afterward he was installed as pastor of the Quincy Free Apostolic Lutheran Church which he had attended in 1899. He held this post until 1945 when he resigned. The Basi's then moved back to Centerville,

Washington, where their children lived. In November 1946, Wilhelmina Basi died. Wilhem lived until March 1951, and died in Centerville at the age of 81.

Carl, also, felt called to religious work. He always had kept in close touch with his cousin, and when Basi resigned from the Quincy church Sacariasen replaced him. He continued preaching in the church from time to time, even after he retired, until the middle 1950's. In 1958, a feature story in the Portland *Journal* led to bringing Sacariasen and his journal together again. He gave his permission to have it translated, and to tell the story that has now been told. Sacariasen died in Portland in August, 1966.

NOTES

[1]IDTP:AK, Record Group 48, Rolls 8 and 9. Jan. 4, Dec. 21, 1901; Jan. 7, 1902-Dec. 15, 1903.

[2]Nichols, Jeannette Paddick, *Alaska: A History of its Administration, Exploitation, and Industrial Development During Its First Half Century Under the Rule of the United States,* Cleveland: The Arthur H. Clark Company, 1924. p. 167.

[3]IDTP:AK, 48:8 Letter, E.A. Oerter to Ethan A. Hitchcock, March 13, 1901; F.H. Gambell, M.D. to Interior, May 11, 1901; Letter T.A. Goler to Brady, Oct. 19, 1901; W.J. McDonnell to Brady, April 22, 1903.

[4]C.O., Ft. Liscum to Frederick Funston, Cdr. Pacific Division, Mar. 3, 1904. IDTP:AK 48:9.

[5]Lomen, *Fifty Years in Alaska*, p. 15; 39-42: Brady to Interior, August 18, 1900, IDTP 48:7.

[6]Wickersham, James, *Old Yukon Tales-Trails-and-Trials*, Washington, Washington Law Book Company, 1938.

[7]Nichols, *Alaska*, p. 108; 167.

[8]Higginson, Ella, *Alaska: The Great Country*, New York: The MacMillan Company, 1926. p. 504.

[9]San Francisco, *Chronicle*, November 6, 1962.

[10]Bellingham *Herald* (wire service accounts) January 17, February 28, March 30, April 21, July 1, 1921.

[11]Lomen, Carl J. *Fifty Years in Alaska*.

[12]Letter, Root to Interior, March 1, 1901. IDTP:AK, 48:8

[13]Correspondence: *Reports*, Bertholf to Harris (Interior Department) August 4, 1901; Pierce to Interior, October 7, 1901, Jackson to Harris, September 5, 1901. IDTP:AK, 48:8

[14]Treasury to Interior, August 31, 1901, IDTP:AK, 48:8.

[15]Letter, G.L. Mickeljohn, Ass't. Sec. of War to Interior, April 28, 1899; Harris to Interior, December 3, 1901, IDTP:AK, 48:8.

[16]D.H. Jarvis to Sheldon Jackson, May 14, 1902. IDTP:AK, 48:9.

[17]Secretary of Agriculture to Interior, April 7, 1903; John Rosene to Jackson, April 22, 1903. IDTP:AK 48:9.

[18]Report, Harris to Interior, December 18, 1901, IDTP:AK 48:8.

[19]F.H. Gambell to Interior, May 11, 1901. IDTP:AK 48:8.

[20]Lomen, *Fifty Years in Alaska*, p. 124; "Influenza at Nome," *Seattle Times*, March 19, 1919. This story claimed that 750 people died between Nome and Cape Prince of Wales during the epidemic. It also noted (April 15, 1919) that Mary Antisarlook was caring for dozens of children orphaned by the "flue." [*sic*].

[21]Lomen, *Fifty Years in Alaska*, p. 52ff; Critchfield, Howard J., "Seward Peninsula," *Economic Geography*, 25:4, October 1949, p. 281; Sonnenfeld, J., "An Arctic Reindeer Industry: Growth and Decline," *The Geographical Review*, 49:1, January 1959, pp. 76-94.

[22]Ray, Dorothy Jean, "Sheldon Jackson and the Reindeer Industry of Alaska," *Journal of Presbyterian History*, 43:2. June 1965; "Lomen Controversy," *Lopp Papers*, University of Oregon Library.

[23]Sonnenfeld, "Arctic Reindeer Industry," p. 85.

[24]Lomen, *Fifty Years in Alaska*, p. 252.

[25]Interview, H.G. Tornensis with the author at Poulsbo, Washington June 4, 1978.

BIBLIOGRAPHY

Primary Sources:

Basi, Wilhelm, *Diary on 1898 Yukon Rescue*, Finnish-American Historical Society of the West, Historical Tract Issue, 6:4, September 1971.

Lopp, William T., *Lopp Papers*, University of Oregon Library, Eugene, Oregon.

National Archives Microfilm Publications. *Interior Department Territorial Papers; Alaska 1869-1911.* "Letters Received Relating to the District of Alaska."

Sacariasen, Carl Johan, *Reiseminder i Alaska*, (Translated from the Norwegian by Agnes Hendrickson Sjogren.) Typewritten. Unpublished manuscript in The Center for Pacific Northwest Studies, Western Washington University, Bellingham, Washington.

Secondary Sources:

Books & Monographs

Andrews, Clarence Leroy, *The Story of Alaska,* The Caxton Printers, Ltd., Caldwell, 1940.

Andrews, Clarence Leroy, *The Eskimo and His Reindeer in Alaska.* The Caxton Printers, Ltd., Caldwell, (Idaho), 1939.

Brower, Charles D., *Fifty Years Below Zero, a Lifetime of Adventure in the Far North*, Dodd, Mead & Company, New York, 1942.

Cameron, Mrs. Charlotte, *A Cheechako in Alaska and Yukon*, T.F. Unwin, London, 1920.

Carlson, Leland H., *An Alaskan Gold Mine, The Story of No. 9 Above*, Northwestern University Press, Evanston, 1951.

Clausen, Clarence A., editor and translator, "Life in the Klondike and Alaska Gold Fields, " *Norwegian-American Studies and Records*, Volume XVI, Norwegian-American Historical Association, Northfield, 1950.

Colby, Merle, *A Guide to Alaska, Last American Frontier*, Federal Writers Project, The Macmillan Company, New York, 1939.

Cook, Warren L., *Flood Tide of Empire: Spain and the Pacific Northwest, 1543-1819*, Yale University Press, New York, 1973.

Dictionary of American Biography, Dumas Malone, ed., "Sheldon Jackson," Charles Scribner's Sons, 1932 v. 9.

Davis, Mary Lee, *Sourdough Gold, The Log of a Yukon Adventure*, W.A. Wilde Co., Boston, 1933.

Davis, Mary Lee, *Uncle Sam's Attic. The Intimate Story of Alaska,* W.A. Wilde Co., Boston, 1930.

Friedel, Frank, *The Splendid Little War*, Dell Publishing Company, Inc., 1962.

French, L.H., *Nome Nuggets, Some of the Experiences of a Party of Gold Seekers in Northwestern Alaska in 1900*, Montross, Clarke and Emmons, New York, 1901.

Freuchen, Peter, *Arctic Adventure, My Life in the Frozen North* , Farrar & Rinehart, Incorporated, New York, 1935.

Galbraith, John S., *The Hudson's Bay Company as an Imperial Factor, 1821-1869*, The University of California Press, Berkeley, 1957.

Grinnell, Joseph, *Gold Hunting in Alaska*, David C. Cook Publishing Company, Chicago, 1901.

Gruening, Ernest, *The State of Alaska*, Random House, New York, 1954.

Harrison, E.S., *Nome and Seward Peninsula*, Metropolitan Press, Seattle, 1905.

Higginson, Ella, *Alaska, the Great Country*, the Macmillan Company, New York, 1926.

Hines, John Chesterfield, *Minstrel of the Yukon,* Greenberg, New York, 1948.

Hynding, Alan, *The Public Life of Eugene Semple: Promoter and Politician of the Pacific Northwest,* University of Washington Press, Seattle, 1973.

Johnshoy, Dr. J. Walter, *Apaurak in Alaska, Social Pioneering Among the Eskimos, Translated and Compiled from the Records of the Reverend T.L. Brevig, Pioneer Missionary to the Eskimos of Alaska from 1894 to 1917,* Dorrance & Company, Philadelphia, 1944.

Lanier, McKee, *The Land of Nome,* Grafton Press, New York, 1902.

Lantis, Margaret, *Human Problems in Technological Change, A Casebook,* Russell Sage Foundation, New York, 1952.

Lazell, J. Arthur, *Alaska Apostle, The Life Story of Sheldon Jackson,* Harper & Brothers, New York, 1960.

Lomen, Carl J., *Fifty Years Ago in Alaska,* David McKay Company, Inc., New York, 1954.

McElwaine, Eugene, *The Truth About Alaska, the Golden Land of the Midnight Sun,* Regan Printing House, Chicago, 1901.

McLain, John Scudder, *Alaska and the Klondike,* McClure, Phillips & Company, 1905.

Miller, Max, *The Great Trek, the Story of the Five-Year Drive of a Reindeer Herd Through the Icy Wastes of Alaska and Northwestern Canada,* Doubleday, Doran & Company, Inc., Garden City, (N.Y.) 1936.

Morgan, Edward E.P., and Woods, Henry F., *God's Loaded Dice, Alaska, 1897-1930,* The Caxton Printers, Ltd., Caldwell (Idaho), 1948.

Nichols, Jeannette Paddock, *Alaska, A History of Its Administration, Exploitation, and Industrial Development During its First Half Century Under the Rule of the United States,* The Arthur H. Clark Company, Cleveland, 1924.

Ray, Dorothy J., *The Eskimos of Bering Strait, 1650-1898,* The University of Washington Press, 1975.

Stewart, Robert Laird, *Sheldon Jackson, Pathfinder and Prospector of the Missionary Vanguard in the Rocky Mountains and Alaska,* Fleming H. Revell Company, New York, 1908.

Underwood, John J., *Alaska, An Empire in the Making,* Dodd Mead & Company, New York, 1928.

White, Helen M., *The Tale of A Comet and Other Stories,* Minnesota Historical Society Press, St. Paul, 1984.

Wickersham, Hon James, *Old Yukon Tales--Trails--and Trials,* Washington Law Book Company, Washington, 1938.

Winslow, Kathryn, *Big Pan-Out,* W.W. Norton & Company, Inc., New York, 1951.

Secondary Sources:

Journal Articles

Andrews, Clarence Leroy, "Alaska's First Educator," *Alaska Life*, 6:9, September 1943.

Andrews, Clarence Leroy, "Driving Reindeer in Alaska," *Pacific Northwest Quarterly*, 26:2, April 1935, pp. 90-93.

Andrews, Clarence Leroy, "Reindeer in Alaska," *Washington Historical Quarterly*, 10:3, July 1919, pp. 171-176.

Andrews, Clarence Leroy, "Reindeer in the Arctic," *Washington Historical Quarterly,* 17:1, January 1926, pp. 14-17.

Andrews, Clarence Leroy, "William T. Lopp," *Alaska Life,* 7:8, August 1944, pp. 52-54.

Arestad, Sverre, "Reindeer in Alaska," *Pacific Northwest Quarterly,* 42:3, July 1951, pp. 211-223.

Arnell, P.B., "The Wreck of the Bark *Alaska,"Alaska Life,* 11:2, February 1948.

Bertholf, Lieutenant Ellsworth P., "The Rescue of the Whalers; A Sled Journey of 1600 Miles in the Arctic Regions," *Harper's Magazine,* June 1899, pp. 3-24.

Carlson, Leland H., "The First Mining Season at Nome, Alaska--1899," *The Pacific Historical Review,* XVI:2, May 1947, pp. 163-175.

Carlson, Leland H., *Nome, From Mining Camp to Civilized Community, Pacific Northwest Quarterly*, 38:3, July 1947, pp. 163-175.

Carlson, Leland H., "The Discovery of Gold at Nome, Alaska," *The Pacific Historical Review* XV:3, September 1946, pp. 259-278.

Critchfield, Howard J., "Seward Peninsula," *Economic Geography,* 25:4, October 1949.

Grosvenor, Gilbert Hovey, "Reindeer in Alaska," *National Geographic Magazine,* 14:4, April 1903, pp. 127-249.

Hawkes, Ernest William, "Transforming the Eskimo Into a Herder," *Anthropos Ephemeris,* 1913, pp. 359-362.

Hinckley, Ted. C., "Sheldon Jackson as Preserver of Alaska's Native Culture," *Pacific Historical Review*, XXXIII:4, November 1964. pp. 411-424.

Lomen, Carl Joys, "The Camel of the Frozen Desert," *National Geographic Magazine,* 30:12, December 1919.

Montgomery, Maurice, "The Murder of Missionary Thornton," *Pacific Northwest Quarterly* 54:4, October 1963, pp. 167-73.

Murray, Keith A., "Dr. Jackson and the Dawson Reindeer," *Idaho Yesterdays,* 2:1, Spring 1958, pp. 8-15.

Ray, Dorothy Jean, "Sheldon Jackson and the Reindeer Industry of Alaska," *Journal of Presbyterian History*, 43:2, June 1965, pp. 71-77.

Seppala, Leonard and Thompson, Raymond, "Gold-Stakers and Claim Jumpers," *Alaska Sportsman,* 27:6, June 1961, pp. 8-10.

Sonnenfeld, J., "An Arctic Reindeer Industry: Growth and Decline," *The Geographical Review,* 49:1, January 1959. p. 76-94.

Government Documents:

52 Cong., 1 Sess., *Congressional Record*, May 23, 1893; 52 Cong., 2 Sess. S Misc. Doc. #22, "Report on Introduction of Domestic Reindeer Into Alaska," 1893.

53 Cong., 3 Sess., *Senate Executive Document #92*, "Introduction of Domestic Reindeer Into Alaska."

54 Cong., 1 Sess., *Senate Document #111*, "Introduction of Domestic Reindeer Into Alaska," Jackson Report; Kjellmann Report.

54 Cong., 2 Sess., *Senate Document #49*, Jackson Report, "Introduction of Domestic Reindeer Into Alaska," 1896.

55 Cong., 2 Sess., *Congressional Record*, Dec. 16, 18, 1897; *Senate Document #14*, "Alaska Gold Fields," 1897; *Senate Document #30*, Jackson Report, "Introduction of Domestic Reindeer Into Alaska," 1897.

55 Cong., 3 Sess., *House Document #5*, Jackson Report, "Report of the Commissioner of Education," 1898. "Commission to Lapland; *Senate Document #34*, Jackson Report, "Report on the Introduction of Domestic Reindeer Into Alaska, with maps and illustrations," "Relief of the Whalters Imprisoned in the Ice Near Point Barrow"; *Senate Document #172*, U.S. Geological Survey, "Explorations in Alaska in 1898."

56 Cong., 1 Sess., *Senate Document #236*, "Preliminary Report on the Cape Nome Gold Region, Alaska," 1899; *Senate Document #245*, "9th Report on Reindeer in Alaska," P.H. Gambell, M.D., "Resident Physician's Report," "Eaton Station Logbook," Jackson Report, "The Introduction of Domestic Reindeer Into Alaska," 1899.

56 Cong., 2 Sess., *House Document #511*, "Report of the Cruise of the U.S. Revenue Cutter *Bear* and the Overland Expedition for the Relief of the Whalers in the Arctic Ocean from November 27, 1897 to September 13, 1898;" *House Document #547*, Brooks, Alfred H. Richardson, George B. Collier, Arthur J., and Mendenhall, Walter C., "Reconnaissances in the Cape Nome and Norton Bay Regions, Alaska, in 1900."

75 Cong., 1 Sess., *House Report #1188,* "Reindeer in Alaska."

76 Cong., 1 Sess., *House Document #174,* "Department of Interior Supplemental Appropriation, 1940."

Newspapers:

Bellingham, (Washington) *Herald.*

Nome *Gold Digger.*

Port Townsend *Morning Leader.*

San Francisco *Chronicle.*

Seattle *Post-Intelligencer.*

Seattle *Times.*

APPENDIX

LIST OF REINDEER HERDERS

Abrahamsen, Jeremias, (Cook--St. Lawrence Island)
Andersen, John
Andersen, Per
Andersen, Sofie
Anti, Larsen (died April 1900)
Bahr, Anders Aslaksen (married Hedly Redmyer's daughter)
Bahr, Ole Olsen (plus wife and two children)
Bals, Aslak Johansen (plus wife and two children)
Bals, Nils Persen (plus wife and one child)
Balto, Anders Johannesen (plus wife and two children)
Balto, Samuel Johannesen
Basi, Wilhelm (Sacariasen's cousin)
Berg, Ole G.
Berg, Peder (Agent for Englestadt at Unalakleet)
Biti, Anders Klemetsen
Biti, Marit
Boino, Klemet Persen
Bongo, Isak Andersen
Eira, Johan Eriksen
Eira, Beret N.
Eira, Marit Persdatter
Eira, Mathias Aslaksen
Gaup, Aslak Aslaksen (plus wife and child)
Greiner, Otto
Hansen, Amund
Hansen, Johan Hilmar
Hatta, Ida Johansdatter
Hatta, Isak Johannsen
Hatta, Jacob Larsen (plus wife and two children)
Hatta, Lars Larsen
Hatta, Ole Klemetsen

Hatta, Per Johannesen
Hermansen, Alfred (and wife)
Johannesen, Johan Peter ("Stalogorgo") The herb doctor.
Johannsen, Peter
Johansen, Johan M.
Johnsen, Anders
Josefsen, Anders
Josefsen, Samuel
Kjeldsberg, Emil
Kjeldsberg, Magnus
Kjeldsberg, Thoralf (from Kaafjord--knew some English)
Klemetsen, Nils (went to Teller in 1901)
Klemetsen, Matthias
Krogh, Ole
Larsen, Lauritz
Leinen, Otto M. (plus wife and four children)
Lindeberg, Jafet (gold discoverer--Pioneer--Wild Goose Mining Co.)
Losvar, Johan (cook)
Nakkila, Mikkel J. (one of the successful miners--sold claim for $55,000)
Nango, Johan Peter Johannsen (wife and two small children)
Nikkila, Isak Samuelsen (shot self while hunting)
Nilima, Alfred Samuelsen (went to Kotzebue in 1901)
Nilsen, Klemet (from Karasjok--a Lapp boy)
Olesen, Ole
Paulsen, Olai
Persanger, Per Josefsen
Pulk, Ole Johansen (plus wife and two children)
Rapp, Ole M.
Ravna, Johannes Aslaksen
Rist, Johan Peter (plus wife and one child)
Rist, Per Aslaksen, (one of the original group from Lapland)
Redmyer, Hedley E. (hired in Seattle)
Sacariasen, Carl Johan (cook)
Samuelsen, Hans
Sara, Nils Persen (plus wife and five children)

Siri, Hans Andersen
Siri, Per Nilsen
Spein, Per Mathesen
Stensfjeld, Ole Johansen (almost washed overboard on *Manitoban*)
Stefansen, Lauritz
Suhr, Karl O. (snowblinded on way to Nome)
Tornensis, Isak Mikklesen
Tornensis, Johan Islaksen (and wife). (Partner of Nikkala)
Tornensis, Johan Speinsen
Tornensis, Margretha (and two children)
Utsi, Anders Persen
Vestad, Ivar Persen
Wiig, Rolf (storekeeper)

238

LIST OF SPONSORS

Henry & Frances **ADAMS**, Bellingham

A.A. & Helen **ANDERSON**, Lopez Island

Mr. & Mrs. Roy E. **ANDERSON**, Bellingham

Frank C. **BROOKS**, Bellingham

Sene R. **CARLILE**, Bellingham

H. Eldridge **CARR**, Bellingham

Reverend Richard & Elizabeth **COLE**, Millbrae, CA

Sandra **CONWAY**, Sunnyvale, CA

Joseph **COONS**, Bellingham

Curtis G. **CORTELYOU**, Bellingham

Albert H. **CULVERWELL**, Blue Jay, CA

Larry **DELORME**, Bellingham

John & Anne **DUNCAN**, Malott, WA

Melvin & Elsie **FARISS** Glendale, CA

Richard & Pat **FLEESON**, Bellingham

Orville **GARRETT**, Bellingham

Humphrey & Isabel **GRIGGS**, Bellingham

Reverend T. **MURDOCK** & Miriam M. **HALE**, Washington VT

Kris & Jean **HAMILTON**, Bellingham

Mr. & Mrs. Robert L. **HANCOCK**, Coupeville, WA

Loren E. **HATCHER**, Omak, WA

Leslie & Orpha **HEDRICK**, Tigard, OR

Dr. Ted. C. **HINCKLEY**, San Jose, CA

James H. **HITCHMAN**, Bellingham

Dr. & Mrs. Eric **JOHNSON**, Bellingham

Dr. & Mrs. Richard **JONES**, Bellingham

Sam & Barbara **KELLY**, Bellingham

William B. **KLEIHEGE**, Bellingham

Dorothy **KOERT**, Bellingham

Dr. Paul & Mildred **KOPER**, Jenkintown, PA

Mr. & Mrs. Harold **LAUT**, Bellingham

Robert & Jane **LAWYER**, Bellingham

A. Robert **MASON**, San Jose, CA

Florence **McBEATH**, Bellingham

Clarence & Gloria **MILLER**, Bellingham

Howard & Jeanne **MITCHELL**, Bellingham

Robert & Marilyn **MONAHAN**, Bellingham

David C. **MORSE**, Bellingham

James D. **MOORE**, Sedro Woolley, WA

Hal J. **MURRAY**, Portland, OR

Neal & Elsie **NOORLAG**, Oak Harbor, WA

Mr. & Mrs. Gus **OKERLUND**, Bellingham

Darline **PEHHALURICK**, Moclips, WA

Mr. & Mrs. John E. **PERGIEL,** Portland, OR

Alice E. **POSTELL,** Portland, OR

James B. **RHOADS,** Bellingham

Dr. & Mrs. Norman **RICHARDSON,** Bremerton, WA

Ralph & Eleanor **RINNE,** Bellingham

Carl **SCHULER,** Bellingham

Maury **SCHWARTZ,** Bellingham   .

James W. **SCOTT,** Bellingham

Andrew & Nellie **SMITH,** Bellingham

Lafe & Gertrude **STOCK,** Sekim, WA

Warren & Doris **TAYLOR,** Atlanta, GA

John & Doris **THOMAS,** Bellingham

Manfred & Hally **VERNON,** Friday Harbor, WA

Center for Pacific Northwest Studies, W.W.U.

Department of History, W.W.U.